W9-CHV-357

The Politics of Urban Education in the United States

Education Policy Perspectives

General Editor: Professor Ivor Goodson, Faculty of Education, University of Western Ontario, London, Canada N6G 1G7

Education policy analysis has long been a neglected area in the UK and, to an extent, in the USA and Australia. The result has been a profound gap between the study of education and the formulation of education policy. For practitioners, such a lack of analysis of new policy initiatives has worrying implications, particularly at a time of such policy flux and change. Education policy has, in recent years, been a matter for intense political debate – the political and public interest in the working of the system has come at the same time as the breaking of the consensus on education policy by the New Right. As never before, political parties and pressure groups differ in their articulated policies and prescriptions for the education sector. Critical thinking about these developments is clearly imperative.

All those working within the system also need information on policy-making, policy implementation and effective day-to-day operation. Pressure on schools from government, education authorities and parents has generated an enormous need for knowledge amongst those on the receiving end of educational policies.

This Falmer Press series aims to fill the academic gap, to reflect the politicalization of education, and to provide the practitioners with the analysis for informed implementation of policies that they will need. It offers studies in broad areas of policy studies, with a particular focus on the following areas: school organization and improvement; critical social analysis; policy studies and evaluation; and education and training.

The Politics of Urban Education in the United States

The 1991 Yearbook of the Politics of Education Association

Edited by

James G. Cibulka

University of Wisconsin-Milwaukee

and

Rodney J. Reed

Pennsylvania State University

and

Kenneth K. Wong

University of Chicago

The Falmer Press
(A member of the Taylor & Francis Group)
Washington D.C. • London

UK Taylor & Francis Ltd, 4 John Street, London WC1N 2ET
USA Taylor & Francis Inc., 1900 Frost Road, 101, Bristol, PA 19007

First published 1992

Library of Congress Cataloging-in-Publication data are available on request

A catalogue record for this book is available from the British Library

ISBN 0 75070 0890 cased
ISBN 0 75070 0904 paperback

Set in 11/12 Bembo, by
Chapterhouse Typesetting Ltd, Formby, Lancs.

Cover Design by Caroline Archer

Printed in Great Britain by Burgess Science Press, Basingstoke on paper which has a specified pH value on final paper manufacture of not less then 7.5 and is therefore 'acid free'.

Contents

Acknowledgements

James Cibulka is grateful to Gail Neu for her able editorial assistance in producing this volume. The School of Education at the University of Wisconsin-Milwaukee also generously provided necessary technical and resource support.

About the Editors and Contributors

James G. Cibulka is Professor of Administrative Leadership and Director of the PhD Program in Urban Education at the University of Wisconsin-Milwaukee. His specializations include educational policies, finance and policy, with particular attention to urban schools, private schools, and state–local relations. He was formerly a Senior Research Fellow at the US Department of Education, where he studied educational restructuring. His most recent book (with William Lowe Boyd) is *Private Schools and Public Policy* (Falmer Press).

Rodney J. Reed is Dean of the College of Education, and Pennsylvania Professor of Education at the Pennsylvania State University. His major teaching and research areas include school leadership and management, educational human resources administration and development, urban education, and teacher supervision and evaluation. He is co-author (with James Guthrie) of *Educational Administration and Policy: Effective Leadership for American Education* and *School and College Competency Testing Programs: Perceptions and Effects on Black Students in Louisiana and North Carolina*.

Kenneth K. Wong is Assistant Professor in the Department of Education and the College at the University of Chicago. He is author of *City Choices: Education and Housing* (SUNY Press) and co-author of *When Federalism Works* (Brookings). In 1989–90 he held a Spencer Postdoctoral Fellowship to study the state fiscal role in public education.

Charles E. Bidwell is William Claude Reavis Professor in the Department of Sociology and Education, the College and the Harris School of Public Policy Studies at the University of Chicago. He also is chair of the Department of Sociology. He is nationally known for his work on school organization and has published widely on this subject.

William Lowe Boyd is Professor of Education in the College of Education at the Pennsylvania State University. His specialty in research and teaching is educational policy and politics. He has been a Visiting Fulbright Scholar in Australia and England. He has co-edited numerous volumes, including most recently, *Private Schools and Public Policy* (Falmer Press) and *Choice in Education: Potential and Problems* (McCutchan).

David Colton is a faculty member and Director of the Bureau of Educational Planning and Development at the University of New Mexico. His work in the politics of education field has focused on the financial aspects of urban school desegregation plans. Major activities have included an NIE-funded study of urban school desegregation costs, and consultation involving desegregation planning in Missouri and Minnesota.

Bruce Cooper is Professor of Education Administration and Policy at the Fordham University School of Education. His research has focused on school politics and policy and reform in public and private schools. In addition to other books, he recently co-authored *Taking Charge: State Action on School Reform in the 1980s* (Hudson Institute).

Robert L. Crowson is a Professor of Educational Administration and Policy at the University of Illinois, Chicago. His research interests centre on the study of administrative discretion up and down the organizational hierarchy, from superintendents to principals. He is a Senior Research Fellow with the National Center for School Leadership and the National Center for Education in the Inner-City.

Patricia F. First is an Associate Professor of Educational Law and Policy at the University of New Orleans. Her research interests include law, politics and policy, particularly as they are related to the functioning and evaluation of state and local boards of education. She is the author of *Educational Policy for School Administrators* (1991) and an editor, with Herbert Walberg, of *School Boards: Their Changing Forms and Functions* (1991). She is currently Chair of the Publications Committee of the National Organization for Legal Problems in Education and serves on the editorial advisory committee for West's *Education Law Reporter*.

Carolyn D. Herrington is visiting Assistant Professor in the Department of Educational Leadership and Associate Director of the Center for Policy Studies in Education at Florida State University. She is the author of numerous articles and reports in the areas of politics of education, intergovernmental relations and integration of children's services. She has recently served as primary author of the *Condition of Education in Florida* and *Condition of Children in Florida*.

Barbara L. Jackson is Professor of Education in the Division of Administration, Policy, and Urban Education at the Fordham University Graduate School of Education, New York City. A recent publication is 'Education from a black perspective with implications for administrator preparation programs' in *Leaders for America's Schools*. Research interests include school-based management and shared decision making at elementary schools in New York City, as well as parent involvement.

Richard A. King is Professor, Division of Educational Leadership and Policy Studies, at the University of Northern Colorado. His research interests include the allocation of resources among and within school systems. He recently co-authored with Austin Swanson of SUNY at Buffalo a textbook on the economics and politics of education.

C. Kent McGuire is Program Director for Education at the Lilly Endowment. He is responsible for education reform initiatives in Indiana. He was formerly on the faculty at the University of Colorado at Denver. His expertise is in education, finance, governance, and policy.

Louis F. Miron is currently Assistant Professor of Urban Education and Public Policy and director of the Urban Education Development Laboratory at the University of New Orleans. His research interests centre on the application of critical theory and pedagogy to the solutions of problems in inner city schools which prevent at-risk students from joining the educational mainstream. Among his published articles is 'The moral exercise of power: A post-structural analysis of school administration', in the *Review of Journal of Philosophy and Social Science*.

Martin E. Orland is currently Associate Director for Analysis and Reporting at the National Education Goals Panel, Washington, DC. He has published widely in the areas of public policy analysis, intergovernmental relations and federal and state education policy.

Joel Spring is Professor at the College of Old Westbury, State University of New York. He has written extensively on the politics and history of American education. His forthcoming book is *Images of American Life: A History of Ideological Management in Schools, Movies, Radio, and Television* (SUNY Press).

Thomas B. Timar is an Associate Professor in the Graduate School of Education at the University of California, Riverside. His primary interests are federal and state educational policy and politics, particularly in how they shape the dynamics of institutional change.

Susan Uchitelle is Executive Director of the Voluntary Interdistrict Coordinating Council in St Louis. She has focused on urban and metropolitan school desegregation issues and implemented the most extensive voluntary interdistrict student transfer programme to date. Research and written activities have included work on school choice in the public sector, alternatives to suspension and student assessment.

Joseph G. Weeres is Chair of the Education Faculty at the Claremont Graduate School. His teaching and research focus on educational administration, educational politics, and educational policy.

Robert K. Wimpelberg is Associate Dean of the College of Education and Associate Professor of Educational Administration at the University of New Orleans. His research interests span the micro-politics of the principalship to the policy influences of national commission reports. He is currently Treasurer of the Politics of Education Association. His most recent published work is the chapter, 'The inservice development of principals: A new movement, its characteristics, and future', in Thurston and Lotto's *Advances in Educational Administration* (1990).

Martin E. Orland is currently Associate Director for Analysis and Reporting at the National Education Goals Panel, Washington, DC. He has published widely in the areas of public policy analysis, intergovernmental relations and federal and state education policy.

Joel Spring is Professor at the College of Old Westbury, State University of New York. He has written extensively on the politics and history of American education. [illegible]

[illegible]

INTRODUCTION

The politics of urban education in the United States: introduction and overview

James G. Cibulka, Rodney J. Reed and Kenneth K. Wong

Urban education has become a public policy concern once again. After the tumult of the 1960s, several forces pushed urban education off the policy agenda. Enrolment drops, recession and decay of some city economies, a growing social backlash against 'liberal social programmes', shrinking economic and political power among cities in Congress and state capitals – all played their part in shaping the neglect of urban schools in the 1980s. Also contributing to this inattention was the general disillusionment about education as a tool for social mobility after James Coleman published *Equality of Educational Opportunity* in 1966. Educators did not begin to formulate a response until the effective schools movement came of age in the late 1970s. The Reagan Administration epitomized this attitude of urban neglect and, in 1991, as this is being written, domestic policy has not changed appreciably.

Nonetheless, a set of counter-forces has begun to cumulate and push urban educational policy to the foreground once more. Educational reform, set in motion more or less officially with the publication of *A Nation at Risk* in 1983, was at first seen as a dangerous paradigm shift which would only contribute to the further neglect of urban schools. The Council of Great City Schools warned as much in its 1987 report *Results in the Making*.

Urban schools have become an important and growing object of attention in the current reform movement. Business concerns about labour shortages were perhaps the dominant factor causing renewed attention to the performance of urban schools. Other factors have contributed as well. State officials are demanding more accountability of all school systems, particularly state testing requirements and accountability reporting systems. While these data have highlighted the reality that the failures of the American educational system reach into virtually every community and every segment of our society, the failures are most conspicuous in many urban school systems.

The deterioration of the quality of life in America's central cities concerns a range of actors, although from different perspectives, so there is little consensus on causes or remedies. Social conservatives worry about moral decay in the inner-city, while fiscal conservatives fret about inefficient and wasteful spending by city bureaucrats. Many on the political left worry instead about the decline of racial harmony and educational opportunity in our cities.

One response to this widening malaise about urban schools has been an increase in demands for governance reforms, such as new ways of selecting urban school boards (e.g. Boston), political decentralization (e.g. Chicago), and educational choice (e.g. Milwaukee). The inability of urban school boards to recruit or keep superintendents began to receive wide media coverage in 1991.

This yearbook, then, comes at a propitious time. It affords scholars interested in

0268–0939/91 $3.00 © 1991 Taylor & Francis Ltd.

urban schools as well as policy makers an opportunity to examine trends and developments affecting these school systems in the United States and to consider how their problems might be addressed effectively.

Overview of the book

Part 1 of the book is entitled 'The Study of the Politics of Education'. In chapter 1 Kenneth K. Wong takes up the theme 'The Politics of Urban Education as a Field of Study: An Interpretive Analysis'. James G. Cibulka follows in chapter 2 with 'Urban Education as a Field of Study: Problems of Knowledge and Power'. Next Joel Spring provides a critical assessment of research on educational politics in 'Knowledge and Power in Research into the Politics of Urban Education' (chapter 3). The final contribution in this first part of the book, co-authored by Joseph G. Weeres and Bruce Cooper, examines 'Public Choice Perspectives on Urban Schools' (chapter 4). Taken together these chapters provide a summary and assessment of our knowledge base on urban education politics and the field of urban education more generally.

Part 2, 'The Political Condition of Urban Schools' shifts to an analysis of the changing socio-political conditions in urban schools, including the causes of changing demands and support. Barbara L. Jackson and James G. Cibulka examine 'Leadership Turnover and Business Mobilization: The Changing Political Ecology of Urban School Systems' (chapter 5). Chapter 6 addresses 'Urban Schools as Organizations: Political Perspectives', by Robert L. Crowson and William Lowe Boyd. Next Thomas B. Timar uses a case-study approach to examine 'Urban Politics and State School Finance in the 1980s' (chapter 7). In chapter 8 Richard A. King and C. Kent McGuire write concerning 'Political and Financial Support for School-based and Child-Centred Reforms'.

Part 3 of the book examines 'Urban School Renewal and Implementation Strategies: Political Implications'. Issues considered in this section include the nature of the policy responses and 'reforms' urban school officials have made to address their problems, the degree of support they enjoy, and political demands for further change. David Colton and Susan Uchitelle examine 'Urban School Desegregation: From Race to Resources' (chapter 9). 'School Decentralization and Empowerment' is the focus of chapter 10, by Rodney J. Reed. In chapter 11 Carolyn D. Herrington and Martin Orland analyse 'Politics and Federal Aid to Urban School Systems: The Case of Chapter One'. In the final chapter of this section, Louis F. Miron, Patricia F. First, and Robert K. Wimpelberg examine 'Equity, Adequacy and Educational Need: The Courts and Urban School Finance'.

In the Epilogue (Part 4) Charles E. Bidwell draws together the various emphases and themes of the volume. His contribution is entitled 'Toward Improved Knowledge and Policy on Urban Education'.

POLITICS OF EDUCATION ASSOCIATION YEARBOOK 1991, 3–26

PART 1: THE STUDY OF THE POLITICS OF EDUCATION

1 *The politics of urban education as a field of study: an interpretive analysis*

Kenneth K. Wong

Researchers in the field of urban education politics have much in agreement – they refute the notion of bureaucratic insulation in school policy making, connect the school to its broader political and economic community, and address the effects of school governance on race relations, governmental legitimacy and political representation. At the same time, approaching the field with different disciplinary backgrounds and substantive interests, researchers have offered competing frameworks in analysing school politics. In my view, disagreements and consensus within the field can be better appreciated if the diverse approaches and their substantive findings are understood in the proper context of the school policy organization – the way power is allocated between the top of the system and the school site and the way clientele are involved in schooling decisions. In this partial review of the literature, I shall propose an integrative framework that specifies the circumstances under which different kinds of politics occur. The final section will explore research and policy implications.

Introduction

Three decades ago, our understanding of the politics of urban education began to shift from the view that the school system was an autonomous organization to the perspective that external political and economic forces substantially shaped school policy. At one time, the 'bureaucratic insulation' model prevailed (Eliot 1959, Katz 1987, Callahan 1962, Peterson 1976, Bidwell 1965, Weick 1976, Rogers 1968). It depicted the school system as a complex bureaucratic structure. The organization's insiders enjoyed autonomy from outsiders' influence because the former possessed the expertise and the information on how the system operated. Activities performed at each level of this multi-layered, loosely coupled organization were connected by strong professional identification and standard operating procedures. School professionals determined the use of most resources, exercised control over curricular and instructional matters, designed the administrative organization, and recruited the staff. School politics, according to this view, was primarily embedded in the organizational milieu.

We no longer wholly subscribe to the notion of an insulated system. Over the past three decades, the scholarship in the politics of education has called into question whether the school system is indeed impermeable (Layton 1982, Burlingame 1988, Boyd 1976, Peterson 1976, Wirt and Kirst 1982, Mitchell 1988, Scribner 1977, LaNoue 1982). To many political analysts, school autonomy is far from complete. Increasingly, external political and economic forces are found to shape school finance, leadership succession, the student population, racial desegregation and issues related to the education of the disadvantaged. Taken as a whole, this scholarship has much in agreement – it refutes the notion of bureaucratic insulation in school policy making, connects the school to its broader political and economic community, and addresses the effects of school governance on race relations, governmental legitimacy and political representation. School politics, in other words, goes beyond the bureaucratic structure.

Diversity in the field

Scholarship in the politics of urban education, however, is marked by significant intellectual cleavages. Approaching the field with different disciplinary backgrounds and substantive interests, researchers have offered competing frameworks in analysing school politics. Three examples come to mind. First, the field is split over whether school politics is unique. In a review of the literature, Paul Peterson (1974) argued that school politics is not much different from other domestic policy domains. On a routine basis, educational policy features a low level of citizen participation, a central board that serves as an agent of legitimation and a lot of direct influence from a small group of professional staff. However, the mayor and other public officials are expected to be actively involved in school (as well as other policy) affairs when 'the issue has major budgetary implications, generates a widespread community controversy, or involves the jurisdiction of other local agencies' (Peterson 1974: 365). In contrast, some analysts consider the character of educational issues as an important determinant. While public education is generally embedded in the progressive tradition of standardization and professionalism, different issues are found to have generated varying levels of community conflict. Greater confrontation is seen in budgetary decisions and school closure than in curriculum design (Boyd 1976, Boyd 1979, Kirst and Walker 1971, Cibulka 1983). The funding and implementation of redistributive programmes encounter more opposition than programmes on general educational quality (Lowi 1964, Peterson *et al.* 1986).

Second, there is disagreement over the extent to which influence on school decisions is widely distributed. The 'elitist' framework centres on how the community's economic and political elites closely dominate school policymaking (McCarty and Ramsey 1971, Spring 1988, Bachrach and Baratz 1962, Kirby *et al.* 1973, Hunter 1953, Stone 1976). The 'pluralist' perspective, however, focuses on how the teachers' union, community organizations and other interest groups bargain with the district administration on budgetary, curricular and other key issues (Dahl 1961, Grimshaw 1979, Wirt and Kirst 1982, McDonnell and Pascal 1979, Cole 1969).

Third, as the trend of urban decline became increasingly apparent in the late 1960s and early 1970s, a new generation of analysts began to challenge the proposition that local political forces determine school policy. According to the economic constraint perspective, urban districts are not altogether free to do what they prefer because they, unlike nation-states, cannot regulate the flow of productive resources (e.g. labour and investment). Given the pervasiveness of structural economic constraints, districts are expected to act rationally and use resources in a calculative manner (Peterson 1981). Indeed, whether urban policy making is shaped by economic constraint or political forces is currently vigorously debated among urban researchers (see Wong 1990).

Chapter's objectives

These competing frameworks testify to the growth and diversity of the politics of education field. Yet, in choosing one framework over another, researchers tend to undermine the contribution of their analytical counterparts and overlook what both sides have in common. In my view, disagreements and consensus within the field can be better appreciated if the diverse approaches and their substantive findings are understood in the proper context of the school policy organization. Toward this objective, I shall propose an integrative framework that specifies the circumstances under which different kinds of politics occur and how these political patterns can be informative in our selection of the appropriate analytical approaches. In this chapter, I shall first construct the synthesized framework. Making use of the current literature, I shall then specify and substantiate the different kinds of school politics that I believe characterize the urban district. The final section will explore research and policy implications.

Proposing an integrative framework

To construct a framework that would integrate diverse perspectives, I distinguish two sets of institutional arrangements on school governances: (1) the way power is allocated between the top of the system and the school site, and (2) the way clientele (e.g. parents, unions and businesses) are involved in schooling decisions. First, the distribution of power within the school organization can be understood in terms of the concepts of centralization and decentralization (or shared authority). For analytical purposes, centralization is used here to suggest a top-down approach where the central board and its bureaucracy hold authority over a wide range of issues, including union bargaining, taxing and spending, programme evaluation, data collection, implementation of federal and state legislation, textbook adoption and recruitment of the professional staff. In a decentralized system where authority is shared between the central administration and the schools, however, the latter enjoys substantial discretion in the use of its own funds, the recruitment of the principal (and perhaps, the instructional staff), curricular design, parental involvement and community services.

The balance of power between the organizational apex and the school is likely to interact with the ways parents and other clients are involved in the school policy system. Parental (clientele) participation can be distinguished in terms of two primary forms. First, parents and other clients involved in the political process to select candidates for the central board and the school-site council, lobby government officials and vote on taxing and spending issues. Through these political activities, clients gain access to the decision-making bodies at different levels of the district organization. Second, market-like mechanisms are also available to parents. Parents and other clients can behave like consumers choosing educational service providers. These mechanisms include individual choice of public schools in other districts, magnet schools in the district and non-public schools. As consumers, parents affect school policy (e.g. leaving the neighbourhood public schools) without having to be involved in the political and electoral process.

Parental participation and the distribution of power in the school organization are likely to yield jointly four kinds of politics, as depicted in table 1. These are (a) the politics of organizational maintenance and adaptation (cell A in table 1), (b) the politics of shared decision making (cell B), (c) the politics of exiting (cell C), and (d) the politics of competition (cell D). Our understanding of each kind of politics comes from the literature in the field of educational politics. The politics of organizational maintenance and adaptation draws on the literature on the school board and its relationship with the school superintendent, the development of the school bureaucracy, the implementation of federal programmmes, interest group politics and political representation. The politics of shared governance is illuminated by the scholarship in site-based management, parental empowerment and other decentralization experiments in big-city districts. The politics of exiting is closely related to studies of the political economy of urban schools, school closing in the context of enrolment decline and the politics of school finance. Finally, the discussion of the politics of competition is based on studies on schooling choice, magnet school programmes in public schools, educational vouchers and the private versus public school debate.

Table 1. An integrative framework on the four patterns of urban school politics

	Authority structure in the School Policy Organization	
	Centralized at the top	*Decentralized at the school*
Forms of clientele(parental) participation		
Political channels	Politics of organizational adaptation (A)	Politics of shared governance (B)
Market-like mechanisms	Politics of exiting (C)	Politics of competition (D)

The four kinds of politics, though covering a wide range of topics, are not meant to be exhaustive in summing up the literature on the politics of urban education. Among the topics not included in my analysis are: the school as an agent of political socialization (Greenstein 1965, Almond and Verba 1965, Gutmann 1987, Easton and Dennis 1969, Jennings and Niemi 1974); the politics of reforming the teaching profession and the administrative staff (Hannaway and Crowson 1989, Lortie 1975); state reform and its implementation (Odden and Marsh 1989, Timar and Kirp 1988, Fuhrman 1988, Wong 1991); educational assessment and evaluation (Fuhrman and Malen 1991); curricular and instructional strategies (Barr and Dreeben 1983, Oakes 1985); multicultural and Afro-centric curriculum (Banks 1988, Olneck 1990); post-secondary education (Orfield 1990); micro-politics of the school (Blase 1991, Ball 1987); and suburban school politics (Minar 1966, Boyd 1975, McCarty and Ramsey 1971).

Although it does not cover the entire field, the integrative framework serves two important purposes. First, it captures the current intellectual movement in the field of urban education. Currently, our analytical shift has taken two directions that are clearly reflective of the new reality in school governance. The first tendency is to move away from the top of the school system (i.e. central authority) and focus on school sites. The 'traditional' bureaucratic structure that preserves insiders' autonomy is gradually transformed into a more decentralized configuration with greater accountability at the neighbourhood level. It has shifted some authority to school sites and parent councils. The central bureaucracy is expected to give fewer commands and to provide more technical support for the local staff and parents. The second trend suggests that researchers not only examine the political role that parents and other clients have played in influencing school policy but also recognize that parents can act as consumers in the educational marketplace. The notion of bureaucratic control is clearly weakened as urban schools introduce market-like mechanisms, such as schooling choice. Consequently, in the 1990s, the urban district may be seen as consisting of diverse governing structures that are bound together by a less 'dictatorial' central bureaucracy.

Second, the integrative framework offers a balanced understanding of school politics – identifying both unity and disagreement in the research. In this regard, the variety in governing arrangements within the urban school system represents a critical development in the politics of education. We can no longer fully understand school politics by focusing our research effort at the top of the system (i.e. the school board, the central office and the superintendency). Nor can we gain an accurate view of the complexity of city schools by just looking at the school and its immediate neighbourhood. In order to understand changing school politics, we need to examine in a more systematic manner the variety of governing structures – with their differing degrees of centralization and different forms of client participation – within the school policy organization. Let us now turn to each of the four political patterns.

Politics of organizational maintenance and adaptation

The 'traditional' politics of organizational adaptation – bureaucracy responds incrementally to competing demands from interest groups – is most likely to be found where the district's central office enjoys substantial authority and where parents and other clients use political channels to exercise their influence. The best evidence on this kind of politics comes from three bodies of literature: (1) studies that examine democratic practices in the development of a central school bureaucracy, (2) analyses of the management of competing interest groups, and (3) those that look at the district's response to social change. As a whole, the three sets of literature ask three important questions about centralized authority: (1) How democratic is urban school governance? (2) How successful are schools in managing competing external interests? and (3) How do urban schools address the needs of disadvantaged pupils? The scholarship in urban school politics has offered different perspectives to each of these issues.

Views on democratic governance

There are two broad understandings on the district's centralized governance and its ability to address clientele demands. While one set of studies sees the school bureaucracy as insulated from external influences, the other finds diverse political representation and bargaining.

A closed system of elites: The first approach sees the school system as a largely autonomous organization that responds to external demands according to its own pace. The development of a central school authority since the progressive era seems to provide the basis for such a view. Between the turn of the century and the 1920s, school governance shifted from neighbourhood-based councils to city-wide school boards. The central office bureaucracy emerged as the locus of power in developing rules to allocate resources, in recruiting teachers and administrators and, in the name of expertise, insulating the conduct of curricular and instructional affairs from external (lay) influences (Tyack 1974, Katz 1987, Cuban 1990, Callahan 1962). Enjoying increasing autonomy from external forces, the school system developed an organizational capacity to serve its own organizational interest (i.e. maintenance and expansion).

By the late 1960s and the early 1970s, Zeigler and Jennings (1974) found that public school governance was largely closed to lay influence. The isolated system seemed alien to democratic practices. Zeigler and Jennings' study focused on the top of the system in a nationally representative sample of 186 boards with a total of 1130 respondents. They found limited evidence to suggest that school districts operate 'responsive and responsible governance' even at a time of heightened concern about citizen participation in the 1960s (p. 242). Instead, in school board selection, they found that 'competition is limited, sponsorship and pre-emptive appointments common. Challengers to the status quo are infrequent; incumbents are but rarely challenged and more rarely still defeated. There are often no issue differences at all in an election, and when there are they seldom deal with the educational program, per se' (p. 245). The superintendency was seen as the centre of power. 'Our overall conclusion is that boards are likely to become spokesman for the superintendent to the community; their representational roles are reversed, and the superintendent becomes the dominant policy maker' (p. 250). Thus, Zeigler and Jennings observed a serious gap between the public beliefs on democratic control and the reality of school decision making. A similar degree of non-responsiveness was found in a study of administration-lay communications in 11 American and Canadian districts by Tucker and Zeigler (1980).

Professional insulation also suggests class and racial inequity in school governance. From the elitist perspective, the community's economic and political elites have exercised control over school policy making (McCarty and Ramsey 1971, Spring 1988, Kirby *et al.* 1973). Indeed, Hays (1964) found service centralization and standardization during the progressive era had tempered political representation of the lower class and failed to improve elite accountability. In assessing representation in 104 big-city school boards during the post-reform 1916 period, Bowles and Gintis (1976) found that while businessmen constituted 45% of all board membership, workers occupied only 9% of all seats (see also Katz 1987). Moreover, studies of New York and other cities showed that the central bureaucracy was not responsive to minorities (Rogers 1968, Fantini *et al.* 1970, Orfield 1969, Schrag 1967). Stability in the socio-political make-up of board members seldom leads to policy innovation (Cistone 1975).

A system of pluralistic representation: In contrast to this notion of an insulated system, analysts see the school board and the central administration moving toward political openness. Leadership succession and policy shift may be brought about by changes in the larger community. Lutz (1970) and Lutz and Iannaccone (1978) suggested a symbiotic relationship between school leadership and community preferences. Tyack and Hansot (1982) argued that the tasks for educational leaders have changed three times as the existing social order was replaced by a new one between 1820 and 1980. While the common-school crusaders of the 19th century mobilized support for public schools, the 'social engineers' of the early 20th century sought legitimacy for their expertise, developed the culture of social efficiency, and placed school 'above politics'. Beginning in the 1960s, according to Tyack and Hansot, educational leaders had to reconcile their professional ideology with racial and social conflict.

Even during the height of his political power in the 1960s, Chicago's Mayor Richard J. Daley appointed representatives from the opposition (i.e. pro-reform forces) to the school board and refrained from direct interference in the selection of the school superintendent. These 'pluralistic' appointment practices at the top of the system, according to Peterson (1976), were closely related to the institutionalization of the 1946 reform – recruitment of a professional superintendent from the outside and establishment of an advisory commission on school board nominations. Seeing direct political control over schools as electorally costly, Daley adhered to the process of pluralist bargaining in school leadership selection. Consequently, the pluralistic school board often engages in policy disagreement. Board members with diverse political beliefs tend to engage in intense conflict both among themselves and with the school superintendent over such controversial issues as racial desegregation (Peterson 1976) and retrenchment (Cibulka 1983, Boyd 1983).

Related to the issue of greater accountability is the argument that minority representation in the school organization is crucial in providing benefits for minority students in the classroom. Using data from the US Office of Civil Rights in districts with at least 15,000 students and 1% black, Meier *et al.* (1989) examined the practice of second-generation discrimination in the classroom following the implementation of a school desegregation plan. They found that black representation on the school board has contributed to the recruitment of black administrators, who in turn have hired more black teachers. Black teachers, according to this study, are crucial in reducing the assignment of black students to classes for the educable mentally retarded. Black representation in the instructional staff also reduces the number of disciplinary actions against black students and increases the latter's participation in classes for the gifted. Similar findings on Hispanic students were presented in a study of 35 large urban districts (Fraga *et al.* 1986). Thus, leadership changes may trigger organizational changes that affect school services for a particular group of clientele.

How central authority manages interest groups

The central authority has to deal with well-organized competing interests. Again, the literature suggests at least two understandings. On the one hand, researchers find the school system can benefit from interest-group activities as it incorporates the latter's demands. On the other hand, studies show that urban schools are increasingly threatened by organized interests, such as the taxpayers' revolt and the teachers' unions.

Incorporating competing interests: School responsiveness to its diverse clients is seen in the development of an increasingly professionalized system. In his study of three central-city districts from 1870 to 1940, Paul Peterson (1985) talked about the 'politics of institutionalization', where clients who had previously been excluded from school services gradually gained admission to the system. Competition among various interests and diverse actors shaped the organizational development of schools. Conflicts were generated by competition among status groups due to ethnic, racial and religious cleavages, as in the 19th and the mid-20th centuries. Class conflict, however, dominated school politics in the first decades of the 20th century. Given the diverse sources of political conflict, no single interest group was found to prevail in all school issues. Thus, the three case studies suggested that the business elites prevailed in taxation issues, while the working class organizations exercised substantial influence over compulsory education. In vocational education, compromise was found.

While diverse actors and interests contributed to an expanding school system in the three cities, the real winners were the school system and its changing clientele. To be sure, there was self-interest involved in the process. After all, the system did gain in prestige, political support and organizational capacity. But, as Peterson (1985) argued, 'this self-interest was disciplined by a concomitant concern for the public interest and, in any case, was readily distinguishable from the class interests of corporate elites' (p. 207). These middle-class school professionals were just as likely to co-operate with trade-union leaders and working-class groups as well as big businesses in the popularization of the educational system during this period. The urban public school system practised the politics of non-exclusion, gradually expanding services from the middle class to the low-income populations, and from the native stocks to various immigrant and racial groups. In his study of the Chicago Teacher Union, Grimshaw (1979) also found that school administrators and school programmes benefited more during the period of reform governance than in the years of machine dominance. Indeed, in central-city school systems, the central bureaucracy has adopted objective, universalistic criteria in distributing resources to neighbourhood schools (Levy *et al.* 1974, Burkhead 1967, Katzman 1971, James *et al.* 1966, Peterson 1981).

Interest groups as autonomous actors: The argument that the school system is capable of accommodating external interests generally undermines the fact that the latter can become autonomous power centres. At times, these actors may threaten the school's interest in organizational maintenance. One major interest is the teachers' union (McDonnell and Pascal 1979). Grimshaw's (1979) study of Chicago's teachers' union suggested that the union has gone through two phases in its relationship with the city and school administration. During the formative years, the union largely co-operated with the administration (and the mayor) in return for a legitimate role in the policy-making process. Cole (1969) also found that union recognition was a key objective in the 1960 teachers' strike in New York City. In the second phase, which Grimshaw characterized as 'union rule', the union became independent of either the local political machine or the reform factions. Instead, it looked to the national union leadership for guidance and engaged in tough bargaining with the administration over better compensation and working conditions. Consequently, Grimshaw argued that policymakers 'no longer are able to set policy unless the policy is consistent with the union's objectives' (p. 150).

Another contending interest the city's schools encounter is an increasingly sceptical taxpaying population, a good portion of which no longer has children in the public schools (Kirst and Garms 1980). The ageing of the city's taxpaying population has placed public education in competition with transportation, hospital and community development over local tax revenues. Discontent with property taxes became widespread during the time of the much-publicized campaign for Proposition 13 in California. According to a 1978 Gallup Poll, when asked to identify their dissatisfaction with various taxing sources for public schools, 52% of the respondents mentioned local property taxes, only 21% cited federal taxes, and just 20% named state taxes (Phi Delta Kappan 1984). Consequently, between 1978 and 1983, of the 67 tax or spending limitation measures on state ballots, 39 were approved (Citrin 1984). Schools, to cope with taxpayer revolt, have to look for additional support from the state (Carroll and Park 1983, Wong 1989).

Adaptation in federal programme implementation

Studies of the implementation of federal programmes for disadvantaged pupils also suggest the importance of bureaucratic adaptation. While there is a consensus on the federal role in redistributive issues, the scholarship is split between two views on local implementation effectiveness – one finds local resistance and the other sees increasing accommodation to the redistributive policy objectives.

The redistributive federal role: Since the Great Society reform of the 1960s, the federal government has clearly focused on social equity issues by promoting racial integration, protecting the educational rights of the handicapped, funding compensatory education and assisting those with limited English proficiency (Peterson *et al.* 1986). These programmes are seen as allocating resources (and legitimacy) to address inequities that primarily arise from class, status and racial cleavages (Lowi 1964, Ripley and Franklin 1984).

The literature on federalism has provided a number of reasons why social redistribution is more likely to be sponsored at the national level (Peterson 1981, Wong 1990, Oates 1972). The federal government enjoys a broader revenue base in which taxes are raised on the ability-to-pay principle. It also represents a constituency with heterogeneous demands. In other words, the national government has both the fiscal capacity and the political resources (often facilitated by interest groups) to respond to social needs. In contrast, localities are more constrained to address social needs because they have a more homogeneous voting constituency, because they need to compete with one another for investment in an open system where businesses and labour can move freely, and because they have a restricted tax base (namely, reliance on land values as a major source of income).

Intergovernmental conflict: Since cities receive substantial federal aid, studies on the politics of urban education have paid particular attention to the implementation of special-needs programmes. There are two understandings of implementation studies. The first set of studies came out in the late 1960s and the 1970s and covered a wide range of policy topics, including compensatory education, bussing programmes to achieve integration and employment programmes in economically depressed communities. They were highly critical of the ways federal programmes operated. In reviewing the complex intergovernmental administrative structure of these programmes, analysts often found confusion, conflict and failure to achieve national social objectives (Murphy 1971, Coleman *et al.* 1975, Pressman and Wildavsky 1973, Martin and McClure 1969, Kirp and Jensen 1985).

The early studies have no doubt raised important political and policy issues. They critically examined the promise and the limits of federal power in social change – whether federal regulations provided the best way to achieve equity objectives, and whether the federal government could overcome obstacles at the subnational level in the delivery of services to the intended beneficiaries. At the same time, these studies have several methodological shortcomings. Most of them based their conclusion on policy failure on a single case, a number of them focused on the initial programme years when implementation problems were highly visible, and virtually all of these studies did not distinguish the programmes that addressed social inequity from those that did not.

Understanding effective implementation: The recent implementation studies tend to overcome methodological shortcomings. First, these studies differentiate the socially redistributive objectives from other purposes in federal programmes. Having made explicit the differences in national purposes, recent research considers intergovernmental conflict as a function of social redistribution goals (Peterson *et al.* 1986, Odden and Marsh 1989, Jung and Kirst 1986).

Programmes that address the disadvantaged often require local governments to reformulate the way services are delivered. Because revenues in these programmes mostly come from the US Congress, the federal government tends to impose numerous and complicated standards on local schools. These regulations are intended to make certain that disadvantaged pupils directly benefit from federal dollars. In compensatory education, for example, local districts are required to use federal funds in schools with the highest concentration of students in poverty, to spend as many local dollars on these schools as on any other school in the district, and to commit at least the same level of local resources as they provided in previous years. In special education, the federal provisions (PL 94-142) give service recipients an official policy-making voice within the service delivery system. The IEP (individualized education plan) provision is designed to allow as much parental participation as possible in evaluation and placement decisions in services for the handicapped. The compensatory education programme requires schools to establish advisory councils composed of parents of children participating in the programme.

There is, as expected, local opposition to federal targeting on disadvantaged pupils. In a study of special-needs programmes in four states and four districts, Peterson *et al.* (1986) found that local districts were tempted, to a greater or lesser extent, to divert funds away from these redistributive programmes to other purposes. Compensatory education funds, for example, were used for general operating purposes that tended to benefit the entire school population. These findings on programme non-compliance are consistent with what the first-generation studies found in numerous education and social programmes. What is not anticipated in the first-generation studies, however, is the extent of local–federal co-operation in programmes that lacked a social equity focus (e.g. vocational education, impact aid programme, and the former ESEA Titles IVB and IVC).

Second, even when they conduct a single case analysis, these studies adopt a longitudinal view. By collecting data from multiple programme years, analysts are able to denote political compromise and programmatic accommodation over time. With the passage of time, a tendency toward increasing intergovernmental accommodation seems to have gradually emerged, as suggested by studies that employed a longitudinal analysis (Kirst and Jung 1982 on Title I, Jung and Kirst 1986, Singer and Butler 1987 on programmes for the handicapped, also see the four-stage process developed by Huberman and Miles 1984). The compensatory education programme, for example, has evolved through three distinct phases (Peterson *et al.* 1986). Originally it was little more than a general federal school aid, with virtually no stipulations attached to the use of funds. Extensive local misuses of these resources prompted the federal government to write tighter regulations. Throughout the 1970s, the programme had acquired an exceedingly well-defined set of rules and guidelines that many state and local officials had difficulty putting in place. Intergovernmental conflict seemed to have tempered by the late 1970s and early 1980s, when federal, state and local administrators worked out their differences.

This transformation from institutional conflict to accommodation has been facilitated by several factors. At the district and school level, a new professional cadre more identified with programme objectives was recruited to administer special programmes, and local officials became more sensitive to federal expectations. At the federal level, policy makers began to doubt whether detailed regulations, tight audits and comprehensive evaluations were unmixed blessings. With the state agency serving as an active mediator, appropriate changes and adjustments were made. Over time, administrators developed programme identifications that transcended governmental boundaries, and a commitment to a co-ordinated effort gradually emerged. As institutional accommodation occurs, local professionals begin to direct more attention to instructional issues, such as whether pullout practices are educationally sound (Knapp 1983, Hill 1977, National Institute of Education 1977).

The pace of moving toward federal–local co-operation in the management of special programmes is not uniform. There are significant variations among districts. This leads to the third methodological characteristic of the recent studies – the use of comparative cases (this can be multiple schools, districts and/or states). Researchers are able to take into consideration variation in local context – specifying sources of local compliance and sources of local resistance. Wong (1990) found that local reform in redistributive services depends on the district's fiscal conditions, political culture and the policy making autonomy of the programme professionals. More severe and prolonged conflict is likely to be found in districts with a weak fiscal capacity and a programme apparatus that is subject to strong political (machine-style) influence. A combination of these fiscal and political circumstances tends to hinder local reform toward redistributive goals. At the other end of the continuum is a district with strong fiscal capacity, autonomous programme professionals and, most of all, teacher commitment to policy objectives (on linking site-level variables to the design of macro policy, see McLaughlin 1987, Elmore 1980, McLaughlin and Berman 1978). In these circumstances, one expects to find rapid transformation from the conflictual to the accommodative phase in special-needs programmes. This institutional process of adaptation is a necessary condition – targeted resources to the needy, for example – for instructional and academic improvement in disadvantaged schools.

Politics of shared decision making

Shared decision making in school policy has taken different forms. In the aftermath of *Brown* and during the Civil Rights movement of the 1960s, reformers began to focus on bureaucratic responsiveness to minorities (Levin 1970, Rogers 1968, Fantini *et al.* 1970, Crain 1968). Beginning in the 1960s and throughout the 1970s, the growth in teacher professionalism has directed the public's attention to site-level decision making because principals and teachers are seen as possessing the knowledge and the technology to improve student performance. At the same time, the federal government began to require citizen advisory bodies at the programme sites in compensatory education and special education (Peterson *et al.* 1986). In the 1980s, parent empowerment at the school sites gained widespread support from reform interest groups, businesses and elected officials (Guthrie *et al.* 1988). Community involvement is further facilitated by state mandates on performance reporting on a school-by-school basis. By the 1990s, virtually all major urban districts have some form of shared governance where parents and community representatives participate in the decision-making structure at the school sites. Examples of these governance arrangements include the New York-style community control; site-based management in Dade County, Rochester, and Salt Lake City; and the Chicago experiment in establishing a locally elected parent council in each school.

The research in the politics of decentralization has examined several key issues: (1) What are the varieties of shared governance? Shared governance differs from district to district in terms of the degree of power-sharing between the central administration and the school sites, the locus of discretionary authority (i.e. subdistrict or school), and the relative role of the professional staff and the lay (parent) representatives (Brown 1990, Guthrie and Reed 1991, Pierce 1978, Levin 1970). (2) Do parents have substantive power in making major decisions at the school site? (3) What are the effects, if any, of school-site governance on educational improvement? Naturally, our knowledge is uneven on each of these issues. As discussed below, we know more about the first two issues than the third one.

Decision-making in shared governance

When school professionals dominate: School professionals often exercise a great deal of control even in decentralized governance. The process of decentralization does not necessarily lead to parent empowerment. When given the opportunity, parents (particularly from low-income, minority groups) do not always exercise their political rights. As demonstrated by the low level of citizen participation in local elections, citizens' choices are often not readily discernible (Verba and Nie 1972, Dahl 1961). Substantial variation in the quality of political involvement also exists among different occupational and socio-economic groups. The electoral strength of minority groups, for example, is often tempered by their low level of registration and turnout. Katznelson (1981) observed a continuation of an uneven distribution of electoral strength among various ethnic communities in the decentralized New York system even after the black protest movement. In each of the five school board elections in North Manhattan during the 1970s, the 'old' neighbourhood groups, of predominantly Jewish and Irish population, continued to dominate the electoral outcomes, thereby maintaining a substantial majority over the 'new' groups in the black and Hispanic neighbourhoods. In recent years, school election in the 31 decentralized districts in New York has continued to attract very low turnouts.

Even when the community and parents are included in school governance, their authority in personnel issues is seriously challenged by the teachers' union. This was most evident in the intense conflict between the union and the community governing board in the Ocean Hill–Brownsville experimental district in New York City during the late 1960s. When the locally elected board fired ten teachers, the union responded with what came to be the first of a series of major strikes. After several strikes and numerous incidents that escalated racial conflict in the community, a state supervisory board was created to protect teachers' union rights from any community board decisions (Meranto 1970, Ravitch 1974). Personnel matters that were related to collective bargaining were taken outside the local governing body under a revised notion of community governance in New York. The Ocean Hill–Brownsville district was incorporated as part of a larger community district, which constituted one of the 31 districts in the decentralized school system. Another controversial decentralization experiment was Detroit, where the central board shared powers with eight regional boards between 1969 and 1982. Early on, the public rejected attempts to use decentralization to improve racial desegregation. Over their tenure, the decentralized boards were charged with corruption and inefficiency (Campbell *et al.* 1985, Grant 1971). Finally, the system was recentralized in 1982.

Union rights and electoral barrier notwithstanding, parental participation can be further constrained by institutional arrangements. The best example of parents' limited influence in school-site decisions is provided by Malen and Ogawa (1988). Based on an in-depth analysis of eight schools in Salt Lake City, the two researchers concluded that decentralized governance did not 'substantially alter the relative power' relationship between the school principal and the parents. Their study suggested several constraints on parental power. First, the site-level partnership consisted of two structures: one for the principal and staff, and the other for both professionals and parents. Naturally, the professionals dominated decision making because they controlled the agenda, maintained privileged access to information on school operation and possessed expertise knowledge. Second, parents were not given the discretionary power over the bulk of the school expenditures. They were not involved in the hiring (or firing) of the principal, and only occasionally were they asked to evaluate the performance of the school staff. Third, parents were not elected, but received 'invitations' from the principal to participate (on co-optation, see Jennings 1980). Consequently, parent-members shared similar values with the principal and acted primarily as supports of 'system maintenance' (see also Mann 1974). Similar findings of limited parental impact are suggested in an earlier review by Boyd and Crowson (1981). In federally funded compensatory education, parent advisory councils also have modest impact on programme design and implementation (McLaughlin and Shields 1986, Wong 1990).

When parents are empowered: The best recent effort to make sure that parents are indeed the key decision makers is found in the local school council in the Chicago Public Schools. Following a long legislative process, the 1988 Chicago School Reform Act (P.A. 85-1418) mandates comprehensive reforms in school governance (Wong and Rollow 1990). The current school reform in Chicago represents an opportunity for parents, school staff and community groups to work together on educational improvement. The reform is designed to restore public confidence by granting parents substantial 'ownership' over schools. To enhance accountability, the central office has decentralized policy making to locally elected parent councils and the principal at the school site. The 11-member council consists of six parents (i.e. the majority), two community representatives, two teachers, and the principal. There is also one student member at the high school level. The first council election in 1989 seems to have provided for a fair representation of various minority groups in the school system.

Members of the local council are given substantial authority – they can hire and fire the principal, allocate school funds and develop school improvement plans. With training and support from business and public interest groups, local councils have written their by-laws, approved current school budgets and successfully reviewed the principals' contract. The first major exercise of parental power was demonstrated in the decision on the principalship, a leadership position that would advance educational improvement. Of the 276 principals (representing half of the schools in the system) who were up for review in March 1990, 82% were retained in a new 4-year contract (see Designs for Change 1990). Councils that were dominated by racial minorities retained their white principals at a high rate of 78%. However, principals who failed to get contract renewal were more likely to hold 'interim' positions in predominantly Hispanic schools. In these neighbourhoods, community groups seemed particularly active in pushing for the selection of candidates who promised to be more responsive to their needs, such as solving the problem of overcrowding in the classroom.

Linking shared governance to school improvement

There is a dearth of empirical studies on the connection between democratic governance and urban school improvement, particularly when parents do gain substantive power. Those who studied community control generally painted an unfavourable picture – patronage, low voters' turnout, mixed staff morale and politicized leadership (see earlier discussion). In strong disagreement with most of the observations on the Ocean Hill–Brownsville community control experiment, Fantini *et al.* (1970) saw positive results. They found that the district was able to fill leadership positions with minorities, to develop a reform climate of community input to schools and to implement innovative programmes that were designed to improve educational performance. Furthermore, in a longitudinal study of the decentralization experience in New York City, Rogers and Chung (1983) concluded that locally elected boards (those that were reflective of racial and ethnic composition of the communities) were more effective in managing ethnic succession in schools because these boards were more politically stable and enjoyed greater legitimacy. Their eight case studies also suggested that, in the longer run, decentralized boards were able to tackle education programming and staff development (including raising staff morale).

It is too soon to know whether Chicago's experiment in parental empowerment will lead to better student performance. Schools are only in their early years of reform and are still in the process of incorporating new mechanisms of governance. Principals, parents, teachers and other key actors are learning more about the new organizational life, and are seeking ways to work with one another (see Brown 1990, Clune and White 1988). In an 11-school survey, Ford (1991) found that principals find it a challenge to balance their role as a supervisor/manager and as a partner in the parent-dominated Local School Council. The success of institution-building is critical to school improvement. Yet the process is likely to be uneven – constrained by neighbourhood differences in socio-economic resources, the availability of competent and dedicated principals, the commitment of parents and the supply of a good teaching force, particularly among racial minorities. In a study of three Chicago high schools, Cibulka (1991) observed significant differences in community support for the principals (see also Summerfield 1971, Minar 1966, Boyd 1976). With variation from school to school, the local parent council may regain public trust at the school–community level. In the long run, new governing practices may substantially shape the organizational life within school, e.g. faculty–parent–community relationship in curricular planning. Parent participation on locally elected councils may even stimulate positive feelings towards school life, which would lead to better attendance rates and higher student and teacher morale. If successful, Chicago reform may revive public education in inner-city neighbourhoods.

Politics of exiting

City schools are adversely affected by the politics of exiting – where schooling choice made by individual families has accumulated a pattern of middle-class migration from central-city schools (Hirschman 1971, Tiebout 1956). The literature has examined the effects of exiting on urban schools from two perspectives. The first set of literature, the popular approach, looks at the socio-economic disadvantages of the urban district in the context of suburbanization. The second perspective, which is gaining attention in recent years, considers the political influence of urban districts in the competition for state funding. Both perspectives agree that exiting politics has put central-city schools in an increasingly disadvantageous position.

The socio-economic challenge for urban schools

Due in part to white flight, urban schools generally have experienced noticeable decline in their white enrolment since the early 1970s. This is especially evident in major metropolitan areas, where schools in outlying suburban communities are predominantly white and those in central cities primarily serve minority, low-income pupils (Orfield 1988). In the late 1980s, over 60% of blacks and over 70% of Hispanics enrolled in predominantly minority schools. Hispanic students became more segregated between 1968 and 1986. Exiting also intensifies community conflict over school closure (Cibulka 1983). Consequently, in *City Limits* Paul Peterson (1981) argued that a bifurcated system of education exists between the central city and the surrounding suburbs. While suburban schools are serving a developmental function that would enhance the economic well-being of their stable communities, central-city schools are largely redistributive. The latter shifts resources from the taxpaying population to the non-taxpaying group, a fiscal practice that tends to further reduce its competitive position with suburban schools and non-public institutions.

The concentration of disadvantaged pupils in urban districts has become an important issue in several lawsuits that have challenged the state funding system (Guthrie *et al.* 1988, Carroll and Park 1983, Wong 1991). The needs of urban districts have received mixed responses from the court. In 1974, four of the largest cities in New York (i.e. New York, Buffalo, Rochester and Syracuse) joined the lawsuit as plaintiffs–intervenors in *Levittown* v. *Nyquist*. The four cities argued that the state-aid formula had overstated their taxable wealth but understated their educational burden. Four sets of overburden were cited: (1) municipal service costs due to higher needs of city populations for police, fire, welfare and other services; (2) higher operating costs in urban schools; (3) higher absenteeism costs, thus reducing state aid based on attendance instead of on enrolment; and (4) higher concentration of the disadvantaged in city schools (Berke *et al.* 1984, Fox 1989). In 1982, the Court of Appeals of New York overturned the rulings of the lower courts and ruled that those funding inequities did not violate either the federal or the state constitutions. Funding reform, the court ruled, remained the responsibility of the state legislature. In addition, policy analysts remain sceptical of the overburden concept. For example, a three-state study provided evidence that cities have access to a broader revenue base and that a portion of a city's tax burden can be exported to non-city residents (Brazer and McCarty 1986).

Problems in urban schools, however, have gained recognition in a 1990 state court ruling. In *Abbott* v. *Burke*, the New Jersey Supreme Court unanimously ruled that the state's school finance system was 'unconstitutional as applied to poorer urban school districts'. In arriving at its unanimous decision, the court compared a group of 28 poorest urban districts (which included Newark, Camden and Paterson) with a group of 54 affluent suburban districts. The latter's taxable property valuation per pupil was almost six times that of the former. The rich districts were able to spend 40% more on their pupils than the less affluent districts. Consequently, the educational quality differed, according to the court. In Camden, a poorer district, there was one computer for 58 children, while in Princeton, an affluent district, there was one computer for eight children. Foreign language instruction began at 9th grade in Jersey City but started in preschool in well-off Montclair (*New York Times* 10 June 1990). Consequently, the court directed the legislature to address the special educational needs of the poorer urban districts so that their funding would be increased to become 'substantially equivalent to the average of that of property-rich suburban districts' (Goertz and Goertz 1990, Wong 1991).

Declining political influence of urban schools

Exiting decisions of middle-class families and businesses not only weaken the tax base for city schools but they also reduce the political influence of the urban district in the state legislature. The latter is illustrated in the city–suburban contention over aid to the disadvantaged in the state legislature (Cronin 1973, Berke *et al.* 1984). In Illinois, for example, the 1978 legislature reduced the weights assigned to poor students which, in effect, decreased state aid to inner-city schools. Of the 86 lawmakers who voted for the bill, 85 represented districts outside the City of Chicago. In contrast, 47 of the 64 legislators who voted against the measure came from both major parties in Chicago. Regional cleavages tend to undermine funding support for central-city schools (Wong 1989).

Coalition building for targeted funding for the urban disadvantaged pupils is difficult when the state lawmakers have to deal with competing interest groups. During the fiscally stressed 1980s, special-needs interest groups (e.g. bilingual-education advocacy groups) were less influential than taxpayers who wanted to reduce their tax burden. Instead, broad-based coalitions in support of 'omnibus' legislative packages seemed crucial to state funding decisions (McLaughlin and Catterall 1984). Under enormous public pressure for lowered taxes, the Arizona legislature adopted a comprehensive school reform package in a 1980 special session. This legislation was approved after extensive bargaining among more than 100 interest groups that came from the taxpaying community, the professional sector and municipalities (Webb 1981). In other words, groups that represent the special-needs student populations find it difficult to operate effectively in a retrenchment climate.

Politics of competition

Choice within the public sector

As governmental institutions, urban schools are facing several key policy challenges – retention of middle-class families, racial integration, service provision for children of poverty and improvement in student performance, among others. To meet these challenges, urban school districts have developed a set of 'mediated choice programmes' – student schooling choice mediated by a complex selection process. They are often referred to as magnet programmes. According to a major study conducted in 1983, there were over 1100 magnet schools in 130 urban districts of more than 20,000 students (Blank *et al.* 1983). By 1989, there were over 2500 magnet schools, of which 60% operate at the elementary level (US Secretary of Education 1989). Among the big-city districts with prominent magnet programmes are Milwaukee, Houston, Los Angeles, Chicago, San Diego and Cincinnati. New York's District 4, which includes Spanish Harlem, has made choice mandatory for its 23 junior high schools since 1983.

The most important feature of choice in public schools is that it combines market-like mechanisms for parents with a decentralized authority system. Magnet schools or programmes within a school are distinguished by academic specialties, such as the fine arts, maths and science, and foreign languages. Enrolment in these programmes is not restricted by the regular attendance boundaries. Instead, admissions are governed by racial requirements and other selective criteria and by the fact that non-public schools are not part of the arrangement. In many districts, schools enjoy discretion in pupil selection, using criteria that include entry-test results, parental agreements, teacher recommendations and other measures of a student's fitness to enrol in a particular programme.

Choice programmes are controversial. Opposition to magnet programmes has been based on concerns over equal educational opportunities and the perpetuation of elitism (Levin 1987, Moore and Davenport 1990, Witte 1990, Raywid 1985). Magnet programmes tend to 'cream off' better students and other resources out of their neighbourhood schools (Downs 1970). Local residents may perceive that the conversion of their neighbourhood school to a choice programme deprives them of direct access to their community-based service institution (Metz 1986). Questions have been raised on the implementation of a system-wide choice plan – distribution of school information to all parents, transportation cost and compliance with civil rights provisions. In short, choice programmes may come into conflict with other restructuring efforts in public schools (Cibulka 1990) and may destabilize school governance (Weeres 1988).

Institutional functions of choice programmes

Major shortcomings notwithstanding, choice programmes have become quite effective in addressing the institutional and political needs of the urban district. First, magnet schools and a voluntary student-transfer policy serve an important role in bringing about racial integration without aggravating racial conflict. In her analysis of desegregation activities in 119 districts, Christine Rossell (1990) argues that voluntary plans are a more effective means to achieve the goal of racial integration. In arriving at this conclusion, Rossell refutes the conventional wisdom as well as her own earlier position that mandatory reassignment is the only way to achieve desegregation and denies that parental choice would hinder socially desirable objectives. Compared with mandatory plans, voluntary magnet programmes are found to be superior in equity, efficiency and effectiveness.

Rossell cites three sets of evidence to support her claim. First, the voluntary plan is more equitable because it 'empowers both black and white parents and is preferred by both races' (p. 211). In a mandatory reassignment plan, both black and white parents exercise no choice unless they exit the public school system. Second, the voluntary plan is more efficient because 'the ratio of students assigned to students enrolled' is high (p. 208). In mandatory plans, on average, as many as half of the white students assigned to predominantly minority schools failed to attend. Third, a voluntary plan is more effective because it produces greater interracial exposure, which is defined as the proportion of white students in an average minority child's school. This indicator is chosen because it is more sensitive to white enrolment, i.e. interracial exposure decreases as white enrolment declines.

Central to the success of voluntary plans is parental choice. From Rossell's perspective, white parents can be motivated to send their children to predominantly black schools if they are given sufficient incentives. In this regard, magnet programmes that are endowed with additional resources are pivotal. In an extensive examination of the 355 magnet curricula in a 20-district sub-sample, she found that there is virtually no difference in the percentage of whites attending magnet programmes that are located in minority neighbourhoods between the two types of plans. On average, 37% of white students were enrolled in the voluntary plans of specialty curricula in minority locations as compared with 32% in the mandatory plans. In other words, parental choice seems to be as effective as mandatory reassignment in accomplishing racial integration. These findings are consistent with the conclusions suggested in a number of studies on magnet programmes in the urban district (Armor 1989, Raywid 1985, Alves and Willie 1987).

Second, as suggested above, choice programmes are often established to retain a middle-class presence in city schools. While Hirschman and other policy analysts argue that reform in public schools, like other 'monopolized' public services, is not likely to be driven by the exit of their clientele, the emergence of choice programmes seems to offer a counter-example. A good example is the Six School Complex in Washington, DC. Located in a community that has become increasingly upper middle class in character, the six elementary schools were faced with closure due to declining enrolment in 1974. To keep these schools open, well-organized parent groups worked with the district to convert the schools to magnet programmes. The boundaries of the schools were combined to create one attendance area, with parents being able to choose from among the schools' unique curricular offerings on a space available basis. In 1987, 63% of the Complex's enrolment came from the more affluent neighbourhoods (Jones 1988). Furthermore, choice programmes seem to help reverse the 'exiting' trend in some districts. In Buffalo, for example, choice programmes were used to retain white pupils as well as to attract students from non-public schools. Between 1977 and 1986, over 2800 pupils left the non-public sector to enrol in Buffalo's choice programmes. Whites comprised four out of five of the new enrollees (Rossell 1987). In Chicago, the opening of Whitney Young Magnet High School in 1975 was clearly designed to complement the city's urban renewal efforts (Campbell and Levine 1977). The specialized curriculum in magnet schools can match the needs of the local labour market (Borman and Spring 1984).

Third, choice programmes are innovative efforts to improve educational quality. Chubb and Moe (1990) have conducted a systematic study to link school autonomy (from electoral control) to student performance (also see Coleman and Hoffer 1987, Boyd and Walberg 1990). The two researchers see public schools as far too responsive to external political demands. They argue that 'public schools are governed by institutions of direct democratic control' (p. 67). These institutions are 'inherently destructive of school autonomy, and inherently conducive to bureaucracy' (p. 47). In their view, educational governance is an open system where political interests have successfully expanded the bureaucracy and proliferated programmatic rules to protect their gains.

Using the High School and Beyond data for 1982 and 1984 and the Administrator and Teacher Survey data for 1984, Chubb and Moe found that politics and bureaucracy do not contribute to the desirable forms of school organization that link to higher academic performance of their students. Instead, the more market-oriented non-public schools are far more likely to produce what they call effective organizations. These high-performance schools, mostly non-public, can be distinguished from low-performance schools (mostly urban public): 'Their goals are clearer and more academically ambitious, their principals are stronger educational leaders, their teachers are more professional and harmonious, their course work is more academically rigorous, and their classrooms are more orderly and less bureaucratic' (p. 99). Consequently, Chubb and Moe suggest parental choice in education as a way to eliminate the adverse effects of democratic politics and bureaucracy.

The Chubb and Moe perspective has generated a great deal of controversy. Sceptics point to their argument's heavy reliance on the 116 items in five sets of tests that took 63 minutes to complete (pp. 72–74, see Kirst 1990). In fact, their analysis focused on interschool variation on gains over a total of 23 items between the sophomore and the senior years. As Kirst (1990) pointed out in a review, 'Using a 1980–82 limited content coverage test is a very weak basis for judging the potential effects of these 1983–90 curricular or any other reforms'. The Chubb and Moe argument also largely ignores the enormous variation among tracks and classes within a school (Dreeben and Barr 1988, Oakes 1985).

The Chubb and Moe recommendation on transforming public education into a market-place seems to be supported by several studies on choice programmes. It should be noted that the early voucher experiment in Alum Rock produced no discernible difference in students' academic outcomes between choice and non-choice programmes (Capell and Doscher 1981). Evaluation of recent choice programmes, however, offers some evidence that connects choice (i.e. student self-selection and site-level governance) to educational improvement. As a 1982 report observed, magnet schools have expanded their initial focus on racial balance to include 'an emphasis on providing quality education or educational options for the district' (Fleming *et al.* 1982, also see Raywid 1985). Using a longitudinal data set on Buffalo's ten early childhood magnet programmes, two analysts concluded that beginning in the third project year, students in these programmes 'systematically perform at a statistically significant and higher level in both reading and mathematics than do the control-group comparisons' (Haskins and Alessi 1989). Better student performance was said to be linked to better curricular planning, greater parental involvement, higher level of racial integration and more effective instructional practices. The real challenge is whether similar student gains can be accomplished when the small-scale choice programmes become system-wide policy.

Conclusions

What is particularly striking in this partial review of the politics of education is the fact that diverse governing structures co-exist within the urban school system. As suggested in the proposed integrative framework, one finds choice programmes in the midst of a powerful central bureaucracy in the urban district. One also sees dedicated parents vigorously involved in site-level governing councils while others continue to exit to the nearby district or the non-public sector. Thus, the urban school organization consists of diverse structures that are distinguishable by their particular kind of politics. To understand the totality of the politics of urban education, one clearly needs to differentiate both the balance of power between layers within the school policy organization as well as the ways parents and other clients exercise their influence in school affairs.

The integrative framework also suggests that the urban district is moving away from centralized governance. Decentralization represents an institutional response to policy challenges. There are, however, varieties in decentralized governance. In districts where minority representation and accountability become important issues, decentralization may be the appropriate response. Districts that are required to achieve racial integration may choose to implement magnet programmes. To stem the outmigration of middle-class parents, schooling choice may be instituted. In other words, these structural changes are not likely to disappear but instead will become institutionalized.

Indeed, differentiated political patterns exist within the urban district because they serve important institutional functions. This becomes apparent when one considers eliminating one or more of these patterns. If the politics of organizational maintenance and adaptation (cell A in table 1) is eliminated, the school system will no longer possess an institutional memory. It will lack policy enforcement capacity (such as on civil rights issues) as well as its ability to conduct programme evaluation. The district will lose its co-ordinative functions in mediating rival interests and will depart from the concept of universalism in service provision. Likewise, an elimination of the politics of shared governance and community control (a cell B-type authority structure) will weaken accountability and may temper fair representation at the neighbourhood level. If the politics of exiting (cell C) no longer exists – a public school system that does not allow residents to exit – an important and fundamental right in our democracy will be compromised. Indeed, in *Pierce v. Society of Sisters* the Supreme Court has affirmed the private schools' right to provide services. Finally, if the urban district does not allow for the politics of competition (cell D), schools may not be able to promote racial integration, middle-class retention, and curricular innovation in a less costly manner.

In sum, diversity in governing structures will remain for some time and will continue to shape our understanding of urban school politics. Indeed, institutional diversity challenges policy makers to address two sets of questions – what are the major functions that the public school system serves and what kind of institutional and political arrangements would best serve those functions? As a growing field of study, scholarship in the politics of urban education will continue to provide a useful groundwork for formulating solutions to these critical policy issues.

Note

This is a revised version of a paper delivered at the 1991 Annual Meeting of the American Political Science Association, The Washington Hilton, 29 August–1 September 1991. The author acknowledges research support from the Culpeper foundation.

References

ALMOND, G. and VERBA, S. (1965) *The Civic Culture: Political Attitudes and Democracy in Five Nations* (Boston: Little, Brown and Co).

ALVES, M. and WILLIE, C. (1987) 'Controlled choice assignments: a new and more effective approach to school desegregation', *The Urban Review*, 19 (2), pp. 67–88.

ARMOR, D.J. (1989) 'After busing: education and choice', *The Public Interest*, 95 (Spring), pp. 24–37.

BACHRACH, P. and BARATZ, M. (1962) 'The two faces of power', *American Political Science Review*, 56, pp. 947–952.

BALL, S. (1987) *The Micro-Politics of the School: Towards a Theory of School Organization* (London: Methuen).

BANKS, J. (1988) *Multiethnic Education: Theory and Practice* (Boston: Allyn & Bacon).

BARR, B. and DREEBEN, R. (1983) *How Schools Work* (Chicago: University of Chicago Press).

BERKE, J., GOERTZ, M. and COLEY, R. (1984) *Politicians, Judges and City Schools: Reforming School Finance in New York* (New York: Russell Sage Foundation).

BIDWELL, C. (1965) 'The school as a formal organization', in J. March (ed.) *Handbook of Organizations* (Skokie: Rand McNally) pp. 972–1022.

BLANK, R.K. *et al.* (1983) *Survey of Magnet Schools: Analyzing A Model for Quality Integrated Education* (Washington, DC: James H. Lowry and Associates and Abt Associates).

BLASE, J. (ed.) (1991) *Politics of Life in Schools* (Newbury Park, CA: Corwin Press, Sage).

BORMAN, K. and SPRING, J. (1984) *Schools in Central Cities* (White Plains, NY: Longman).

BOWLES, S. and GINTIS, H. (1976) *Schooling in Capitalist America* (New York: Basic Books).

BOYD, W.L. (1975) *Community and Status Group Conflict in Suburban School Politics* (Beverly Hills: Sage).

BOYD, W.L. (1976) 'The public, the professionals and educational policy making: who governs?', *Teachers College Record*, 77 (4), pp. 539–577.

BOYD, W.L. (ed.) (1979) 'Declining school enrollments: politics and management', *Education and Urban Society*, 11, pp. 275–431.

BOYD, W.L. (1983) 'Rethinking educational policy and management: political science and educational administration in the 1980's', *American Journal of Education*, (November), pp. 1–29.

BOYD, W.L. and CROWSON, R. (1981) 'The changing conception and practice of public school administration', in D.C. Berliner (ed.) *Review of Research in Education*, Vol. 9 (Washington, DC: American Educational Research Association), pp. 311–373.

BOYD, W.L. and WALBERG, H. (1990) *Choice in Education: Potential and Problems* (Berkeley: McCutchan).

BRAZER, H. and MCCARTY, T. (1986) 'Municipal overburden: an empirical analysis', *Economics of Education Review*, 5, pp. 353–361.

BROWN, D. (1990) *Decentralization and School-Based Management* (London: Falmer).

BURKHEAD, J. (1967) *Input and Output in Large-City High Schools* (Syracuse: Syracuse University).

BURLINGAME, M. (1988) 'The politics of education and educational policy: the local level', in N.J. Boyan (ed.) *Handbook of Research on Educational Administration* (New York: Longman), pp. 439–451.

CALLAHAN, R. (1962) *Education and the Cult of Efficiency* (Chicago: University of Chicago Press).

CAMPBELL, C. and LEVINE, D. (1977) 'Whitney Young Magnet High School of Chicago and urban renewal', in D. Levine and R. Havighurst (eds) *The Future of Big-City Schools* (Berkeley: McCutchan Publishing), pp. 139–149.

CAMPBELL, R. *et al.* (1985) *The Organization and Control of American Schools*, 5th edn (Columbus, Ohio: Charles E. Merrill Publishing).

CAPELL, F. and DOSCHER, L. (1981) *A Study of Alternatives in American Education, Vol. VI: Student Outcomes At Alum Rock 1974–1976* (Santa Monica: Rand Corporation).

CARROLL, S. and PARK, R. (1983) *The Search for Equity in School Finance* (Cambridge, MA: Ballinger).

CHUBB, J. and MOE, T. (1990) *Politics, Markets and America's Schools* (Washington, DC: Brookings Institution).

CIBULKA, J. (1983) 'Explaining the problem: A comparison of closings in ten US Cities', *Education and Urban Society*, 15 (2), pp. 165–174.

CIBULKA, J. (1990) 'Choice and the restructuring of American education', in W. L. Boyd and H. Walberg (eds) *Choice in Education: Potential and Problems* (Berkeley: McCutchan), pp. 43–62.
CIBULKA, J. (1992) 'Local school reform: The changing shape of educational politics in Chicago', in K. Wong (ed.) *The Politics of Policy Innovation in Chicago* (Greenwich, CT: JAI Press).
CISTONE, P. J. (ed.) (1975) *Understanding School Boards* (Lexington, MA: Lexington).
CITRIN, J. (1984) 'Introduction: The legacy of Proposition 13', in T. Schwadron (ed.) *California and the American Tax Revolt* (Berkeley: University of California Press), pp. 1–69.
CLUNE, W. and WHITE, P. (1988) *School-based Management Institutional Variation, Implementation and Issues for Further Research* (New Brunswick, NJ: Center for Policy Research in Education).
COLE, S. (1969) *The Unionization of Teachers: A Case Study of the United Federation of Teachers* (New York: Praeger).
COLEMAN, J. S. *et al.* (1975) *Trends in School Desegregation 1968–73* (Washington, DC: Urban Institute).
COLEMAN, J. S. and HOFFER, T. (1987) *Public and Private High Schools* (New York: Basic Books).
CRAIN, R. (1968) *The Politics of School Desegregation* (Chicago: Aldine).
CRONIN, J. (1973) *The Control of Urban Schools* (New York: Free Press).
CUBAN, L. (1990) 'Reforming again, again, and again', *Educational Researcher*, 19 (1), pp. 3–13.
DAHL, R. (1961) *Who Governs?* (New Haven: Yale University Press).
DESIGNS FOR CHANGE (1990) *Chicago Principals: Changing of the Guard* (Chicago: Author).
DOWNS, A. (1970) 'Competition and community schools', in H. Levin (ed.) *Community Control of Schools* (New York: Clarion Book), pp. 219–249.
DREEBEN, R. and BARR, R. (1988) 'The formation and instruction of ability groups', *American Journal of Education*, 97 (1), pp. 34–64.
EASTON, D. and DENNIS, J. (1969) *Children in the Political System: Origins of Political Legitimacy* (New York: McGraw-Hill).
ELIOT, T. H. (1959) 'Toward an understanding of public school politics', *American Political Science Review*, 52, pp. 1032–1057.
ELMORE, R. (1980) 'Backward mapping: implementation research and policy decisions', *Political Science Quarterly*, 94 (4), pp. 601–616.
FANTINI, M., GITTELL, M. and MAGAT, R. (1970) *Community Control and the Urban School* (New York: Praeger).
FLEMING, P. *et al.* (1982) *Survey of Magnet Schools: Interim Report* (Washington, DC: James H. Lowry & Associates).
FORD, D. (1991) *The School Principal and Chicago School Reform: Principals' Early Perceptions of Reform Initiatives* (Chicago: Chicago Panel on Public School Policy and Finance).
FOX, J. N. (1989) 'School finance and the economics of education: an essay review of major works', *Educational Evaluation and Policy Analysis*, 11 (Spring), pp. 69–83.
FRAGA, L., MEIER, K. and ENGLAND, R. (1986) 'Hispanic Americans and educational policy: limits to equal access', *Journal of Politics*, 48, pp. 850–876.
FUHRMAN, S. (1988) 'State politics and education reform', in J. Hannaway and R. Crowson (eds) *The Politics of Reforming School Administration* (Philadelphia: Falmer), pp. 61–75.
FUHRMAN, S. and MALEN, B. (1991) *The Politics of Curriculum and Testing* (London: Falmer).
GOERTZ, R. and GOERTZ, M. (1990) 'The Quality Education Act of 1990: New Jersey responds to Abbott v. Burke', *Journal of Education Finance*, 16 (1), pp. 104–114.
GRANT, W. (1971) 'Community control vs. integration: the case of Detroit', *The Public Interest*, 24 (Summer), pp. 62–79.
GREENSTEIN, F. (1965) *Children and Politics* (New Haven: Yale University Press).
GRIMSHAW, W. (1979) *Union Rule in the Schools* (Lexington: D. C. Heath).
GUTHRIE, J. and REED, R. (1991) *Educational Administration and Policy: Effective Leadership for American Education* (Englewood Cliffs, NJ: Prentice Hall).
GUTHRIE, J., GARMS, W. and PIERCE, L. (1988) *School Finance and Education Policy*, 2nd edn (Englewood Cliffs, NJ: Prentice Hall).
GUTMANN, A. (1987) *Democratic Education* (Princeton: Princeton University Press).
HANNAWAY, J. and CROWSON, R. (eds) (1989) *The Politics of Reforming School Administration* (London: Falmer).
HASKINS, G. and ALESSI, S. (1989) 'An early childhood center developmental model for public school settings', *Teachers College Record*, 90 (3), pp. 415–433.
HAYS, S. (1964) 'The politics of reform in municipal government in the progressive era', *Pacific Northwest Quarterly*, 55 (October), pp. 157–169.

HILL, P. (1977) *Compensatory Education Services*, Report Prepared for the US Office of Education (Washington, DC: Department of Health, Education and Welfare).

HIRSCHMAN, A. (1971) *Exit, Voice, and Loyalty* (Cambridge: Harvard University Press).

HUBERMAN, M. and MILES, M. (1984) *Innovation Up Close* (New York: Plenum).

HUNTER, F. (1953) *Community Power Structure* (Chapel Hill: University of North Carolina).

JAMES, H. T., KELLY, J. A. and GARMS, W. (1966) *Determinants of Educational Expenditures in Large Cities of the United States* (Palo Alto, CA: School of Education, Stanford University).

JENNINGS, M. K. and NIEMI, R. (eds) (1974) *The Political Character of Adolescence: The Influence of Families and Schools* (Princeton: Princeton University Press).

JENNINGS, R. (1980) 'School advisory councils in America: frustration and failure', in G. Baron (ed.) *The Politics of School Government* (New York: Pergamon Press).

JONES, J. (1988) 'The six school complex: a "cluster" provides choice', *Equity and Choice*, (Winter), pp. 31–38.

JUNG, R. and KIRST, M. (1986) 'Beyond mutual adaptation, into the bully pulpit: recent research on the federal role in education', *Educational Administration Quarterly*, 22 (3), pp. 80–109.

KATZ, M. B. (1987) *Reconstructing American Education* (Cambridge: Harvard University Press).

KATZMAN, M. (1971) *The Political Economy of Urban Schools* (Cambridge, MA: Harvard University Press).

KATZNELSON, I. (1981) *City Trenches* (New York: Pantheon).

KIRBY, T., HARRIS, T. R. and CRAIN, R. (1973) *Political Strategies in Northern School Desegregation* (Lexington: Lexington Books).

KIRP, D. and JENSEN, A. (1985) *School Days, Rule Day* (Philadelphia: Falmer).

KIRST, M. (1990) 'Review of politics, markets and America's schools', *Politics of Education Bulletin*, Fall.

KIRST, M. and GARMS, W. (1980) 'The political environment of school finance policy in the 1980s', in J. Guthrie (ed.) *School Finance Politics and Practices – The 1980s: A Decade of Conflict* (Cambridge: Ballinger), pp. 47–75.

KIRST, M. and JUNG, R. (1982) 'The utility of a longitudinal approach in assessing implementation: a thirteen-year view of title I, ESEA', in W. Williams *et al.* (eds) *Studying Implementation: Methodological and Administrative Issues* (New York: Chatham House), pp. 119–148.

KIRST, M. and WALKER, D. (1971) 'An analysis of curriculum policy-making', *Review of Educational Research*, 41, pp. 479–509.

KNAPP, M. *et al.* (1983) *Cumulative Effects of Federal Education Policies on Schools and Districts* (Menlo Park, CA: SRI International).

LANOUE, G. R. (1982) 'Political science', in H. E. Mitzel *et al.* (eds) *Encyclopedia of Educational Research* (Washington, DC: American Educational Research Association), Vol. 3, pp. 1421–1426.

LAYTON, D. (1982) 'The emergence of the politics of education as a field of study', in H. L. Gray (ed.) *The Management of Educational Institutions* (Barcombe, Lewes, UK: Falmer), pp. 109–126.

LEVIN, H. (ed.) (1970) *Community Control of Schools* (New York: Clarion).

LEVIN, H. (1987) 'Education as public and private good', *Journal of Policy Analysis and Management*, 6 (4), pp. 628–641.

LEVY, F. *et al.* (1974) *Urban Outcomes* (Berkeley: University of California Press).

LORTIE, D. (1975) *Schoolteacher* (Chicago: University of Chicago Press).

LOWI, T. (1964) 'American business and public policy, case studies and political theory', *World Politics*, July, pp. 677–715.

LUTZ, F. W. (ed.) (1970) *Toward Improved Urban Education* (Worthington, OH: Charles A. Jones).

LUTZ, F. W. and IANNACCONE, L. (eds) (1978) *Public Participation in Local School Districts* (Lexington, MA: Lexington).

MALEN, B. and OGAWA, R. (1988) 'Professional-patron influence on site-based governance councils: a confounding case study', *Educational Evaluation and Policy Analysis*, 10 (4), pp. 251–270.

MANN, D. (1974) 'Political representation and urban school advisory councils', *Teachers College Record*, 75 (3), pp. 279–307.

MARTIN, R. and MCCLURE, P. (1969) *Title I of ESEA: Is It Helping Poor Children?* (Washington, DC: Washington Research Project of the Southern Center for Studies in Public Policy and the NAACP Legal Defense of Education Fund).

MCCARTY, D. and RAMSEY, C. (1971) *The School Managers: Power and Conflict in American Public Education* (Westport: Greenwood).

MCDONNELL, L. and PASCAL, A. (1979) *Organized Teachers in American Schools* (Santa Monica: Rand).

MCLAUGHLIN, M. (1987) 'Learning from experience: lessons from policy implementation', *Educational Evaluation and Policy Analysis*, 9 (2), pp. 171–178.

McLaughlin, M. and Berman, P. (1978) *Federal Programs Supporting Educational Change Vol. 8: Implementing and Sustaining Innovation* (Santa Monica: Rand).
McLaughlin, M. and Catterall, J. (1984) 'Notes on the new politics of education', *Education and Urban Society*, 16 (May), pp. 375–381.
McLaughlin, M. and Shields, P. (1986) 'Involving parents in schools: lessons for policy', paper prepared for the Conference on Effects of Alternative Designs in Compensatory Education, Washington, DC, June.
Meier, K., Stewart, J. and England, R. (1989) *Race, Class and Education* (Madison: University of Wisconsin Press).
Meranto, P. (1970) *School Politics in the Metropolis* (Columbus: Charles E. Merrill).
Metz, M. (1986) *Different By Design: The Context and Character of Three Magnet Schools* (New York: Routledge and Kegan Paul).
Minar, D. W. (1966) 'The community basis of conflict in school system politics', *American Sociological Review*, 31 (4), pp. 822–834.
Mitchell, D. (1988) 'Educational politics and policy: the state level', in N. J. Boyan (ed.) *Handbook of Research on Educational Administration* (New York: Longman), pp. 453–466.
Moore, D. and Davenport, S. (1990) 'Choice: the new improved sorting machine', in W. L. Boyd and H. J. Walberg (eds) *Choice in Education: Potential and Problems* (Berkeley: McCutchan), pp. 187–223.
Murphy, J. (1971) 'Title I of ESEA: the politics of implementing federal education reform', *Harvard Educational Review*, 41 (February), pp. 36–63.
National Institute of Education (1977) *Administration of Compensatory Education* (Washington, DC: US Department of Health, Education and Welfare).
Oakes, J. (1985) *Keeping Track: How Schools Structure Inequality* (New Haven: Yale University Press).
Oates, W. (1972) *Fiscal Federalism* (New York: Harcourt Brace Jovanovich).
Odden, A. and Marsh, D. (1989) 'State education reform implementation: a framework for analysis', in J. Hannaway and R. Crowson (eds) *The Politics of Reforming School Administration* (London: Falmer), pp. 41–59.
Olneck, M. (1990) 'The recurring dream: symbolism and ideology in intercultural and multicultural education', *American Journal of Education*, 98 (2), pp. 147–174.
Orfield, G. (1969) *The Reconstruction of Southern Education: The Schools and the 1964 Civil Rights Act* (New York: John Wiley).
Orfield, G. (1988) 'Race, income and educational inequality: students and schools at risk in the 1980s', in Council of Chief State School Officers, *School Success for Students at Risk* (Orlando: Harcourt Brace Jovanovich).
Orfield, G. (1990) 'Public policy and college opportunity', *American Journal of Education*, 98 (4), pp. 317–350.
Peterson, P. E. (1974) 'The politics of American education', in F. N. Kerlinger and J. Carroll (eds) *Review of Research in Education*, Vol. 2 (Itasca: F. E. Peacock), pp. 348–389.
Peterson, P. E. (1976) *School Politics Chicago Style* (Chicago: University of Chicago Press).
Peterson, P. E. (1981) *City Limits* (Chicago: University of Chicago Press).
Peterson, P. E. (1985) *The Politics of School Reform 1870–1940* (Chicago: University of Chicago Press).
Peterson, P. E., Rabe, B. and Wong, K. (1986) *When Federalism Works* (Washington, DC: Brookings Institution).
Phi Delta Kappan (1984) *Gallup Polls of Attitudes Toward Education, 1969–1984: A Topical Summary* (Bloomington, IN: Phi Delta Kappan).
Pierce, L. (1978) *School Site Management* (Aspen, CO: Aspen Institute for Humanistic Studies).
Pressman, J. and Wildavsky, A. (1973) *Implementation* (Berkeley, CA: University of California Press).
Ravitch, D. (1974) *The Great School Wars* (New York: Basic Books).
Raywid, M. A. (1985) 'Family choice arrangements in public schools: a review of literature', *Review of Educational Research*, 55 (4), pp. 435–467.
Ripley, R. and Franklin, G. (1984) *Congress, the Bureaucracy, and Public Policy* (Homewood, IL: Dorsey Press).
Rogers, D. (1968) *110 Livingston Street* (New York: Random House).
Rogers, D. and Chung, N. (1983) *110 Livingston Street Revisited: Decentralization in Action* (New York: New York University Press).
Rossell, C. (1987) 'The Buffalo controlled choice plan', *Urban Education*, 22 (3), pp. 328–354.
Rossell, C. (1990) *The Carrot or the Stick for School Desegregation Policy* (Philadelphia: Temple University Press).
Schrag, P. (1967) *Village School Downtown* (Boston: Beacon).

SCRIBNER, J.D. (ed.) (1977) *The Politics of Education: Part 2*. The 76th Yearbook of the National Society for the Study of Education (Chicago: University of Chicago Press).
SINGER, J. and BUTLER, J. (1987) 'The education of all handicapped children act: schools as agents of social reform', *Harvard Educational Review*, 57 (2), pp. 25–38.
SPRING, J. (1988) *Conflict of Interests* (New York: Longman).
STONE, C. (1976) *Economic Growth and Neighborhood Discontent* (Chapel Hill: University of North Carolina Press).
SUMMERFIELD, H.L. (1971) *The Neighborhood-based Politics of Education* (Columbus, OH: Charles E. Merrill).
TIEBOUT, C. (1956) 'A pure theory of local expenditures', *Journal of Political Economy*, 64 (October), pp. 416–424.
TIMAR, T. and KIRP, D. (1988) *Managing Educational Excellence* (Philadelphia: Falmer).
TUCKER, H.J. and ZEIGLER, L.H. (1980) *Professionals Versus the Public* (New York: Longman).
TYACK, D. (1974) *The One Best System* (Cambridge: Harvard University Press).
TYACK, D. and HANSOT, E. (1982) *Managers of Virtue* (New York: Basic Books).
US SECRETARY OF EDUCATION (1989) *Educating Our Children: Parents & Schools Together* (Washington, DC: Department of Education).
VERBA, S. and NIE, N. (1972) *Participation in America* (New York: Harper and Row).
WEBB, L.D. (1981) 'The role of special interest groups in the shaping of state educational policy relative to school finance: a case study', *Journal of Education Finance*, 7 (Fall), pp. 168–188.
WEERES, J. (1988) 'Economic choice and the dissolution of community', in W. Boyd and C. Kerchner (eds) *The Politics of Excellence and Choice in Education* (London: Falmer).
WEICK, K. (1976) 'Educational organizations as loosely coupled systems', *Administrative Science Quarterly*, 21, pp. 1–9.
WIRT, F. and KIRST, M. (1982) *Schools in Conflict* (Berkeley: McCutchan).
WITTE, J. (1990) 'Understanding high school achievement: after a decade of research, do we have any confident policy recommendations?', paper delivered at the 1990 Annual Meeting of the American Political Science Association, San Francisco.
WONG, K. (1989) 'Fiscal support for education in American states: the "parity-to-dominance" view examined', *American Journal of Education*, 97 (4), pp. 339–357.
WONG, K. (1990) *City Choices: Education and Housing* (Albany: State University of New York Press).
WONG, K. (1991) 'State reform in education finance: territorial and social strategies', *Publius: The Journal of Federalism*, 21 (3), pp. 125–142.
WONG, K. and ROLLOW, S. (1990) 'A case study of the recent Chicago school reform', *Administrator's Notebook*, 34 (5 and 6).
ZEIGLER, L.H. and JENNINGS, M.K. (1974) *Governing American Schools* (North Scituat, MA: Duxbury).

POLITICS OF EDUCATION ASSOCIATION YEARBOOK 1991, 27–43

2 *Urban education as a field of study: problems of knowledge and power*

James G. Cibulka

A review of the scholarship on urban education indicates that the knowledge base is disputed in fundamental ways and is fragmentary, reflecting educational research generally. Further, many promising practices remain unadopted or poorly implemented, further reinforcing the knowledge-base problem. The political organization of urban schools (centralized bureaucracy, standardized resource allocation rules and bureaucratic incentives) poses a major obstacle to improving this knowledge base. Correspondingly, the task of generating better knowledge of how urban schools can work must overcome several political problems such as the strength of bureaucracies and their allies; the narrow orientation of consumer-oriented reform demands, and the resource inadequacies of urban schools. Restructuring proposals do not address these interlocking impediments. Dramatic improvements in urban schools cannot be expected without attention to how the knowledge base can be improved.

The study of urban education emerged as a field of study in its own right during the 1960s, reflecting a national interest in the problems of poverty, civil rights demands and the plight of our cities. During the 1970s explicit concern about urban educational issues *per se* gradually decreased. The 1990s promise to be a decade in which urban education issues re-emerge as a central concern of researchers and policy makers. High rates of school failure and underachievement, particularly for poor children and those of colour, have focused attention on how to improve urban schools.

Because of this renewed interest, in this chapter I ask what, if anything, the knowledge base on urban education has taught us which might guide future research and policy directions. In the concluding section of the chapter, I turn to the relation between this knowledge base and the political structure and control on our urban school systems. In particular, I address why there appears to be a misfit between these organizational structures and the knowledge requirements for improving urban schools.

Characterizing the knowledge base and its use

Any careful review of the knowledge base on urban schools[1] is likely to lead us to several conclusions:

1. that the knowledge base is disputed in fundamental ways;
2. that the knowledge base is fragmentary, reflecting educational research generally;
3. that despite the limitations of this knowledge base, many promising practices are unadopted or poorly implemented, and there appears to be meagre experimentation in a vast number of urban schools.

I take up each of these themes in turn.

0268–0939/91 $3.00 © 1991 Taylor & Francis Ltd.

A disputed knowledge base

About the only aspect of our knowledge of urban schools which is not disputed is that many of them are quite unappealing places to work and study. Many studies capture the high level of conflict, stress and boredom in a large number of urban schools, e.g. Grant 1988, Louis and Miles 1990, MacLeod 1987. (There also was a large body of critical literature in the 1960s such as Hentoff 1966, Holt 1964, Kozol 1967, Rogers 1969.)

Beyond the descriptions these reports offer, however, the diagnoses of what is wrong can vary dramatically. For example, while Grant offers a generally sympathetic portrayal of teachers' behaviour and their aspirations for their students, MacLeod and others paint a more negative picture of teacher behaviour. Indeed, some decades ago Havighurst (1966) documented how the social origins of teachers and their career preparation contributed to their negative attitudes toward students, particularly when working with African-American youth. The continuing shortage of minority teachers aggravates this problem (Task Force on Teaching as a Profession 1986). Teachers, however, are quick to point to the many constraints on their behaviour – heavy teaching loads, lack of resources, administrative pressure to dilute standards, lack of family support and a host of other factors.

One way to characterize this debate is whether school organization or social background is more responsible for the problems of urban schools. This debate has not been resolved by the status attainment literature in educational sociology (Alexander *et al.* 1978, Wolfe 1985, and many others). From the perspective of left libertarians such as Spring (1989) and research studies informed by critical theory (e.g. Willis 1977), the larger opportunity structures of society, particularly for occupational status, are a key ingredient in explaining school failure for the poor children of colour.

Unfortunately, when we turn to an assessment of specific programmatic reforms, this same Gordian knot appears; there is confusion over the diagnosis and treatment appropriate to urban schools, as the examples below will illustrate.

Compensatory education: Since the 1960s there have been serious debates about the wisdom of compensatory education strategies.[2] Originally the controversy swirled around characterizations of poor children as 'culturally deprived' (Riessman 1962). Critics charged that this amounted to 'blaming the victim'. While this pejorative label has been abandoned, compensatory programmes still begin from the sometimes implicit premise that educationally disadvantaged children possess untapped and unrealized motivations for school which require special intervention. This notion of differences remains a major source of controversy in research on urban disadvantaged children.

The major compensatory education programme Chapter 1 has shown modest results in improving learning outcomes for educationally disadvantaged children. The Sustaining Effects study (Carter 1984) showed positive results only for the lower elementary grades, a finding similar to the OERI National Assessment of Chapter 1 (Kennedy *et al.* 1986). A number of researchers have attributed student performance improvements in some areas of the National Assessment of Educational Progress (NAEP) to Chapter 1 (e.g. Murnane 1988). There is evidence that students in the programme, on average, get greater exposure to direct academic instruction than other students (Rowan *et al.* 1986). This factor has been shown to improve student learning (e.g. Cooley and Leinhardt 1980). The problem is that Chapter 1 is an extremely diverse programme with many service delivery models. Researchers debate whether programme effects are due to Chapter 1's organization and administration, or to variations in instructional quality. One is left with very little guidance as to what specifically works and why. Recently, attention has turned to schoolwide programmes, but there is not conclusive evidence that these will show superior student outcomes compared with service delivery models conventionally applied in this programme.[3]

Desegregation: This educational reform strategy is disputed also. Desegregation policy is the prime example. After decades of effort, many urban school systems remain highly segregated (Orfield and Montfort 1988). Critics (e.g. Ravitch and Armor 1978) charge that bussing has contributed to white flight, has reduced parental involvement and school autonomy, and is costly.

The literature on how school desegregation affects the school achievement of African-American students is inconclusive. Some reviews of the literature find small gains in achievement resulting from 1 to 2 years attendance at racially mixed schools (e.g. Crain and Mahard 1978). Yet others, e.g. Bradley and Bradley (1977) conclude that achievement gains cannot be assumed. On a more optimistic note, white student achievement is unaffected, and positive effects for African-American students are most likely where desegregation is required by official policy, where students begin their schooling in desegregated school settings, and where cumulative gains are measured (Cook 1979: 428). Crain and Mahard (1983) find positive effects outweighing losses in a strong majority of cases, and Watcher (1988) comes to the same conclusion. Yet if self-esteem of African-American children is an outcome measure, rather than scores on standardized tests, some reviewers have found no trend apparent (Epps 1978), while others find negative effects on self-esteem more frequently than positive effects.

It is worth noting that compensatory education has sometimes been a strategy used to complement desegregation court orders. Additional resources have been given to schools which remain segregated and are outside the court order, in order to improve the quality of education at those sites. Thus, while compensatory education and desegregation are very different strategies, in practice they sometimes are employed together.

Empowerment: Another reform strategy which has been advocated is empowerment. In the 1960s this was referred to as 'black power' and later 'brown power', while more recently it has re-emerged in proposals for an 'Afro-centred curriculum'. Emphasis on building indigenous institutions within communities of colour has a long history, particularly among African-Americans.

Ogbu's (1974, 1978, 1988) and Fordham and Ogbu's (1986) analysis of the 'cultural discontinuity' between African-American children and most schools serves to explain why an empowerment perspective may address a major part of the problem. Because African-Americans are an involuntary minority in American society, racial stratification can influence negatively the way these students and their parents are treated by teachers and administrators. Also, students reduce their aspirations and performance so as not to act white or in order to cope with their perceived limited economic chances in American life. Thus, as members of an 'oppositional culture' African-American children suffer pervasive disadvantages which reach beyond the institutional characteristics of specific schools they attend, but which are more deeply rooted in their social status. From Ogbu's perspective, this is why more limited strategies which focus on the developmental deficiencies of African-American children, the nature of the peer group, or the character of specific schools all have had so negligible an impact on the problem of school failure and low-performance by African-American children.

Community control was much debated in the 1960s and early 1970s, as one means of addressing the issues which Ogbu subsequently articulated. Yet given the challenge to established authority and power which the community control concept represented as well as to the traditional integration goals of the civil rights movement, the actual experiments with the community control concept were exceedingly limited and amounted to schemes of partial political decentralization in Detroit and New York. In fact, the recent creation of local school councils at each Chicago public school (Hess 1990) moves much further towards community empowerment than any previous decentralization reforms in urban schools. Given the fact that there have been no pure experiments with community control, few conclusions can be drawn about its salutary effects on students. The recent Temporary State Commission on New York City School Governance was created to review the governance of the city's schools because of widespread dissatisfaction with the educational results and governance of the community districts. Clearly, a goal of such reforms has been to provide access to jobs and resources for local communities, but sometimes at the cost of considerable graft.

Purely defined, compensatory education, desegregation and empowerment have very different philosophical assumptions. Compensatory education assumes that educationally disadvantaged children suffer from a learning deficit when they enter school, which must be closed through one or another remedial strategies. Desegregation, on the other hand, focuses more on the improved learning opportunities for children of colour when they are educated in desegregated environments, owing to their access to greater school resources than are historically available in segregated schools, and to assumed positive peer group effects. Finally, empowerment strategies emphasize first the need to afford poor, minority children greater cultural awareness before they will be motivated to learn effectively, as well as complementary efforts to build ethnic/racial community power through the schools. In truth, these competing paradigms for urban education never have been resolved and remain as contested today as when they emerged in the 1950s and 1960s.

Effects of tracking: Tracking in American schools has been strongly criticized, e.g. Oakes 1985. Summarizing the literature and prevailing belief Hallinan (1987) points out that disproportionately large numbers of low-income and minority students are relegated to these low tracks and ability groups, compared with a greater proportion of higher income and white students in high tracks or ability groups. However, given that tracking is such a pervasive feature of American schools, it has its defenders. (For an overview of these reviews and their orientation, the reader is referred to Oakes 1985.) Nor is there agreement that schools which track less perform better. A good example is the debate on this between Coleman *et al.* (1982) as well as Coleman and Hoffer (1987) and their critics (for a summary see Haertl *et al.* [1988]). Catholic high schools may track less but their superior achievement effects for minority pupils are disputed. Even if there were more agreement on the effects of tracking, its impact on the internal organization of schools is far from clear. (For a summary of what is known and efforts at new model-building, see the entire volume edited by Hallinan 1987.) One reason for the absence of consensus is that there are many types of tracking systems and practices. Further, the relation between such internal features as tracking and key outcomes such as moral development needs further attention (Bidwell 1987). Obviously, the paucity of conclusive research in this area diminishes the confidence we can have in its application to the reform of urban schools.

Effective schools: For approximately 15 years after the publication of the Coleman report (1966), it was argued that schools could do little to reverse the effects of family background on student achievement. The effective schools literature, as articulated by

Brookover *et al.* 1979, Edmonds 1979, 1986, Klitgard and Hall 1974, Lezotte and Bancroft 1985, and others countered this pessimism. However, the research has been heavily criticized on conceptual and methodological grounds (Brophy and Good 1986, Murphy *et al.* 1985, Purkey and Smith 1983, Rosenholtz 1985, Rowan *et al.* 1983), including the subjectivity of criteria used to identify effective schools. Despite its common-sense appeal, this literature does not offer a simple formula for school improvement (Purkey and Smith 1983). Nor are its findings on how to influence student and teacher behaviour at the classroom level altogether conclusive (Murnane 1983).

An initial problem is that the effective schools characteristics which fit elementary settings, where the model was developed, do not necessarily apply to high schools. A number of studies (e.g. Bryk *et al.* 1989, Grant 1981, Lightfoot 1983, Rutter *et al.* 1979, Mortimore *et al.* 1988, Sizer 1984, Wehlage *et al.* 1989) provide suggestive findings that may contribute to an effective schools model for secondary settings. Among these are a reduced reliance on tracking, an institutionalized capacity to help students with problems, and a strong emphasis on caring. Yet at this stage in its development, this literature is far from conclusive.

A second problem in the effective schools literature is that typically it has ignored the importance of the school's social context (Wimpelberg *et al.* 1989). Schools serving predominantly low-income or minority populations possess different characteristics from those serving higher income clientele (Hallinger and Murphy 1986).

Karweit (1986) argues that many schools serving low-income or minority students are lacking in the nine characteristics used to identify effective schools. If correct, then the problem may be that many urban school systems have not properly implemented this model. Yet the lack of dramatic improvements in student achievement at many urban schools which have at least nominally adopted an effective schools approach illustates that school improvement strategies may be inadequate. For one, the heavy emphasis on learning basic skills, as distinct from higher-order reasoning abilities, may reinforce the problem of low expectations which often is said to plague educational strategies for the urban poor.

A third shortcoming of the effective schools literature is its neglect of individual differences among children (Epstein 1988). She points out that Weber's (1971) original work on this topic had paid much more attention to the diverse needs of students.

Indeed, other approaches to effective schools have emerged in recent years which incorporate different characteristics from the nine basic ones in the effective schools literature. Comer's (1980, 1987, 1988a, 1988b) well-known experiments in two New Haven, Connecticut elementary schools emphasize the child's psychological development, particularly by closing the gap between home and school with positive interactions between school staff and parents, team management and other features. Thus, Comer places much more emphasis on the developmental needs of each child and on extensive parent involvement than the mainstream effective schools literature.

Levin's (1988) accelerated schools approach also departs from earlier effective schools literature by focusing on the strengths of disadvantaged students rather than their deficits. His approach uses a variety of innovative pedagogical and curricular techniques to accelerate the learning process, such as oral and artistic expression, appropriate learning materials, peer tutoring and co-operative learning.

Recently, a body of consensus has emerged that we really do know what works, if we will only make the necessary investments. This was initiated from outside the educational establishment by Schorr (1988), who wished to counter conservative critiques of the Great Society social programmes by Murray (1984) and others. Investment in early childhood programmes, parent involvement and co-ordinated service delivery approaches are at the centre of this consensus. Yet it would be more accurate to characterize these and related approaches as 'promising practices' (Oakes 1987) rather than as conclusive research evidence. A brief discussion of these additional reform nostrums will illustrate this point.

Early childhood programmes: A wide range of data has accumulated to show that maternal child and health programmes improve later school performance and are cost-effective (e.g. Weitzman *et al.* 1982, Wolfe 1985), although the national picture of infant health is not encouraging and has deteriorated (Hughes *et al.* 1986). Perhaps the best known early childhood programme is Head Start. After the initial Westinghouse study (Granger *et al.* 1969) failed to document lasting positive effects, the more recent CSR, Inc. review of all studies (McKey *et al.* 1985) found positive short-term effects on cognitive and socio-emotional development and long-term effects on physical development. Gamble and Zigler (in press) criticize the meta-analysis in this review as failing to discard studies with weak designs, thus leading to the allegedly erroneous conclusion that cognitive and affective gains for participating students 'wash out' or level off. David Weikert's (1989) highly publicized Perry Preschool Program claims long-term benefits, although it is based on a small sample with attrition and other methodological problems (Zigler 1987). While early childhood programmes are now accepted as a good investment, particularly to raise the learning readiness of poverty children, the fact is that research has not established clearly what benefits are associated with children having particular needs exposed to different delivery systems. For instance, it is quite possible that public school models such as four-year-old kindergarten will be less effective than the comprehensive, developmental approach of Head Start.

Parent involvement: There is a large body of literature on parent involvement, much of which reports on single experiments and lacks tight evaluation designs. Major reviews of the literature on parent education indicate that, for the most part, increased parent involvement in school is associated with improved student performance (Epstein 1987, Henderson 1987). However, a number of studies indicate that parent involvement activities in low-income settings, while leading to some achievement gains, do not close the achievement gap. (For a review of these studies, see McAllister 1991). Parental involvement in homework can be negative (Cooper 1989). Inasmuch as these negative findings obtain among populations similar to those found in many central-city schools, the cause of the deviant results is especially important to isolate. However, because of limitations in the research designs, it is not possible to pinpoint why these negative results occur. Administrators' and teachers' low expectations are blamed in some research (Chrispeels 1991). Many parent involvement programmes delegate tasks to parents without seeking their active collaboration (Seeley 1991).

Integrated service delivery: A compelling case can be made for integrating or at least co-ordinating a range of social services through schools. Advocates argue that it is more effective both for the client (students or their family members) and the providers of care (Kirst and McLaughlin 1989). Clients have 'one-stop shopping' where a range of needs can be met, while providers can communicate more effectively thereby reducing red tape, contradictory requirements, service gaps and the like. This approach is appealing to some because it is likely to be more cost-effective than duplicative, fragmented service delivery systems currently in place.

Despite these advocacies, there is next to no research evidence that this approach will make a major difference in the quality of central city education. We are at the 'too early to tell' stage with a scattered number of experiments in place and only promising practices to report (Levy and Copple 1989).

Choice: Another area which has engendered considerable interest in recent years is experimentation with school choice. Despite spirited defence of choice arrangements by Chubb and Moe (1990), the solid evidence that this approach will work is non-existent. Their own study has been criticized on methodological grounds (Glass and Matthews 1991, Witte 1990).

Two principal prototypes for advancing the argument for greater choice are magnet/specialty schools and private schools. Unfortunately, research evidence does not establish that the magnitude of performance advantage at these schools is sufficiently large to label them a success or that their superior performance is due to the school as opposed to a selection effect. Blank *et al.* (1983) and Blank (1989) found magnet schools to have superior achievement. Yet critics (e.g. Moore and Davenport 1990) point to selective magnet schools as a new form of the sorting machine. Coleman, Hoffer, and Kilgore (1982) and Coleman and Hoffer (1987) argue the superiority of private schools, particularly in advancing the achievement of minorities. However, their findings have been subject to much controversy (an excellent summary of the debate is contained in Haertl *et al.* 1988). James (1991) reviews international findings which point to the likelihood of superior performance by private schools even after selection effects are controlled for, but doubts that this factor ever can be measured satisfactorily.

Site-based management: Another governance reform which decentralizes, this time through administrative delegation, is site-based management. To date, however, there is little conclusive evidence that this will improve achievement. Despite promising findings in New York City's District 4 (Fliegel 1989), other experiments with site-based management have failed to yield noticeable results. Miami's programme actually increased staff turnover and thus far has no apparent achievement effects (Collins 1991). Malen and Ogawa's (1988) review of Salt Lake City's experiment also lists many implementation problems, which indicate the complexities associated with this reform. It may be that conditions which made this reform successful in the private sector do not automatically transfer to schools. While it would be too early to dismiss site-based management as a failure, its potential for success is far from guaranteed.

Bilingual instruction: An important issue in urban education is how to provide effective instruction to the growing number of limited-English proficiency (LEP) children enrolled in the public schools. (This is not exclusively an urban phenomenon to be sure, particularly in states such as California with large in-migrations of foreigners and a large Hispanic population.)

Research tends to support the effectiveness of bilingual education programmes (e.g. Willig 1985, Wong-Fillmore and Valdez 1986). However, considerable controversy arises when these programmes are viewed not as temporary transitional devices to move the student to English proficiency (e.g. English-as-a-Second Language Program) but rather as bilingual maintenance programmes. The controversy surrounding how best to serve LEP children illustrates how value conflicts confound efforts to develop a sound knowledge base to improve practice.

To summarize thus far, we have reviewed briefly a large number of areas of research as they bear on our knowledge base in urban education. In virtually all of these areas the knowledge base is sharply contested or too poorly developed to be conclusive.

The fragmentation of knowledge

A second observation which may be made about the study of urban education is that it cannot be called a coherent body of knowledge. Apart from the fact that there is little knowledge about which we can speak confidently, there is a serious problem of fragmentation of inquiry. As others also have observed, education is not a discipline, despite decades of efforts to make it so by pedagogists, educational psychologists and other specialists (Clifford and Guthrie 1988). It is more accurately portrayed as a field of study informed by a variety of disciplinary traditions. Hence, the divisions among boundaries of knowledge are quite severe, and they are extremely dysfunctional to the improvement of practice. In political science it is quite harmless for some scholars to specialize in international relations and others in American politics; these are branches of knowledge which can proceed relatively independently of one another without detrimental consequences. Not so in the professions, where informed practice requires breadth of knowledge and a synthesis of perspectives.

Not all specialization is harmful, of course. In law it is altogether appropriate that some should specialize in civil law, others in criminal law, and still others in tax law. But problems of teaching and learning are not so easily disentangled. Pedagogy should be informed by psychology as well as anthropology, administration as much by ethics or political philosophy as by organizational studies. Yet for reasons having a great deal to do with political power, or aspirations thereto by would-be educationists, knowledge has remained segmented. Administrators wished to distance themselves from curriculum and instruction because it was dominated by women. Educational psychologists wished to identify themselves with the scientific rigour of psychology rather than with others in their own field. These internal struggles for status within an emergent profession eventually erected dysfunctional barriers which still plague programmes of professional preparation and research inquiry. This problem of fragmentation has been aggravated by the low regard in which education professors are held by many of their university peers, prompting periodic efforts by scientists and social scientists to influence what is taught in schools of education. The paucity of research monies available to many social scientists impels them to seek extramural funding in educational research, although few do more than dabble, merely reinforcing the problem of fragmentation.

The problems generated by the balkanization of our knowledge base in education are particularly apparent in urban education, which is after all a *context* within which the entire field of education must be refocused. Problems of student motivation and human development, as Comer's innovations illustrate, are central to restructuring urban schools, but these are inseparable from the organization of teaching and learning and the practice of administration. Similarly, administrative efforts to decentralize to the school site are unlikely to lead to more than trivial changes without a much broadened conception of administrative leadership. Improved accountability through greater assessment of student performance must avoid the pitfalls and abuses of large-scale standardized testing, which frequently have been used against the best interests of the urban poor and children of colour rather than as tools to help them reach their full potential. Even within educational psychology, the field's dominant paradigm, test and measurement arguably has dwarfed psychological theory as a foundation for educational research (Travers 1983).

Utilization of knowledge

I come now to a third observation about knowledge of urban education, particularly its application in the schools. There is an old maxim, unfortunately not greatly exaggerated, that it takes 30 years for a new idea to make its way into the classroom. Despite a plethora of experiments, evaluations, innovative pilot programmes and the like, schools have remained quite impervious to the use of new information to inform practice. School systems constantly adopt new programmes, which promptly run into implementation problems. This is documented by the literature on problems of change in schools (e.g. Sarason 1990), and the literature on implementation (e.g. Rand Corporation 1974, McLaughlin 1990). The explanations of these problems of knowledge utilization span a wide range of fields – organizational theory, communication theory, information theory, cognition, evaluation utilization (Riehl, *et al.* 1991), as well as political science, economics, anthropology and other fields. In the next section I focus this literature by contrasting two alternative lines of explanation for why the knowledge base on urban schooling remains poor and its application in schools so inadequate.

Explaining the 'knowledge-base problem' in urban schools

It is useful to begin with the assumption that all individuals have limited tolerance for accepting change, subject to a variety of personal factors such as cognition, prior education and information, personality and values, and others. This receptivity to new information is, moreover, influenced by the social context within which the individual finds oneself, here the social context of the workplace itself. Organizational decision structures, processes and cultures, as well as the system of authority, power and status are important aspects of this social context surrounding the individual. Thus, it is at the level of organization that we shall direct our attention here.

Dissemination of knowledge as a problem

This view of the knowledge-base problem is essentially that urban school personnel (teachers, administrators and others) lack access to additional information on how to improve practice. This is a diffusion-of-innovations perspective which initially was associated with Rogers (1983). The individual is the adopter, and the essential problem is to get the information accessible to that individual. Such views continue to hold currency. For example, Natriello *et al.* (1990: 141) argue, in a generally very thoughtful book on schooling for disadvantaged children, that addressing their problems is less a matter of will than of serious gaps of information available to teachers and administrators, among others. Improved information, they assert, would eventually result in improved educational services for all students.

Such diffusion of information approaches to innovation in schools suffer from a number of shortcomings. First, as the Rand study (1974) pointed out, this model does not fit schools well, where goals of an innovation are unclear, where treatment frequently is unspecified, and where the adopter is not an individual but instead a social system with powerful norms and practices. To be sure, the diffusion-of-innovations perspective does capture a part of the problem. There are large numbers of teachers who work in schools where access to new knowledge and innovation is rare. The difficulty is that to portray the problem as one of transmitting knowledge more effectively greatly understates the magnitude of the barriers to innovation in schools.

Political organization as a knowledge problem

These barriers are better understood as rooted in the political organization of urban school systems. Three interlocking aspects of this political organization are powerful impediments to improving the knowledge base: centralized bureaucracy, standardized resource allocation rules and the system of bureaucratic incentives.

Centralized bureaucracy: The bureaucratization of urban school systems has been a much discussed phenomenon. Diagnoses of the dysfunctions of these bureaucracies emphasizes how overregulation leads to goal displacement as well as the inefficiencies which stem from large bureaucracies. Another serious problem which typically is overlooked is *the negative impact on knowledge utilization and production*. The model of scientific management which reigned in the early 1900s, upon whose premises urban school bureaucracies were built (Callahan 1962, Tyack 1975) is now antiquated. This closed-system model assumed that management had the knowledge of what to produce and how best to produce it, which was to be carried out through a hierarchical chain of command. This no longer fits the realities of most private firms, where frequent changes both in technology and in market demands require decentralized management strategies. Performance is monitored through output standards rather than detailed day-to-day regulation of work processes.

Urban school systems face similar environmental challenges to those of private firms. Their clientele, and hence their 'markets' are changing. Levels of expected student performance have risen with the globalization of economic competition. Yet these systems are saddled with archaic bureaucratic structures which seek to regulate from the top what is to be taught, methods of instruction, how schools are to be organized and so on. Most urban school bureaucracies possess weakly developed and poorly co-ordinated infrastructures to assess student and school performance, to conduct research and evaluation, and to target staff development.

The modest knowledge base we possess in education, particularly as it applies to urban schools, never was well served by this scientific menagement model. If little is known, better to foster conditions under which widespread experimentation will prevail. A decentralized research and development approach would better fit these conditions. Instead, urban school systems set up centralized staff development, research, and evaluation units.

The loosely coupled character of these bureaucracies only compounds these dysfunctions. Schools enjoy autonomy to resist central bureaucrats but have no organizational support system in place to encourage more experimentation at the local school.

University relationships to the schools for the most part continue to be built on a centralized R&D model. As new knowledge is produced in higher education settings, it is passed down to practitioners in local schools, usually with the central office acting as intermediary. Efforts to develop more collaborative interaction between univerity researchers and school systems are rare (for an exception see Cooley and Bickel 1986).

Standardized resource allocation rules: A concomitant problem is that centralized bureaucracies use universalistic norms to allocate resources, because ostensibly this is fair.

When pupil needs were assumed to vary little, as was the case for many decades in urban education, horizontal equity could be defended as a legitimate principle in resource allocation rules. Such professional rules, supposedly based on application of technical expertise, also serve to protect bureaucrats against charges of favouritism.

It is immediately apparent, however, that these universalistic norms of standardized treatment are part of the problem, since they are required by a centralized bureaucratic system to legitimate itself. This in turn discourages local variation in the deployment of resources, since they are formula-driven and frequently leave little room for local discretion.

Any large organization must develop allocation rules. Short of breaking up the organization, some methods must be devised which determine how fairly to allocate resources from the command centre to the operating units. Yet there are many ways to accomplish this short of standardized allocation rules. Urban school systems evolved these standardized formulas as part of the scientific management system where the command centre made all important decisions.

Bureaucratic incentives: It is sometimes pointed out, following the loosely coupled logic, that individual schools still have enormous discretion to experiment if they want to. This implies that teachers or administrators are unwilling to take risks. Such a diagnosis ignores the central point that most of the bureaucratic incentives push against greater experimentation. First, the compensation system has no relationship to student outcomes or efforts to improve those outcomes. Second, the very poor instructional information systems (Bank and Williams 1987) and evaluation units available in most urban school systems discourage use of data to compare performance of schools or units within schools. Third, research units in urban school systems are not designed to encourage experimentation and data-based decision making. Their role is largely symbolic, serving to provide a ritualistic assurance that appropriate attitudes about decision making and professional competence exist (Feldman and March 1981). Indeed, there is little integration between instruction, evaluation and staff development functions in most central offices, much less co-ordination of these to principals and teachers (Bank 1982). Finally, the levels of staffing in most schools create severe impediments to experimentation, because teachers are expected to instruct large numbers of students and have little free time. Slack resources either are not available or are not deployed effectively to release them for conferences and other professional development activities. Until serious efforts are made to improve the quality of the school as a professional workplace, greater experimentation is not likely to occur. In short, there are powerful disincentives in educational bureaucracies, both monetary and non-monetary, for improving our knowledge base on urban education and thus creating the preconditions for improved student performance. As long as this system of incentives is in place, it helps maintain the legitimacy of the centralized bureaucracy and the standardized allocation rules discussed above.

To recap then, it is the political organization of urban schools which poses a major obstacle to improving the knowledge base in urban education. Centralization of the bureacratic enterprise, rules for resource allocation and the nature of bureaucratic incentives all play a mutually reinforcing role in perpetuating this problem.

Conclusion

The task of generating a better knowledge of how urban schools can work more effectively is a threefold political problem. First, it requires dislodging powerful bureaucratic forces, institutionalized in law and protected by the interests of administrators, teachers' unions, and other producers of urban schooling. These interests are able to influence boards of education through the information they provide to board members and through their access to selection processes for board members. There is much literature in the politics of education which documents the way educational bureaucracies and their allies influence policy outcomes far beyond their official role as merely implementers of policy (e.g. Zeigler *et al.* 1974, Rogers 1969, Peterson 1976).

Second, when consumers mobilize to favour their particular interests, they generally demand specific benefits for their group. This is done to counter the free-rider problem (Olsen 1971) and to increase the likelihood of a favourable outcome, since it is easier to win a narrow concession for a specific group (distributive politics) than to argue for a broad policy which authorities are more likely to interpret as requiring redistribution of authority or resources. The problem here is not that providers dominate consumers but rather that coalitions of consumers rarely form to demand broadly redistributive policies which would improve consumer influence over decision making. A new categorical programme or targeted perquisite merely extends the legitimacy of the centralized bureaucracy with its standardized allocation rules; the appearance of responsiveness is maintained by showing willingness to make exceptions to the standardized rules.[4]

Third, improving learning opportunities for urban disadvantaged children is likely to require additional resources. Spending in central-city school systems is far below most suburban systems with fewer pupil needs, and in many states cities spend less than the state average, even after adjusting for differences in poverty concentration between the city and the state as a whole (Cibulka forthcoming). While the research on spending and educational achievement admittedly has yet to establish a credible relationship between the two, productivity improvements in urban school systems are not likely alone to negate the need for additional spending. This cannot be accomplished without some degree of resource redistribution from higher spending suburban and rural districts. Even the federal government, which is more likely to succeed in redistributive policies (Peterson 1981, Peterson *et al.* 1986) than states or localities, is inclined to dilute the redistributive aspects of Chapter 1 by spreading the services thin, giving it the quality of a pork-barrel distribution. Thus, while the basic obstacles to an improved knowledge base on urban schooling come from bureaucratic impediments, it is also the case that the financing inequality in schooling between cities and suburbs is a key cause. This is embedded in the politics of race and class and cannot be ignored as an important part of this policy problem.

Given these formidable political obstacles to improving the knowledge base, it might be asked whether the major restructuring strategies now under way have much promise. Taken singly, each has too narrow a perspective on the scope of the knowledge dimensions of the problem. Teacher professionalization and site-based management, for instance, do attempt to undo the dysfunctional elements of centralized bureaucracy and create a wider zone of discretion for allocation of resources at the school level. For the most part, however, they avoid the political problem of incentives discussed earlier, a matter which performance accountability reporting, and also choice, do address, although they, too, tend to underplay a number of intractable political problems.

Further, none of these reform nostrums adequately addresses the need for greater research and development and the conditions which will foster this. In that regard President George Bush's *America 2000* reform plan is a welcome addition to the reform agenda by focusing on efforts to create new models of schooling through R&D mechanisms. The plan makes some attempts to relate the threads of reform – national testing, choice, etc., to one another, but still falls far short of a comprehensive strategy for reform.

Still another political impediment to true reform of our urban schools is the use of school reform for political symbolism. Overly simplistic plans which play well on headlines and news bites are largely symbolic, and symbolism is a durable output of our political system (Edelman 1985). Yet symbolic politics, by their nature, are designed principally to regain public confidence for a political regime, not to alter institutional performance. Until reforms address more directly how to create the conditions within urban schools which will permit a new knowledge base to be discovered and applied, most of the restructuring movement can be viewed as political symbolism.

Finally, urban education as a field of study needs to be reconceptualized so that it is less disjointed and constrained by the various research traditions within education. If research is to fulfil its old but largely unrealized promise of informing practice, scholars of education will have to reconstruct their research agenda. This need is as urgent as are reforms in urban schools themselves.

Notes

1. There is a serious problem disentangling research findings so that they speak clearly to urban children and the conditions in urban schools. Much of the research literature on educationally disadvantaged children, or children of colour relies heavily on data drawn from urban settings. Yet many children with these characteristics are located outside central cities. Moreover, some would argue that urban should really mean everything which happens in a metropolitan context. Given the impossibility of isolating research findings or reaching consensus on what urban means, in this chapter I settle for approximations. Specifically, I review findings pertaining to educationally disadvantaged children, and children of colour as indicative of our knowledge base in urban education. Because of space limitations this review is illustrative rather than comprehensive. For more complete treatments, several excellent reviews are Boyd 1991, Natriello *et al.* 1990, Oakes 1987.
2. Because of the extensive nature of this literature, only a few citations are offered. For a full review and extensive citations, see Jaynes and Williams (1989: 329–389).
3. For a fuller discussion of Chapter 1 see Chapter Eleven by Herrington and Orland herein.
4. It may be that the relatively recent resurgence of business interest in the schools will alter the narrow scope of demands consumers traditionally have made on the schools (since businesses see themselves as consumers of the workers schools produce) and force changes in bureaucratic influence, allocation rules and bureaucratic incentives.

References

ALEXANDER, K. L., COOK, M. and MCDILL, W. L. (1978) 'Curriculum tracking and educational stratification: Some further evidence', *American Sociological Review*, 43, pp. 47–66.

BANK, A. (1982) 'Can evaluation plus staff development equal school improvement?' *The Journal of Staff Development*, 3(1), pp. 170–181.

BANK, A. and WILLIAMS, R. C. (eds) (1987) *Information Systems and School Improvement: Inventing the Future* (New York: Teachers College Press).

BIDWELL, C. (1987) 'Moral education and school social organization', in M. Hallinen (ed.) *The Social Organization of Schools* (New York: Plenum Press), pp. 205–217.

BLANK, R. K. (1989) 'Educational effects of magnet schools', paper presented at the Conference on Choice and Control in American Education, University of Wisconsin, Madison, WI.

BLANK, R. K., DENTLER, R. A., BLATZALL, D. C. and CHABOTAR, K. (1983) *Survey of magnet schools: Analyzing a model for quality integrated education* (Chicago, IL: James H. Lowry and Associates).

BOYD, W. L. (1991) 'What makes ghetto schools succeed or fail?', *Teachers College Record*, 92(3), pp. 331–362.

BRADLEY, L. and BRADLEY, G. (1977) 'The academic achievement of blacks in desegregated schools': A critical review', *Review of Educational Research*, 47(3), pp. 399–499.

BROOKOVER, W., BEADY, C., FLOOD, P., SCHWEITZER, J. and WISENBAKER, J. (1979) *School Social Systems and Student Achievement: Schools Can Make a Difference* (New York: Praeger).

BROPHY, J. and GOOD, T. J. (1986) 'Teachers' behavior and student achievement', in M. C. Wittrock (ed.) *Handbook of Research on Teaching* (New York: Macmillan).

BRYK, A. S., LEE, V. and SMITH, J. B. (1989) 'High school organization and its effects on teachers and students: An interpretive summary of the research', paper presented at the Conference on Choice and Control in American Education, University of Wisconsin, Madison, WI.

CALLAHAN, R. (1962) *Education and the Cult of Efficiency* (Chicago: University of Chicago Press).

CARTER, L. F. (1984) 'The sustaining effects study of compensatory and elementary education', *Educational Researcher*, 13(7), pp. 4–13.

CHRISPEELS, J. H. (1991) 'District leadership in parent involvement: Policies and actions in San Diego', *Phi Delta Kappan*, 72(5), pp. 367–371.

CHUBB, J. E. and MOE, T. M. (1990) *Politics, Markets and American Schools* (Washington, DC: Brookings).

CIBULKA, J. G. (forthcoming) 'Demographic diversity in urban schools', in J. G. Ward (ed.) *Who Pays for Student Diversity?* (Santa Monica, CA: Sage).

CLIFFORD, G. J. and GUTHRIE, J. W. (1988) *Ed School* (Chicago: University of Chicago Press).

COLEMAN, J. S., CAMPBELL, E. Q. and others (1966) *Equality of Educational Opportunity* (Washington, DC: US Government Printing Office).

COLEMAN, J. S. and HOFFER, T. (1987) *Public and Private High Schools: The Impact of Communities* (New York: Basic Books).

COLEMAN, J. S., HOFFER, T. and KILGORE, S. (1982) *High School Achievement: Public, Catholic, and Private High Schools Compared* (New York: Basic Books).

COLLINS, R. A. (1991) 'Projectwide impact of school-based management on selected indicators over 3 years', paper presented at the annual meeting of the American Educational Research Association, Chicago.

COMER, J. P. (1980) *School Power: Implications of an Intervention Project* (New York: Free Press).

COMER, J. P. (1987) 'New Haven's school-community connection', *Educational Leadership*, 44(6), pp. 13–16.

COMER, J. P. (1988a) 'Educating poor minority children', *Scientific American*, 259(5), pp. 42–48.

COMER, J. P. (1988b) 'Effective schools: Why they rarely exist for at-risk elementary schools and adolescent students', in *School Success for Students At-Risk: Analysis and Recommendations of the Council of Chief State School Officers* (Orlando, FL: Harcourt Brace Jovanovich), pp. 72–88.

COOK, S. W. (1979) 'Social science and school desegregation: Did we mislead the Supreme Court?', *Personality and Social Psychology Bulletin*, 5(4), pp. 420–437.

COOLEY, W. W. and BICKEL, W. E. (1986) *Decision-oriented Educational Research* (Boston: Kluwer-Nijhoff).

COOLEY, W. W. and LEINHARDT, G. (1980) 'The instructional dimensions study', *Educational Evaluation and Policy Analysis*, 2, pp. 7–26.

COOPER, H. (1989) 'Synthesis of research on homework', *Educational Leadership*, 47(3), pp. 85–91.

CRAIN, R. L. and MAHARD, R. E. (1978) 'Desegregation and black achievement: A review of the research', *Law and Contemporary Problems*, 42(3), pp. 17–56.

CRAIN, R. L. and MAHARD, R. E. (1983) 'The effect of research methodology on desegregation achievement studies: a meta-analysis', *American Journal of Sociology*, 88(5), pp. 839–854.

EDELMAN, M. (1985) *The Symbolic Uses of Politics* (Urbana: University of Illinois Press).

EDMONDS, R. (1979) 'Effective schools for the urban poor', *Educational Leadership*, 37(1), pp. 15–24.

EDMONDS, R. (1986) 'Characteristics of effective schools', in U. Neisser (ed.) *The School Achievement of Minority Children: New Perspectives* (Hillsdale, NJ: Erlbaum).

EPPS, E. G. (1978) 'The impact of school desegregation on the self-evaluation and achievement orientation of minority children', *Law and Contemporary Problems*, 42(3), pp. 57–76.

EPSTEIN, J. (1987) 'Parent involvement: What the research says to administrators', *Education and Urban Society*, 19(2), pp. 119–136.

EPSTEIN, J. (1988) 'Effective schools or effective students: Dealing with diversity', in R. Haskins and D. McRae (eds) *Policies for America's Schools: Teachers, Equity, and Indicators* (Norwood, NJ: Ablex).

FELDMAN, M. S. and MARCH, J. G. (1981) 'Information in organizations as signal and symbol', *Administrative Science Quarterly*, 26(1), pp. 171–186.

FLIEGEL, S. (1989) 'Creative non-compliance in east Harlem schools', paper presented at the Conference on Choice and Control in American Education, University of Wisconsin, Madison, WI.

FORDHAM, S. and OGBU, J. (1986) 'Black students' school success: coping with the burden of "acting white"', *Urban Review*, 18(3), pp. 176–206.

GAMBLE, T. J. and ZIGLER, E. (forthcoming) 'The Head Start synthesis project: A critique', *Journal of Applied Developmental Psychology*.

GLASS, G. V. and MATTHEWS, D. A. (1991) 'Are data enough?', *Educational Researcher*, 20(3), pp. 24–27.

GRANGER, R. L., CICIRELLI, V. G., COOPER, W. H., RHODE, W. E. and MAXEY, E. J. (1969) *The Impact of Head Start: An Evaluation of the Effects of Head Start on Children's Cognitive and Affective Development*, Vol. 1 (Athens, OH: Westinghouse Learning Corp. and Ohio University).

GRANT, G. (1981) 'The character of education and the education of character', *Daedelus*, 110(3), pp. 135–149.

GRANT, G. (1988) *The World We Created at Hamilton High* (Cambridge, MA: Harvard University Press).

HAERTL, E. H., JAMES, T. and LEVIN, H. M. (1988) *Comparing Public and Private High Schools: Vol. 1, School Achievement* (New York: Falmer).

HALLINAN, M. (1987) *The Social Organization of Schools* (New York: Plenum Press).

HALLINGER, P. and MURPHY, J. (1986) 'The social context of effective schools', *American Journal of Education*, 94(3), pp. 328–355.

HAVIGHURST, R. (1966) *Education in Metropolitan Areas* (Boston: Allyn and Bacon).

HENDERSON, A. (1987) *The Evidence Continues to Grow: Parent Involvement Improves Student Achievement* (Columbia, MD: National Committee for Citizens in Education).

HENTOFF, N. (1966) *Our Children Are Dying* (New York: Viking Press).

HESS, G. A. Jr. (1990) 'Chicago school reform: What it is and how it came to be', unpublished paper, Committee on Public Policy and Finance, Chicago.

HOLT, J. (1964) *How Children Fail* (New York: Pitman).

HUGHES, D., JOHNSON, K., SIMONS, J. and ROSENBAUM, S. (1986) *Maternal and Child Health Data Book: The Health of America's Children*. (Washington, DC: Children's Defense Fund).

JAMES, E. (1991) 'Private school finance and public policy in cross-cultural perspective', paper delivered at the US Department of Education conference on 'Dollars and Cents of Private Schools', Washington, DC.

JAYNES, G. D. and WILLIAMS, R. M. Jr. (1989) *A Common Destiny: Blacks and American Society* (Washington, DC: National Academy Press).

KARWEIT, N. (1986) 'Elementary education and black Americans: raising the odds', paper prepared for the Committee on the Status of Black Americans, National Research Council, Washington, DC.

KENNEDY, M. M., BERMAN, B. F. and DEMALINE, R. E. (1986) 'The effectiveness of Chapter 1 services' (National Assessment of Chapter 1) (Washington, DC: US Department of Education).

KIRST, M. W. and MCLAUGHLIN, M. (1989) 'Rethinking policy for children: Implications for educational administration', in B. Mitchell and L. C. Cunningham, (eds) *Educational Leadership and Changing Conditions of Families, Communities and Schools* 89th Yearbook, Pt. 2 (Chicago: National Society for the Study of Education), pp. 69–90.

KLITGARD, R. E. and HALL, G. R. (1974) 'Are there unusually effective schools?', *Journal of Human Resources*, 10(1), pp. 90–106.

KOZOL, J. (1967) *Death at an Early Age: The Destruction of the Hearts and Minds of Negro Children in the Boston Public Schools* (Boston: Houghton Mifflin).

LEVIN, H. M. (1988) 'Accelerated schools for at-risk students', Center for Policy Research in Education, Rutgers University, New Brunswick, NJ.

LEVY, J. and COPPLE, C. (1989) *Joining Forces: A Report from the First Year* (Washington, DC: National Association of State Boards of Education).

LEZOTTE, L. and BANCROFT, B. A. (1985) 'Growing use of the effective schools model of school improvement', *Educational Leadership*, 42(8), pp. 23–27.

LIGHTFOOT, S. (1983) *The Good High School: Portraits of Character and Culture* (New York: Basic Books).

LOUIS, K. S. and MILES, M. B. (1990) *Improving the Urban High School: What Works and Why* (New York: Teachers College).

MACLEOD, J. (1987) *Ain't No Makin' It: Leveled Aspirations in a Low-Income Neighborhood* (Boulder, CO: Westview Press).

MALEN, B. and OGAWA, R. T. (1988) 'Decentralizing and democratizing the public schools: A viable approach to reform?', in S. B. Bacharach, (ed.) *Educational Reform: Making Sense of It All* (Boston: Allyn and Bacon), pp. 103–120.

MCALLISTER, S. (1991) 'Can parent involvement lead to increased student achievement in urban schools?, paper presented at the annual meeting of the American Educational Research Association, Chicago.

MCKEY, R. H., CONDELLI, L., GANSON, H., BSRRETT, B. J., MCCKONKEY, C. and PLANTZ, M. C. (1985) *The Impact of Head Start on Children, Families, and Communities* (Washington, DC: CSR).

MCLAUGHLIN, M. (1990) 'The Rand change agent study revised: Macro perspectives and micro realities', *Educational Researcher*, 19(9), pp. 11–16.

MOORE, D. and DAVENPORT, S. (1990) 'School choice: The new improved sorting machine', in W. L. Boyd and H. J. Walberg, *Choice: Potential and Problems* (Berkeley, CA: McCutchan), pp. 187–229.

MORTIMORE, P., SAMMONS, P., STOLL, L., LEWIS, D. and ECOB, R. (1988) *School Matters* (Berkeley, CA: University of California Press).

MURNANE, R. (1983) 'Quantitative studies of effective schools: What have we learned', in A. Odden and L. D. Webb (eds) *School Finance and School Improvement: Linkages for the 1980s* (Cambridge, MA: Ballinger), pp. 193–210.

MURNANE, R. J. (1988) 'Education and the productivity of the work force: Looking ahead', in R. E. Litan, R. Z. Lawrence, and C. L. Schultze (eds) *American Living Standards: Threats and Challenges* (Washington, DC: Brookings), pp. 215–246.

MURRAY, C. (1984) *Losing Ground: American Social Policy 1950–1980* (New York: Simon and Schuster).

MURPHY, J., HALLINGER, P. and MESA, R. P. (1985) 'School effectiveness: Charting professional assumptions and developing a role for state and federal government', *Teachers College Record*, 81(4), pp. 615–641.

NATRIELLO, G., MCDILL, E. L. and PALLAS, A. M. (1990) *Schooling Disadvantaged Children: Racing Against Catastrophe* (New York: Teachers College Press).

OAKES, J. (1985) *Keeping Track: How Schools Structure Inequality* (New Haven: Yale University Press).

OAKES, J. (1987) 'Improving inner-city schools: Current directions in urban district reform', Rutgers University, Center for Policy Research in Education (New Brunswick, NJ).

OGBU, J. (1974) *The Next Generation: An Ethnography of Education in an Urban Neighborhood* (New York: Academic Press).

OGBU, J. (1978) *Minority Education and Caste: The American System in Cross-Cultural Perspective* (New York: Academic Press).

OGBU, J. (1986) 'The consequences of the American caste system', in U. Neisser (ed.) *The School Achievement of Minority Children: New Perspectives* (Hillsdale, NJ: Erlbaum), pp. 19–56.

OGBU, J. (1988) 'Diversity and equity in public education: Community forces and minority school adjustment and performance', in R. Haskins and D. MacRae (eds), *Policies for America's Public Schools: Teachers, Equity and Indicators* (Norwood, NJ: Ablex).

OLSEN, M. L. (1971) *The Logic of Collective Action: Public Goods and the Theory of Groups* (Cambridge, MA: Harvard University Press).

ORFIELD, G. and MONFORT, F. (1988) 'Racial change and desegregation in large school districts: Trends through the 1986–1987 school year', Alexandria, VA: National School Boards Association.

PETERSON, P. E. (1976) *School Politics Chicago Style* (Chicago: University of Chicago Press).

PETERSON, P. E. (1981) *City Limits* (Chicago: University of Chicago Press).

PETERSON, P. E., RABE, B. and WONG, K. (1986) *When Federalism Works* (Washington, DC: Brookings).

PURKEY, S. C. and SMITH, M. S. (1983) 'Effective schools: A review', *Elementary School Journal*, 83(4), pp. 427–452.

RAND CORP. (1974) *A Model of Educational Change*, Vol. 1, Research Report No. R-1589/1-HEW (Santa Monica, CA: Rand).

RAVITCH, D. and ARMOUR, D. J. (1978) 'Busing and "white flight" ', *Public Interest*, No. 53, pp. 109–115.

RIEHL, C., PALLAS, A. M. and NATRIELLO, G. (1991) 'Annotated bibliography: The use of information by educators', Report No. 13 (Baltimore: Johns Hopkins University, Center for Research on Effective Schooling for Disadvantaged Students).

RIESSMAN, F. (1962) *The Culturally Deprived Child* (New York: Harper and Row).

ROGERS, D. (1969) 110 Livingston Street: Politics and Bureaucracy in the New York City Schools (New York: Random House).

ROGERS, E. M. (1983) *Diffusion of Innovations*, 3rd edn (New York: Free Press).

ROSENHOLTZ, S. J. (1985) 'Effective schools: Interpreting the evidence', *American Journal of Education*, 93(3), pp. 352–388.

ROWAN, B., BOSSERT, S. T. and DWYER, D. C. (1983) 'Research on effective schools: A cautionary note', *Educational Researcher*, 12(4), pp. 24–31.

ROWAN, B., GUTHRIE, L. F., LEE, G. V. and GUTHRIE, G. P. (1986) 'The design and implementation of Chapter 1 instructional services: A study of 24 schools' (San Francisco: Far West Laboratory).

RUTTER, M., MAUGHAN, B., MORTIMORE, P., OUSTON, J. and SMITH, A. (1979) *Fifteen Thousand Hours: Secondary Schools and Their Effects on Children* (Cambridge, MA: Harvard University Press).

SARASON, S. B. (1990) *The Predictable Failure of Educational Reform* (San Francisco: Jossey-Bass).

SCHORR, L. (1988) *Within Our Reach: Breaking the Cycle of Disadvantage* (New York: Basic Books).

SEELEY, D. S. (1991) 'Brother, can you paradigm? Finding a banner around which to rally in restructuring schools', paper presented at the annual meeting of the American Educational Research Association, Chicago.

SIZER, T. R. (1984) *Horace's Compromise: The Dilemma of the American High School* (Boston: Houghton Mifflin).

SPRING, J. (1989) *American Education: An Introduction to Social and Political Aspects* (New York: Longman).

TASK FORCE ON TEACHING AS A PROFESSION (1986) *A Nation Prepared: Teachers for the 21st Century* (New York: Carnegie Corporation of New York).

TRAVERS, R. M. W. (1983) *How Research Has Changed American Schools: A History from 1840 to the Present* (Kalamazoo, MI: Mythos Press).

TYACK, D. (1975) *The One Best System: A History of American Urban Education* (Cambridge, MA: Harvard University Press).

WATCHER, K. W. (1988) 'Disturbed by meta-analysis', *Science*, 241 (September), pp. 1407–1408.

WEBER, G. (1971) *Inner-city Children Can Be Taught to Read: Four Successful Schools* (Washington, DC: Council for Basic Education).

WEHLAGE, G. (ed.) (1989) *Reducing the Risk: Schools as Communities of Support* (New York: Falmer Press).

WEIKERT, D. P. (1989) *Quality Preschool Programs: A Long-term Investment* (New York: The Ford Foundation).

WEITZMAN, M., KLERMAN, L. V., LAMB, G., MENARY, J. and ALPERT, J. J. (1982) 'School absence: A problem for the pediatrician', *Pediatrics*, 69(6), pp. 739–746.

WILLIG, A. C. (1985) 'A meta-analysis of selected studies on the effectiveness of bilingual education', *Review of Educational Research*, 55(3), pp.269–318.

WILLIS, P. E. (1977) *Learning to Labour: How Working Class Kids Get Working Class Jobs* (Farnborough, UK: Saxon House).

WIMPELBERG, R., TEDDIE, C. and STRINGFIELD, S. (1989) 'Sensitivity to context: The past and future of effective schools research', *Educational Administration Quarterly*, 25(1), pp. 82–107.

WITTE, J. (1990) 'Understanding high school achievement: After a decade of research do we have any confident policy recommendations?', paper presented at the annual meeting of the American Political Science Association, San Francisco.

WOLFE, B. L. (1985) 'The influence of health on school outcomes', *Medical Care*, 23(10), pp. 1127–1138.

WOLFE, L. M. (1985) 'Postsecondary educational attainment among whites and blacks', *American Educational Research Journal*, 22(4), pp. 501–525.

WONG-FILLMORE, L. and VALDEZ, C. (1986) Teaching bilingual learners, in M. C. Wittrock (ed.), *Handbook of research on teaching*, 3rd edn (New York: Macmillan).

ZEIGLER, L. H., JENNINGS, M. K. and PEAK, T. (1974) *Governing American Schools: Political Interaction in Local School Districts* (North Scituate, MA: Duxbury).

ZIGLER, E. (1987) 'Formal schooling for four-year olds? No', *American Psychologist*, 42(3), pp. 254–260.

POLITICS OF EDUCATION ASSOCIATION YEARBOOK 1991, 45–55

3 Knowledge and power in research into the politics of urban education

Joel Spring

This essay discusses the importance of the relationship between power and knowledge for research into the politics of education. Based on this discussion, the author proposes research questions regarding the poor, effective schools, restructuring, and the influence of business on schools. Of particular concern is the effect of the relationship between power and knowledge on the education of children from poor families, and dominated racial and ethnic groups. In addition, the essay suggests an interrelationship between the political and economic interests of educational researchers and the types of research questions that they ask.

There is a relationship between the political and economic interests of those doing research on the politics of education, and the assumption by these researchers that knowledge is politically neutral. This assumption allows researchers to act as if the most important educational goals are high scores on standardized tests, retention of students and implementation of increased academic requirements. Without questioning the political nature of the knowledge distributed by the schools, researchers can join hands with any group, including the business community and politically oriented foundations, that profess the same educational goals. The assumption of the political neutrality of knowledge provides a safe haven for investigators who want to maximize their sources of support, and maintain access to research sites and networks. The unquestioned assumption of the political neutrality of knowledge creates a situation where the educational researcher acts as a servant of power.

I will illustrate my argument by posing a set of research questions related to the traditional urban school problems of poverty and bureaucracy, and recent research on effective shools. My questions will assume that there is a political dimension to the knowledge disseminated by schools. I will develop these questions by first considering the relationship between knowledge and power. After discussing this relationship and its effect on research questions regarding poverty, I will examine the types of questions asked in research on effective schools, and a spin-off of this research, John Chubb's and Terry Moe's (1990) *Politics, Markets, and America's Schools*. The Chubb and Moe book provides a basis for raising research questions about the wave of political restructuring of schools occurring in the late 1980s and early 1990s. In addition, I will suggest why policy researchers often fail to raise critical issues regarding business domination of urban school reform in the 1980s. The essay will conclude with a discussion of the political and economic interests of educational researchers.

Knowledge, power and poverty

For the purposes of this chapter, I am defining power as the ability to control the actions of other people and the ability to escape from the control of others. This definition

0268–0939/91 $3.00

provides two dimensions to the connection between knowledge and power. One dimension is where the distribution of knowledge (or schooling) is used to control others. The second dimension is where knowledge provides the individual with the ability to gain freedom from the control of others. In this context, political neutrality refers to the assumption that knowledge does not serve as an instrument of power.

Historically, education has been used to control others by distributing knowledge that builds allegiance to ruling elites, and convinces the individual to accept their subordinate position in society and existing power relations. Also, as is currently the case, if knowledge is presented as just a means for getting a job and building a career, then it denies to individuals an education that would increase their ability to raise critical questions about power relationships. In addition, institutional relations can be used to support power relationships. For instance, segregated education in the South was used to keep African-Americans in their place. On the other side of the coin, knowledge, and the institutional mechanisms for its distribution, can be a means for understanding how to free oneself from control, and how to protect oneself from economic exploitation.

The basic research questions when considering the relationship between power and knowledge are:

1. Who is gaining power as a result of the type of knowledge distributed by the educational system?
2. Who is gaining power as a result of the manner in which knowledge is distributed?

Power is also related to economic conditions in the sense that some people will use knowledge to improve their economic situation, while others will attempt to control people for the purpose of economic exploitation. This is an important issue when considering the education of children from poor families, and from dominated racial and ethnic groups.

For instance, economic issues for the poor include problems of employment and distribution of national income. During the 1980s, the rich got richer, and the middle class and poor got poorer. A 1991 report by the US Census Bureau states that between 1984 and 1988 the median income for the most affluent fifth of all households increased by 14% from $98,411 to $111,770, while the median income of all households declined from $37,012 to $35,752. The report also states that white family income is twice that of African-American families, and that the total wealth of white families is ten times that of African-American familes (Pear 1991). Other statistics show a significant change in the distribution of income between 1977 and 1990. During that period, the average pretax income of the richest fifth of the population increased by 9%, while the poorest fifth declined by 5% (Reich 1991:7).

In other words, education for employment can occur in an economy where the real wage for workers is declining and their percentage of the economic pie is remaining the same or declining. Obviously, these conditions are advantageous for businesses which want to maintain or increase profits by reducing labour costs. Under these conditions, the question can legitimately be asked:

> Is the public school system teaching the knowledge and skills needed to help workers stop the erosion of their share of the economic pie?

In other words, is the school system helping people both to gain employment and to protect themselves from economic exploitation?

Also, those concerned about the economic conditions of African-Americans might ask:

> Is the public school system teaching African-American students the knowledge and skills needed to end the disparity between white and African-American family income and wealth?

These questions are related to issues that I will raise regarding research on effective schools. The question for effective schools research could be:

> What factors in schools enhance the learning of knowledge and skills needed for workers to protect their share of national income, and to help traditionally exploited groups, such as African-Americans and Hispanics, gain a greater share of national income?

These questions are directly related to the historic debate about a major concern of research into effective schools, the education of children from poor families. One position in this debate is that poverty is a product of social and economic conditions and, therefore, the elimination of poverty is dependent on educating active citizens who will work to change those conditions. In differing forms, this argument was made by Workingmen's Parties during the common school movement, labour unions in the 19th and early 20th centuries, progressive educators led by John Dewey, social reconstructionists during the 1930s, and most recently by educational philosopher Paulo Freire (Spring 1990, Freire 1970).

In sharp contrast, many members of the business community and conservative educational leaders in the 19th and 20th centuries argued, and continue to argue, that poverty can be eliminated by giving the children of the poor an education that will help them to fit into existing economic and political relationships. This argument persists from the common school movement to the current development of compacts between urban school systems and private industry councils. The emphasis in this argument is on giving students the knowledge and social habits to meet the needs of the business community (Spring 1990).

For the purposes of this essay, it is not important which of these arguments is correct. The important thing is that they represent politically different concepts about what schools should be teaching and how students should be treated. For instance, the argument for political activism stresses the imparting of knowledge that will help individuals protect their political and economic rights, and the socialization of students for political participation. During the common school movement, the Workingmen's Parties campaigned for public schools so that future workers could gain the knowledge necesssary for protecting themselves from exploitation by the rich. Currently, Paulo Freire argues that what students learn and how they learn makes a difference as to whether or not they are economically exploited and politically disenfranchised. On the other side of the coin, during the common school movement the advocates of the Lancasterian system argued that drill and routine in schooling were important in shaping the behaviour of students to meet the needs of the workplace. Similar arguments are currently made by advocates of closer business–school relationships. In these arguments, stress is placed on the needs of the workplace determining the curriculum and socialization in schools.

Effective schools

The assumption that knowledge is politically neutral runs through the research on effective schools, restructuring, and business involvement in education. For instance, most research on effective schools focuses on identifying factors that increase student scores on standardized tests. The assumption is that standardized tests contain a universally agreed body of knowledge that is politically neutral, and that if learned this body of knowledge will be beneficial to all students. The same assumption is made by Chubb and Moe (1990) when they use standardized tests and effective schools research to develop an argument that the best method of improving American schools is through political restructuring. Also, increased business involvement in urban schools is seldom, if ever, analysed according to its effect on the type of knowledge distributed by the schools. It is just assumed that educating future workers for the benefit of business is good for the individual and society.

Consider this issue from the standpoint of effective schools research. The publication in 1979 of Michael Rutter *et al.*'s *Fifteen Thousand Hours* opened the door to a period of optimism about urban education. This book, and later research into effective schools, conclude that administrative leadership in instruction, high teacher expectations, homework, frequent evaluation of students and an orderly school climate improve student achievement (Spring 1991: pp. 100–105). I would argue, however, that just as standardized tests are not politically neutral, the recommendations of effective schools research are not neutral either.

Placed in the context of the historic debate over the education of children from poor families, important issues can be raised about the use of standardized tests in effective schools research. None of these traditional arguments agrees on what students should be taught and, consequently, they do not agree on what knowledge should be measured. For instance, one tradition emphasizes educating students about the importance of labour unions and collective action to protect economic rights, while the other tradition stresses the importance of economic competition and individualism. Even the method of teaching reading is considered a political act by educators such as Paulo Freire and Henry Giroux (Freire 1970, Giroux 1983, Spring 1990).

Viewed from this perspective, a researcher must reject the assumption of political neutrality regarding the knowledge in standardized tests and raise the issue of whose political interests are served by the use of particular tests. In addition, the researcher needs to question the meaning of effectiveness. Are schools effective in educating students for political activism and protection of economic rights or are schools effective in meeting the needs of business?

This question leads to a different research agenda for those investigating effective schools for the urban poor. This research agenda might contain the following questions:

> What factors in schools are effective in educating students from poor families to be politically active and who are able to protect their political and economic rights?
>
> What factors in schools are effective in educating students from poor families to meet the needs of the business community?

The perspective generated by these questions also raises issues regarding the findings of effective schools research. Traditionally, educators advocating political activism stress that education should be based on student interests and participation in the control of the learning environment. The other tradition emphasizes the importance of authority, order and drill in developing the habits needed by the business community. Clearly, the findings of effective schools research support the principles advocated by this latter tradition. While this does not mean that researchers on effective schools are pawns of the business community, it does add another question to our list:

> How do the political values of the researcher affect the definition of effective schooling and its measurement?

The recent movement for Afrocentric education also raises issues regarding the political content of standardized tests and effective schools research. Advocates of Afrocentricity, such as Molefi Kete Asante, argue that African-American children can only benefit from an education that places knowledge in the context of African traditions. An Afrocentric education, it is argued, provides African-American children with a positive sense of self and, consequently, provides motivation to remain in school. Advocates contend that the traditional Eurocentric curriculum reduces a sense of political power by *not* providing African-Americans with a knowledge of their participation in the shaping of the world's culture. In 1990, these arguments supported the creation of a number of cities of public schools organized around an Afrocentric curriculum (Asante 1988).

Whether or not one accepts the arguments supporting Afrocentricity is not important for this discussion. What is important is the link advocates of an Afrocentric curriculum make to the need to prepare students for political participation. From this perspective, the cultural base used to measure school effectiveness is a political decision. Eurocentric tests given to African-American children, according to this argument, are a measure of the degree of subjugation of African-American children. For the advocates of an Afrocentric education, the only appropriate test that would measure the effective education of African-American children would be one based on an Afrocentric curriculum. Therefore, in the context of Afrocentricity, there is no such thing as a politically neutral test.

The arguments for Afrocentricity create more questions about research into effective schools.

> What factors enhance the effectiveness of schools in educating students within a particular cultural tradition?
>
> In the context of the answer to the previous question, does the cultural tradition of the curriculum of a school enhance or reduce the sense of political power of students?

These questions suggest that schools could be effective in teaching a cultural tradition that reduces the political power of students. For example, studies of the history of colonial education suggest that the imposition of a cultural tradition through schooling was an important means for the group in power to maintain power. In particular, the British in India and Africa, and the French in Africa and Asia, imposed their curricula on conquered countries as a means of proclaiming and establishing the superiority of their own cultures, and as a strategy for undercutting the political power of indigenous groups (Carnoy 1974).

Bureaucracy

Similar research questions can be asked regarding Chubb and Moe's *Politics, Markets, & American Schools*. Written in the 1980s, their book reflects the general concern of the period with changing the structure of control of urban schools. At the heart of these changes is increasing control at the school level through site-based management or, as in the case of Chicago, giving control to elected parent councils. In addition, the 1980s and 1990s is a period when the Republican Party along with some liberal groups has actively supported choice in education as a means of changing power relationships. Beginning in the 1980 election, the Republican Party platform advocated support of choice through tuition tax credits (Spring 1991: 200–203).

The Republican agenda is reflected in Chubb and Moe's conclusion that the major hope for American schools is the introduction of a choice plan. From the standpoint of the politics of research, it is not surprising that their study was in part financed by the Republican-controlled US Department of Education which, at the time of their research, was headed by a strong advocate of choice, Secretary of Education William Bennett. Indeed, their major criticism of the schools is the same as that of former Secretary Bennett.

They argue that the primary source of problems for American education is the control exerted by an unwieldy educational bureaucracy (Spring 1988: 54–57).

Of course, liberals and conservatives have attacked bureaucracy as a major source of problems in education. The radical right argued in the 1950s that the educational bureaucracy made the schools havens for Communist thinking by introducing progressive education. The military-defence establishment, led by the developer of the nuclear submarine, Admiral Hyman Rickover, charged the educational bureaucracy with making public schools the weakest link in America's defence against the Soviet Union. On the other hand, in the 1960s, liberals attacked urban educational bureaucracies for promoting racism, segregation and social class discrimination (Spring 1989).

Chubb and Moe believe that the source of the problem is democracy. They write, 'In sum, the politics of democratic control promotes the piece-by-piece construction of a peculiar set of organizational arrangements that are highly bureaucratic' (Chubb and Moe 1990:44). This occurs, they argue, because the uncertainty of democratic policies causes educational leaders to construct bureaucracies as both a means of control and as a means of protection. Surprisingly, the enemy of American education becomes democracy. They describe the construction of bureaucracies in the following manner:

> Direct democratic control stimulates a political struggle over the right to impose higher-order values on the schools through public authority, and this in turn promotes bureaucracy – which is both a crucial means of ensuring that these higher-order values are actually implemented at the school level (by personnel who may not agree with them) and a crucial means of insulating them from subversion by opposing groups and officials who may gain hold of public authority in the future. (Chubb and Moe 1990:167)

Their answer for the problems of American schools is to replace democratic control with control by the free market-place. In other words, they propose choice as a solution. This argument is justified by using the research on effective schools and data collected on changes in high school performance from 1980 to 1982 by the High School and Beyond (HSB) survey. Using this data, Chubb and Moe conclude that improvement in student achievement is directly related to increasing school autonomy or, in other words, eliminating the educational bureaucracy.

Besides the issue of the content of the achievement tests that are used to justify their argument, there is the question of the validity of the research that is used. As Michael Kirst (1990) points out, combining research on effective schools with data from the HSB survey is mixing apples with oranges. Effective schools research is primarily focused on elementary schools while the arguments of Chubb and Moe and the HSB data are focused on high schools. In addition, Kirst questions the HSB data because it is based on five tests containing only 116 items to be completed in 63 minutes. Kirst doubts that high school achievement for grades 10–12 can be judged by such short tests. For instance, the science test for these three high school grades is only 10 minutes in length. In addition, there were no tests for social studies and foreign languages (Kirst 1990).

The flimsy quality of the data used by Chubb and Moe suggests that a knowledge of their political values could be important for understanding their conclusions. Since the data might not prove their conclusions, their study might be considered a political argument rather than a scientific study. At this time, I am unable to chart clearly their particular set of political values.

On the other hand, if we accept the research material as supporting their argument, then we must deal with the issue of content of the tests. Similar to most researchers in the politics of education, Chubb and Moe never discuss the content and values embodied in the tests used by the HSB and by effective schools researchers. Without knowing the content and values in these tests, it is difficult to determine the meaning of effectiveness in their research.

For instance, I doubt that these tests reflect the values and content of an Afrocentric education. Therefore, from the standpoint of supporters of an Afrocentric education, Chubb and Moe do not prove that choice plans will increase the effectiveness of schools in empowering African-American students. Also, one wonders if the tests reflect the content and values of an education that would prepare people to work actively to change the social and economic conditions that create poverty. This raises the important question:

> Do the HSB tests primarily reflect knowledge and values needed for fitting into existing social and economic conditions?

Of course, one could argue that choice plans would allow for the development of schools reflecting a broad range of political and cultural values. This seems unlikely because of increasing control by state governments of academic requirements and the content of instruction by the use of statewide tests. There is nothing in Chubb and Moe's research or conclusions to suggest that choice plans would be more effective in creating these alternative schools as compared with some form of increased democratic control.

Given their assumption of the neutrality of knowledge, Chubb and Moe never ask:

> Who will gain power as a result of turning public schooling over to the forces of the market-place?

What their research data suggest is that choice will enhance the power of those who benefit from the knowledge measured and values contained in the tests used in their research. Personally, I believe that choice plans have the potential for establishing schools that offer truly alternative forms of political and cultural knowledge. But based on their research, I cannot determine if choice plans or democratic control would be the best means for achieving these alternative-type institutions. Given their lack of discussion of this issue, one might conclude after reading their book that choice plans might primarily enhance the power of white, middle and upper middle class, and conservative religious groups.

Given that studies of alternative methods of controlling public education will probably increase during this period of restructuring, it is essential to include research questions on the relationship between power and knowledge. For instance, the following questions might be asked:

> Does the particular change in control (site-based management, parents' councils, choice, etc.) favour the distribution of particular forms of knowledge and values?
>
> Who is gaining power (as I defined power at the beginning of the essay) because of the particular change in control?

Business and urban schools

Questions of this sort should be asked about increased business involvement in education. There seems to be wide acceptance of the idea that if education serves the interests of business then it serves the interests of the individual. The acceptance of business control is dramatically highlighted by the 1991 proposal of the New York City Schools Chancellor, Joseph Fernandez, to provide warranties to business that graduates of the school system will be able to read, write and calculate. If the employer finds the graduate lacking in these skills, the school system promises to provide remedial programmes. Fernandez's proposal was influenced by the wallet-sized 'Guaranteed Employability Certificate' issued by the Prince George's County public school system (Berger 1991).

The uncritical acceptance of ties between business and schools is exemplified by Eleanor Farrar's case study of the Boston Compact between the local private industry council and the Boston public schools. Issued as a report for the Center for Policy Research in Education Studies, the study describes the functioning of the Boston Compact from 1982, the date of its signing, to 1985. The Compact promised jobs for Boston graduates in return for improvements in student achievement. It became a model for similar efforts around the country (Farrar 1988).

Exemplifying the uncritical acceptance of this arrangement is a quote by Farrar from Phil Moskoff of Jamaica Plain High School: '[The Compact] works far better than I imagined.... For students the Compact shows... that there is a connection between school and work.... And it has helped in that a lot of kids who didn't see a concrete value in education, now do' (Farrar 1988:29). The same uncritical acceptance is reflected in Farrar's conclusion: 'In three years, the Boston Compact became a national success story, attracting scores of visitors eager to learn about how to begin similar ventures in their own cities' (Farr 1988:27).

Business influence on state and national educational policy also increased during this period. The Task Force on Education for Economic Growth of the Education Commission of the States was dominated by the heads of leading corporations, such as AT&T, Dow Chemical, Xerox, Ford Motor Company, and IBM. The influential report of this task force, *Action for Excellence*, declares: 'We believe especially that businesses, in their role as employers, should be much more involved in the process of setting goals for education in America' (Task Force on Education for Economic Growth 1983:80). At the level of state government, the business community during this period increased its activity in educational affairs (Spring 1991:176–189).

In the framework of my argument, the question that should be asked is:

> Who is gaining power (ability to control others) as a result of increased business influence over the type of knowledge distributed by the educational system?

To answer this question, one must consider the possible benefits that the business community might wish to gain from school systems. My list of possible benefits is based on the assumption that a major motivating factor in the actions of American business is the desire to increase profits. One way of enhancing profits is to maintain low wages and tax rates. Based on these assumptions, businesses might want public school systems to:

1. educate potential employees at the lowest cost to the corporate taxpayer:
2. reduce the cost of labour by educating a steady stream of employees for particular segments of the labour market;
3. concentrate on skills needed by business;
4. present knowledge as instrumental for work as opposed to knowledge as a means to develop a critical awareness of politics and the economy;
5. socialize the student to be a compliant worker who will not rock the corporate boat;
6. avoid teaching about unionism and collective action as a possible means of improving working conditions and wages, because these would increase labour costs and reduce profits;
7. teach the student a pro-business ideology that would not question increasing concentrations of wealth.

In the context of this list, businesses might want to exert power to make the school system educate employees who can be easily controlled in the workplace and who can be ideologically controlled to support policies that will reduce wages and enhance corporate profits.

To deal with these issues, one would have to decide on what knowledge and skills are required to help workers and exploited groups enhance their economic position in society. I am sure that deliberation of this issue would result in a clear distinction between the knowledge business wants distributed through the schools, and the knowledge workers and dominated groups need to protect themselves from economic exploitation.

Educational researchers as servants of power

Related to the preceding discussion is the question of why researchers avoid these issues by assuming the political neutrality of knowledge. I would argue that the answer to this question can be found in a consideration of the political nature of research. Obviously, a major influence on research is sources of funding. A Republican-dominated Department of Education is not very likely to support research into factors in schooling that could help workers increase their share of national income. The same thing is true of large foundations, such as the Carnegie Corporation and the Ford Foundation. Governments and foundations provide educational research money in the framework of their agendas for the public schools.

In addition, the political values of the researcher influence decisions about research. A white researcher might ask different questions about schools and the curriculum than an African-American committed to empowerment through an Afrocentric education. Different questions might also occur because of dissimilar beliefs about the roles of government and business in society.

Also, research networks might have an influence, because the researcher might be unwilling to ask questions that would offend sources of support and close off access to research sites. For instance, a researcher might avoid questions that would offend school authorities because the researcher needs access to schools and school personnel. Also, school authorities might hesitate before allowing research that might not be approved by some group having influence on the school system.

I believe that because of these factors, the researcher tends to avoid questions of the political nature of knowledge. By putting on blinkers about the content of learning, a researcher into the politics of education can act as if the most important goals are high scores on standardized tests, retention of students and carrying out government policies. Researchers can investigate the effectiveness of policy without raising the question of who is gaining power as a result of that policy.

This situation is well illustrated by the two major groups doing research into the politics of education, the Center for Policy Research (CPRE) and Policy Analysis for California Education (PACE). Both organizations are tied to an interdependent network of government officials, academic researchers and government financial support. Neglecting all concerns about the relationship between knowledge and power, researchers for these groups tend to focus on the relatively safe issue of the effectiveness of implementing government policies and not their consequences as related to the distribution of power.

For instance, PACE has engaged in a number of studies about the impact of educational legislation in California. Assuming that knowledge is politically neutral, PACE researchers investigated the curricular change in California schools by simply determining the percentage change in the number of course sections offered throughout the state (Grossman *et al.* 1985). This study yielded simplistic results such as, between 1982 and 1985 there was a 21% decline in the number of course sections in home economics and a 34% increase in the number of course sections of European history. No analysis of the political content of these courses was performed nor were questions asked about which students would benefit from these changes. It was assumed that these curricular changes would benefit all students.

This type of simplistic educational research finds justification in the application of systems analysis to educational research questions. A leading advocate of this approach is Michael Kirst, the co-director of PACE, major consultant on school finance reform to several state legislatures and holder of many government positions, including president of the California State Board of Education and staff director of the US Senate Subcommission on Employment, Manpower and Poverty. Kirst's use of systems analysis results in a consideration of educational politics as a study of inputs and outputs. Absent from his analysis is the suggestion that inputs into the educational system involve desires for power that extend outside the system. Therefore, in the previously mentioned PACE study of curricular changes in which Kirst was a co-investigator, the problem was simply treated as a matter of inputs (legislative action) and outputs (curricular changes). Questions dealing with who benefits in terms of economic and political power as a result of the type of knowledge disseminated by the schools are not only absent from this study but also from Kirst's co-authored textbook (Wirt and Kirst 1989).

The same lack of critical questioning appears in some investigations of the financing of school reform in the 1980s (Odden 1987). The major questions have been about whether state funding is adequate for supporting educational reform. It is assumed that any increase in financial support for educational reform is good for all students. It is not asked who is benefiting from reform and who is paying the bill. For instance, research might have found that lower income groups are paying a greater share of educational costs for school systems that are being reformed to benefit primarily business and upper income groups.

In fact, I would argue that because of their lack of consideration of the relationship between power and knowledge, researchers for organizations like PACE and CPRE missed one of the most important trends in the 1980s. This was a trend that would have devastating effects on schools in the 1990s. As researchers accepted the educational value of business-sponsored reforms and investigated their implementation, business was quietly withdrawing its financial support of the public school system.

As researchers into the politics of education danced to the tune of government and foundation research money, business and the wealthy reduced their financial support of public schools through reductions in federal and state taxes, and tax abatements in local school districts. After changes in the federal income tax in the 1980s, the income tax on the wealthiest citizens in the USA was the lowest of any industrialized nation in the world. During this same period, many states reduced income taxes on the wealthy and taxes on corporations. At the local level, corporate share of local property tax revenues declined from 45% in 1957 to 16% in 1987. As economist Robert Reich states, 'By the end of the 1980s, the top 1 percent of American earners were paying a combined federal-state-local tax rate of only 26.8 percent, compared with 29 percent in 1975 and 19.6 percent in 1966' (Reich, 1991: 200, 246, 281).

In summary, there is an interrelationship between the political and economic interests of researchers and their research questions. Therefore, the issue of knowledge and power creates a new set of questions about politics and education, and adds to the research agenda questions about the political and economic interests of researchers. Without a consideration of this latter set of questions, we cannot fully understand how the politics of research determines research into the politics of urban education.

References

ASANTE, M. K. (1988) *Afrocentricity* (Trenton: Africa World Press).

BERGER, J. (1991) 'Fernandez proposes placing warranties on graduates in '92', *The New York Times* (5 January 1991), pp. 1, 25.

CARNOY, M. (1974) *Education as Cultural Imperialism* (New York: David McKay Company).

CHUBB, J. E. and MOE, T. M. (1990) *Politics, Markets & Schools* (Washington, DC: The Brookings Institution).

FARRAR, E. (1988) *The Boston Compact: A Teaching Case* (Brunswick, NJ: Center for Policy Research in Education).

FREIRE, P. (1970) *Pedagogy of the Oppressed* (New York: Continuum).

GROSSMAN, P., KIRST, M., NEGASH, W. and SCHMIDT-POSNER, J. (1985) *Study of Curricular Change in California Comprehensive High Schools: 1982–83 to 1984–85*, Policy Paper No. PP85-7-4 (Berkeley: PACE).

GIROUX, H. (1983) *Theory of Resistance* (South Hadley, MA: Bergin & Garvey).

KIRST, M. (1990) 'Politics, markets, and American schools by John E. Chubb and Terry M. Moe', *Politics of Education Bulletin*, 17 (1), pp. 2–3, 8.

ODDEN, A. (1987) 'The economics of financing educational excellence', paper presented to the American Education Research Association, Washington, DC.

PEAR, R. (1991) 'Rich got richer in 80's; others held even', *The New York Times* (11 January 1991), pp. 1, 20.

REICH, R. (1991) *The Work of Nations: Preparing Ourselves for 21st-Century Capitalism* (New York: Alfred A. Knopf).

RUTTER, M., MAUGHAN, B., MORTIMORE, P., OUSTON, J. and SMITH, A. (1979) *Fifteen Thousand Hours* (Cambridge, MA: Harvard University Press).

SPRING, J. (1989) *The Sorting Machine Revisited: National Educational Policy Since 1945* (White Plains: Longman).

SPRING, J. (1990) *The American School 1642–1990*, 2nd Edn (White Plains: Longman).

SPRING, J. (1991) *American Education: An Introduction to Social and Political Aspects*, 5th Edn (White Plains: Longman).

TASK FORCE ON EDUCATION FOR ECONOMIC GROWTH (1983) *Action for Excellence* (Denver: Education Commission of the States).

WIRT, F. and KIRST, M. (1989) *The Politics of Education: Schools in Conflict*, 2nd Edn (Berkeley, CA: Mc Cutchan).

POLITICS OF EDUCATION ASSOCIATION YEARBOOK 1991, 57–69

4 *Public choice perspectives on urban schools*

Joseph G. Weeres and Bruce Cooper

Using public choice theory as a conceptual orientation, the authors argue that politics in urban school districts have differed from those in suburban school districts. Urban school politics have been characterized by relatively well-organized interest groups and weak market controls, although politics in suburban school districts vary also, as a function of the strength of market controls. The strength of these interest groups in city school systems is reflected in school board politics, in the administrative structure and in district policies. Interest group liberalism in urban school districts may be lessening due to the changing educational needs of urban students and due to reformers' efforts to give parents more educational choices. However, the success of market reforms depends on a number of conditions which will be a severe challenge to reformers.

Big-city school districts once again are at the forefront of educational reform. The Chicago public school district has radically decentralized its governance system down to citizen control at the school site level. In other cities, such as Rochester, Hammond, Cincinnati, Louisville, Miami and Pittsburgh, efforts are under way to transform the professional role of teachers (Kerchner *et al.* 1990). Milwaukee has introduced an extensive social choice plan, and a host of other cities are reconsidering the structures by which services are delivered.

The pattern of governance in big cities has not been like that in most suburban school districts. Big-city school districts typically have had more well-organized interest groups, virtually full-time school board members, greater reliance on intergovernmental funding, and larger administrative bureaucracies relative to the number of students. The style of politics that has frequently characterized these districts is what Lowi (1969) termed 'interest group liberalism', the mutual accommodation of well-established interest groups.

In this paper we conclude that the hold of these interest groups on urban public schools may be lessening. Throughout the 1980s, especially during the so-called 'second wave' of school reform from 1986 to 1990, reformers introduced a range of innovations designed to strengthen the school market and to dissaggregate the processes of political governance to give clients in these urban districts greater school options and a stronger say in how schools are run.

These reforms are interpreted in light of a general model of school politics we construct based on work drawn from public choice theory. We first advance the argument that school politics in suburban communities varies systematically as a function of the strength of market controls. The model delineates effects on school board politics, bureaucratic structure and district policies. We then argue that politics in large urban city school districts is a special case of weak market controls coupled with the influence of relatively well-organized interest groups which produces the pattern of politics characteristic of interest group liberalism. We conclude by examining school reforms being implemented in many urban cities designed to restructure this governance system.

Public choice theory

The theoretical perspective we bring to this analysis is drawn from public choice theory. It is perhaps a misnomer to refer to this work as a theory, in the sense of a developed body of hypotheses and constructs. At this stage of its development, it is more of a conceptual orientation: the application of economic reasoning to the study of politics. Many scholars in the field of education have been sceptical of economic models for the study of school politics, for such constructs are perceived as too simplistic, assuming pure individual rationality, perfect information and fully competitive markets. Furthermore, public choice theory often has been expressed by economists in normative terms, leading to invidious distinctions between the qualities of public and private sectors. Public choice theory has another face, however: one that is at once more analytic and less normative, and one which constructs its theoretical postulates on a foundation of assumptions less rarefied that those embodied in classical economics.

This work stems from the recognition by economists that classical economic theory is not a theory of competition but of decentralization (Demsetz 1982, Moe 1984). Classical theory explains how goods are allocated optimally without central control in a market composed of small, autonomous units. It does not explain how actors compete: the strategies they adopt, the ways they organize themselves, the alliances they build with other actors. Work related to these topics has led to the use of more realistic assumptions, and to the development of theoretical arguments potentially useful for enriching our understanding of school politics. For general reviews of public choice theory, see Aranson (1981) and Moe (1984); Boyd (1982) and Michaelsen (1980) discuss some of the literature in relationship to school politics.

A public choice model of school politics

Principal-agent theory, an important construct in the public choice literature, potentially offers a useful way of conceptualizing school politics. Many of the relationships embedded in school politics are agency relationships in which one party (the principal) enters into an agreement with another (the agent) with the hope that the agent will maximize the principal's welfare. The school board, for example, signs a contract with a superintendent with the expectation that the superintendent will serve its interests. The superintendent, in turn, has similar hopes when hiring administrators and teachers. The structure of school politics can be conceived of as a chain of these relationships beginning with the citizen and ending with the teacher.

Alchian and Demsetz (1972), originators of principal-agent theory, point out that these relationships are subject to conflict of interest and information asymmetry. The school board, for example, may locate a qualified school superintendent, but that is no guarantee that the superintendent will not serve his or her own personal interest instead of the board's. Moreover, once on the job, the superintendent will acquire specialized information that can be used to shape board policies, as well as individual board-member perceptions of their agent's own administrative performance (Zeigler and Jennings 1974).

The same control problems manifest themselves within each set of hierarchical links in the chain connecting the citizen to the teacher in the classroom. Williamson (1975), for example, has examined the effects of unobservable information and behaviour on hierarchical control within bureaucratic organizations, such as that which might pertain to the administrator–teacher link. The solution to these control problems, according to principal-agent theory, lies in the institutional and organizational design of monitoring devices and incentives structures that will induce the agent to maximize the principal's welfare within each set of links in the chain.

The market solution

The institutional design of public education at the local level relies mainly on markets for citizens (the principals) to exercise control over their agents. In a seminal paper, Tiebout (1956) pointed out that the proliferation of local political jurisdictions within metropolitan areas creates conditions conducive to market competition. Individuals exercise choice as to residential and business location, and local governments compete with one another to attract businesses and citizens capable of paying taxes and user fees to their communities. Under these conditions, governments fine tune their governmental service packages to make their communities desirable to those most able to purchase those services via local taxes, and individual citizens and businesses shop for communities which provide the most services for the least taxes. Tiebout hypothesized that a perfectly efficient market within large metropolitan areas would result in a distribution of relatively small, internally homogeneous communities, stratified from one another by the median income of residents and the quality of governmental services. Under these circumstances, politics, as we commonly think of it, would simply mediate the economic imperatives of this market competition. Citizens already would be grouped on the basis of choice regarding the governmental services they want and are willing to pay for, thereby diminishing the necessity for political voice. Governments would be constrained by the exit option of citizens and businesses if service delivery packages were not tailored to meet the needs of the citizens they desired to retain and attract. Under these conditions, dissatisfaction theory (Iannaccone and Lutz 1970, Lutz and Iannaccone 1978) would provide a reasonably accurate approximation of the type of school politics that would ensue. As demographic changes occurred in communities, citizens would simply need to express their dissatisfaction with governmental service delivery packages through the election of a new board majority. The board in turn would hire a new superintendent, who would recouple the district's services to meet the needs of its new clients. Politics would be largely regulated by market controls.

Historical political boundaries, legal statutes and transactions costs, however, limit the efficiency of this market. Political jurisdictions are not established solely by the market. The jurisdictional boundaries of big cities, for example, were established prior to the baby boom following the Second World War which fuelled the enormous expansion of the metropolitan area, making the diverse market of local communities possible. State legislatures and county governments also intervene to set annexation rules and conditions for the formation of local governmental units. Equity norms and legal requirements for equal treatment limit the capacity of local governments to tailor service delivery packages to satisfy those citizens in the community who have the most taxpaying capacity (Peterson 1981). Statutes restricting redlining make it more difficult for communities to exclude less capable taxpayers via zoning regulations. Relatively robust transaction costs associated with migrating from one community to the next (realtor fees, closing costs, moving expenses, etc.) constrain the ability of citizens and businesses to optimize their expenditure of tax dollars in purchasing the packages of governmental services offered by various communities. For the less affluent, these transaction costs often are sufficiently high to preclude the exercise of choice.

Hamilton (1983) has estimated that these metropolitan markets operate moderately efficiently. Greater efficiency is achieved at the top end of the income scale, because in these communities taxpayers can most afford the transaction costs associated with emigration and exit. Grubb (1982) found that the demographic composition of communities within metropolitan areas reflected a greater emphasis by citizens on low tax rates than on optimal governmental service delivery packages. Citizens attempted to minimize the high informational costs associated with searching for optimal services by selecting communities with the lowest tax rates relative to the desired demographic composition of the community ('birds of a feather logic').

Public choice theory, consequently, is likely to have sufficient explanatory power to make arguments such as Peterson's (1981) useful, namely, that cities pursue their own economic interest by promoting developmental policies and avoiding redistributive ones. Peterson's related federalism argument has been supported in empirical studies by Vogel (1979), Kearney and Kim (1990), and Schneider and Ji (1990). Schneider (1989) also presents data confirming a range of hypotheses deduced from Peterson's work. (For a contrary perspective, see Sanders and Stone [1987].)

Inefficiencies in the functioning of these metropolitan markets, however, leave plenty of room for more traditional political explanations of governmental behaviour. Wong and Peterson (1986), for example, found that mayoral preferences played some role in how federal block grant revenues were spent even though overall their use resulted in less redistributive social policies. Dreier and Keating (1990) found a similar mayoral influence with respect to housing policy in the city of Boston. Wong (1988) has argued that communities have more political choices than the structural economic constraint model implies because sufficient fragmentation, segmentation and conflict occur among subunits within the city and subareas of policy to constrain the enactment of the collective economic interest of the city. Political actors still want to know which subunits will benefit, by how much, and which will pay the costs.

Effects of market controls on school politics

Analytically, market controls can be conceptualized as a continuum ranging from circumstances where the market functions efficiently to those where such controls are relatively weak. Many factors contribute to the relative efficiency of the market, including ways in which local governments are structured. But since most school districts have similar governmental structures, transactions costs to individuals, particularly the exercise or threat of the exit option, are the primary determinant of market efficiency. District size also is a factor in the capacity of citizens (the principals) to induce their agents (board members, superintendent, and administrators) to serve their interests. As district size expands the costs of participating in the political process also typically increase, because individuals need to mobilize a larger number of other citizens to make their voice effectively heard. Later, when we examine politics in large urban school districts, we will address the effects of district size. For now, though, let us consider the impact of market controls on school politics in the relatively smaller suburban districts. The basic hypothesis advanced is that the pattern of politics which emerges in small districts systematically varies as a function of the strength of market controls, or, conversely, the transaction costs to individuals of market entry and exit.

Table 1 presents the distribution of these effects with respect to school board politics, administrative behaviour and school district policies for districts in which market controls are strong, moderate and weak. Also identified are the demographic characteristics of districts most typically associated with each level of market control. In discussing these effects, we are examining only the influence of market controls. Myriad other factors impinge on school politics in any given community, making the observed patterns more complex than represented by the single variable market control model. School districts also are distributed more evenly along the market control axis than the three types identified in table 1.

Table 1. Effects of market controls on school politics

	Strength of Controls		
	Strong	*Moderate*	*Weak*
Economic status	Affluent	Middle class	Poor
Demographic composition	Homogeneous	Heterogeneous	Homogeneous
Board politics	Trustee	Unstable majorities	Machine-like
Administrative bureaucracy	Professional and administratively efficient	Street-level bureaucrat and moderately efficient	Insular and allocationally inefficient
District policies	Coherent with low divisibility	Disjointed with moderately high divisibility	Disconnected from population and low divisibility
General type	Quasi-private schools	Politicized schools	Monopolist schools

Market controls and socio-economic status

Market controls are likely to be coincident with the socio-economic status of the school district population because transaction costs for individuals vary by income. Affluent citizens can more readily exercise the exit option than the economically poor. Market controls, consequently, will be strongest in the highly affluent communities and become progressively weaker as the socio-economic status of citizens decreases.

Districts with populations at the top and low end of the income scale will be more homogeneous in composition than those in the middle. Citizens who are affluent have the most choices with respect to housing location. They will select communities where their tax dollars will purchase public services exclusively for them, and they have the income to bid up housing prices sufficiently to make their communities of choice relatively homogeneous in socio-economic composition. Homeogeneity at the bottom end of the income scale is achieved because more affluent citizens will not want their tax dollars to support redistributive social programmes for the economically poor (Peterson 1981).

Where market controls are moderate in strength, communities will have a tendency to become more heterogeneous in their socio-economic composition. For middle-class citizens, the transaction costs associated with moving away are just high enough relative to their incomes to make rational calculation of voice and exit ambiguous. Some will decide to stay; others to leave. If the ratio of new homes in a metropolitan area is high relative to existing structures (as it was in the 1950s and '60s), a higher proportion of middle-class citizens will choose the exit option, because housing costs on the periphery tend to be low relative to equivalent units closer to the city centre. But when this ratio become smaller (as it is today because metropolitan areas are larger and population growth has slowed in many areas), then middle-class citizens collectively have fewer choices and, consequently, Tiebout's (1956) sorting process becomes less efficient. These communities often become more heterogeneous economically and ethnically in their population composition as housing and infrastructure age and less affluent and more ethnically diverse citizens begin purchasing or renting available structures (Stahura 1988).

School board politics

Citizen participation in school politics is a function of resources and need. Sharp (1984) has suggested that the joint influence of these two factors on participation is distributed parabolically by income. Affluent citizens have high resources but comparatively low need for governmental services. Many of their wants can be satisfied privately. Citizens who are poor have high need but few resources to make their participation effective. Middle-income citizens have both resources and need, which produces more intense participation.

These varying levels of participation in conjunction with market controls shape school board politics. Where market controls are strong, boards and administrators must design policies responsive to collective community needs or risk the loss of taxpayers. At the same time, affluent citizens are less compelled to demand governmental response to personal needs because many of these can be satisfied privately. Trustee boards emerge under these two conditions. They operate in a zone of indifference sufficient to legislate broad policy for the district. Nominating committees often are used as a monitoring device to ensure that individuals with community policy perspectives are elected to the board.

Moderate market controls produce more politicized boards. Attenuation of the exit option allows boards and administrators greater flexibility to construct school delivery packages divergent from the (hypothetical) collective district interest. This latitude provides different groups of citizens with opportunities to shift district policy towards their special preferences. This slack, coupled with a propensity of middle-class citizens to participate, leads to unstable board majorities, because after one special interest shifts policy off-centre to their advantage another will mobilize to turn it in their direction. Ethnic and socio-economic heterogeneity magnify the tendency towards circular social choice (Weeres 1988).

Weak market controls and low participation permit boards to develop political machine-like characteristics. Where citizens cannot easily exit and do not have the resources to monitor their agents, board members can engage in friends-and-neighbours government. In education, external regulatory controls mitigate these tendencies.

Administrative bureaucracy

These differences in the principal–agent relations of citizens to boards influence the behaviour and allocational efficiency of the administrative bureaucracy. In districts where market controls are strong and trustee government is secure, boards can allow superintendents and administrative personnel considerable professional discretion in operating the schools. The identification of collective goals by the board, the pressure of the market and professional autonomy facilitate allocational efficiency.

Politicized boards and participative citizens, however, closely monitor administrators. This tight coupling produces leaner bureaucracies than perhaps is allocationally efficient, because each expenditure is contested by someone. It also converts the role of the superintendent into that of a politician. Left unattended, circular social choices of boards and participative citizens would trigger exit by many residents from the community, thereby diminishing fiscal and other resources. The superintendent is held accountable for the well-being of the district, and, consequently, must function as a politician to remain in office. The task is to fashion what often turn out to be a set of rolling coalitions in order to constrain the range of policy shifts produced by single-issue board and community participants. The relative power of the board and superintendent, therefore, is not zero-sum: in these communities both are relatively fragile, whereas both the board and superintendent are comparatively powerful under conditions of strong market controls.

Low market controls and machine-like boards produce insular administrative bureaucracies. Board members may intervene to acquire special favours for friends and neighbours, but they also are not compelled by community demands to closely monitor the actions of administrators. Nor do market controls exert much pressure on the administrative bureaucracy to be allocationally efficient. Administrative size, therefore, should display a U-shaped curve (after the relevant controls for revenue, student population, sources of funding, etc.): higher where market controls are weak or strong, and lower where they are moderate.

District policies

Districts which function under strong market controls display most of the characteristics Chubb and Moe (1990) attribute to private schools. The educational service delivery packages that emerge are cohesive and accountable to the collective needs of the community. Trustee boards and professionally autonomous administrators are reluctant to respond to individual client demands that are incompatible with district policy.

Concessions to individual client demands are greater in politicized districts. Slack for meeting these demands is created by the comparatively higher transaction costs (relative to income) for middle-class residents to exercise their exit option. If the community becomes economically heterogeneous in its composition, and new housing construction in the metropolitan area slows, then the product can be subdivided even further, But, more typically, a measure of coherence in the service delivery package is compelled by the market.

Weak market controls allow for monopolist behaviour by school districts. They do not need to respond attentively to client demands either collectively or individually, because transaction costs associated with exit are high relative to the income of residents.

Organized interest groups in big cities

Market controls on big-city school districts are weak. These districts not only have a high percentage of lower socio-economic residents, but their large size increases the costs of citizen influence over board and school district policy. However, the pattern of politics which typically emerges in these districts is altered by the influence of relatively well-organized interest groups.

Much of the literature on big-city politics (Banfield and Wilson 1963, Greenstone and

Peterson 1973, Teaford 1990) reports the presence and influence of comparatively well-organized groups, including business organizations, labour unions, homeowners' associations, ethnic groups and even, in some cities, residual political party organizations. Suburban communities appear to display a more diffuse, less formal type of interest group participation (Schneider 1989). Indeed, McConnell (1966), found that as the size of political jurisdiction increased so did the number and diversity of formally organized groups. Small jurisdictions, he argued, led to the exclusion of minority interests in political bargaining.

Yet, Olson (1965), in his well-known public choice analysis of group formation, advanced a theory that seemed to suggest the reverse: large latent constituencies would have more difficulty organizing than smaller ones. Rational individuals, Olson pointed out, would be discouraged by free-riders who could gain benefits without incurring costs, and by the probability that any individual contribution would not be sufficient to obtain the collective good.

However, more recent experimental research by Oliver, Marwell, and their associates (Oliver *et al.* 1985, Oliver and Marwell 1988, Marwell *et al.* 1988) frames the problem differently, leading to way out of the social trap of free-riding. They note that the cost of a collective good does not necessarily increase with the size of the group: many individuals can partake of the good (e.g. obtaining a new superintendent for the district) without decreasing its supply to others. This, in turn, means that if a small, critical mass organizes to procure the good, they do not have to worry about costs being driven up by free riders. Organizers' benefits are not diminished by the consumption of the good by non-contributors.

Oliver and Marwell go on to hypothesize that critical mass is more likely to be achieved in large groups. As the size of the group increases, the group becomes more heterogeneous in its composition (due to the probability of extreme values in the distribution), and consequently the greater the probability that some critical mass of individuals, who have a great desire to see the collective good produced and who possess resources sufficient to absorb a relatively large share of the start-up costs, will step forward to launch the collective effort. These individuals do not need to procure the entire good. They just must achieve enough of a partial victory to sustain the critical mass and call public and governmental attention to the interests of the larger collective. They then can use the social leverage of the larger unorganized constituency as bargaining chits with governmental agencies. One tactic frequently employed is to precipitate a crisis that temporarily mobilizes latent members as a show of strength (Alinsky tactics). This reasoning is consonant with McConnell's (1966) contention that if a group comprises 10% of a million-person jurisdictional population it is more likely to be represented in an organized form than when it is 10% of ten thousand. It also seems to square with the empirical literature on organized interests in big-city politics. Organized groups form, but still confront relatively severe organizational maintenance needs which influence how they participate (Banfield and Wilson 1963).

Interest group liberalism, which at the outset we indicated characterized school politics in large urban districts, is a function of organized interest groups operating in an environment of weak market controls. The influence of these groups contributes to the shape of school board politics, administrative structure and district policies.

School board politics

In big-city school districts, organized groups (the principals) closely monitor their agents on the board. Individual board members obtain and retain office through the sponsorship of particular organized constituencies (e.g. teachers' union, neighbourhood associations, ethnic advocacy groups, etc.). The close identification of board members with these groups helps ensure their incumbencies, giving big-city school districts relatively stable boards. This stability, in turn, fosters norms of pluralistic exchange that encourage log-rolling. Consequently, demands of organized interests tend to be accommodated in board policy. Citizen preferences which are not represented by organized groups, however, face considerable competition securing a position on the agenda.

Administrative structure

Perhaps the most salient feature of big-city administrative bureaucracies is their large size relative to revenue, student population and the size of the teaching force. Much of the public choice literature attributes this condition to weak market controls and the inability of boards to monitor administrative behaviour. Cibulka (1987), however, has shown that these explanations are not compatible with budgeting behaviour in the ten big-city school districts he studied. Moreover, if interest groups monitored board behaviour closely, board members would have strong incentives to monitor administrators. Many board members, indeed, serve virtually full time and have offices in central administrative headquarters. They have at least the opportunity to monitor, though informational costs for doing so would be relatively high given the size and complexity of administrative structures.

A better explanation for the growth in the size of these bureaucracies perhaps is tied to the log-rolling behaviour of their governing boards. Tullock (1959) has pointed out that where a substantial portion of citizens are not represented by organized constituencies, those who are represented on governing boards have a strong incentive to approve policies which produce at least some collective benefits, because they then can require the entire collective (rather than just themselves) to bear the costs of implementing those policies. The unrepresented who may not want the policies still must pay their share of the costs. Norms supportive of log-rolling magnify the enactment of these types of policies because board members will need the future support of other members for approval of special-interest projects they will offer. Under these conditions, bureaucratic growth is a consequence of the socialization of conflict on the board.

Third-party payments make enactment of policies that result in bureaucratic growth even easier for organized interests and their representatives on the board, because these costs are passed on to taxpayers outside the district. Significantly, a large portion of big-city school district revenues come from intergovernmental revenues. The relatively large number of state representatives with constituencies in big-city jurisdictional boundaries enhances their capacity to raise revenue from state governments. Organized groups within these districts, such as unions, also have the political means to press for larger intergovernmental payments. Big-city districts frequently employ professional lobbyists to sponsor their solicitations from external governmental agencies. Badrkhan (1987) found that big-city school district representatives substantially influenced the formulation of allocation rules whereby vocational education revenues were apportioned.

In smaller districts where market controls are strong to moderate in strength, these revenues do not provide the same opportunities for administrative expansion because citizens can insist that these revenues be expended efficiently. Where market controls are weak and monitoring by boards and citizens slack, senior administrators determine how the monies are spent. But because these bureaucracies are insular, organizational norms will favour the expenditure of these funds evenly across the entire organization, with the major portion going to the school sites where most of the employees are stationed.

The influence of organized interest groups in big-city school districts, however, creates a central office expenditure bias for these revenues. Organized interests and board members want access to the administrators and staff who run the projects they sponsor. Locating the positions funded by these revenues in the central headquarters rather than at dispersed school sites gives organized interests and board members greater opportunities to monitor and influence the administrators of these projects.

The bureaucracy thus partly becomes a reification of log-rolling conflict resolution. This is possibly one reason why large urban districts develop internal labour markets and comparatively powerful organizational cultures. Superintendents are reluctant to go outside the organization for new personnel, when organized interest groups and board members have developed alliances with administrative personnel whom they would like to see retained and promoted.

District policies

District policies reflect the influence of organized interest groups. But because these groups are diverse and typically represent relatively narrow preferences (due to organizational maintenance needs), the patchwork quilt of policies enacted through log-rolling frequently do not result in a coherent educational service delivery package. The tendency of large bureaucracies to proliferate allocational and decision rules also mitigates against responding favourably to individual citizen demands.

Conclusion: the status of urban school reform

The grip of interest group liberalism on urban school politics now appears to be lessening. Internal regional and external global competition are narrowing the economic function of cities, creating a juxtaposition, already evident, of urban renaissance in the form of new office buildings alongside a growing impoverished student population. In many districts, as many as 75% of the students are on free lunch programmes. Interest group liberalism is losing its moral voice as the outcomes of political bargaining and log-rolling appear increasingly disconnected from the educational needs of these students.

Reformers are seeking to challenge the hold of interest group liberalism by restructuring the elements of the governance system which produce it. Enhanced public choice is seen as a means for resolving the dilemma of weak market controls, and enhanced parental voice as a way of contesting the influence of organized special-interest groups.

Many of the reforms of the 1980s, and particularly during the so-called 'second wave' of reform from about 1986 to 1990, centred on efforts to enhance the 'market' qualities of urban education systems (see Doyle *et al.* 1991). In the mostly public sector world of elementary and secondary education, where 90% of provision is already public, the effort was twofold:

1. To extend choice options for parents to enter the private sector through tax credits, tax deductions and voucher plans – *inter-sectoral* options – all of which established a far wider range of education choices to modest and low-income families who traditionally had limited-to-no access to the private school market; and
2. To offer choice *within* the public sector, creating an intra-sectoral market among public schools through such schemes as open enrolment, metro-transfer

> plans, magnet schools, theme schools, alternative schools and even subschools with different programmes within a single existing school.

Another approach has been to strengthen the 'voice' of parents and community through site-based management and local decision making. Here, the argument is that while consumers – particularly poor ones – cannot easily 'buy' their way out, perhaps they can talk the system into responding to their needs. For most parents, being able to have some say in how their own children's schools are run is perhaps sufficient, since the particular school is where the teaching and learning occur – and the 'system' is more of an epiphenomenon than a reality.

Interestingly, some cities worked on 'voice' while eschewing 'exit', including Chicago. Drafters of the Local School Council legislation passed by the Illinois legislature purposely avoided increasing choice out of a strong ideological belief that 'exiting' would enable the elite, white and savvy to change schools while further isolating the poor, non-English-speaking and least able. Moore and Davenport (1990) found that magnet schools (a popular form of public school exit through choice) isolated the middle class from the lower classes and non-white in six major cities, increasing segregation.

Other urban areas have worked at enhancing choice and have put less emphasis on breaking the political bottle-neck that interest group politics involves. And a few cities have tried both decentralization and improved market mechanisms, though no city has moved radically to 'privatize' both the governance (local school-site control) and resources (through vouchers or extensive tax breaks for education costs). In the next wave of reform, President Bush seems to favour 'new kinds of schools', including public-private models which will attempt to strengthen public choice, by giving parents even more options (federally stimulated) and more control through site-based governance.

Public choice theory, which gave rise to these choice and voice proposals, cannot provide a complete picture of likely outcomes of these reform efforts, because the theory projects too narrow a field of vision for viewing the whole of school politics. Analytically, it presents a lower boundary estimate of what is possible. Participants in school politics, however, are more than instrumentally rational creatures pursuing their self-interest, narrowly defined. They want their lives to have substantive meaning, and this desire influences how they participate and what they seek from the political process.

Normatively, public choice theory can inform the debate about educational reform by specifying the conditions under which markets function effectively. Hirschman (1986) has pointed out that the appropriateness of market solutions depends on the presence of four conditions: (1) there are differences in preference that are widely recognized as equally legitimate; (2) citizens generally are knowledgeable about the quality of services and can evaluate and compare them; (3) purchasers can move freely from one supplier to the next, and can learn from experience; and (4) there are many competing providers.

Designing an institutional governance structure for education that simultaneously satisfies these four conditions will be a severe challenge to reformers. Elite private schools and affluent suburban school districts offer a portrait of what can happen when markets function efficiently. But, as we saw during our analysis of suburban school politics, even modest market inefficiencies produce relatively severe untoward effects on school politics in middle and lower income communities, effects which perhaps institutionally reinforce the association between school district socio-economic status and school achievement. The success of efforts to reshape urban school governance around the concepts of greater choice and voice will depend as much on the ingenuity of reformers in scotching market failure as in designing new avenues for access and participation.

References

ALCHAIN, A. and DEMSETZ, H. (1972) 'Production, information costs, and economic competition', *American Economic Review*, 62(4), pp. 777–795.

ARANSON, P. (1981) *American Government: Strategy and Choice* (New York: Winthrop).

BADRKHAN, K. (1987) 'Vocational Education Finance Theories', PhD dissertation, The Claremont Graduate School.

BANFIELD, E. and WILSON, J. (1963) *City Politics* (Cambridge, MA: Harvard University Press).

BOYD, W. (1982) 'The political economy of public schools', *Educational Administration Quarterly*, 18(3), pp. 111–130.

CHUBB J. AND MOE T. (1990) *Politics, Markets, and America's Schools* (Washington, DC: Brookings Institution).

CIBULKA, J. (1987) 'Theories of education budgeting: lessons from the management of decline', *Educational Administration Quarterly*, 23(1), pp. 7–40.

DEMSETZ, H. (1982) *Economic, Legal, and Political Dimensions of Competition* (Amsterdam: North Holland).

DOYLE, D. P., COOPER, B. S. and TRACHTMAN, R. (1991) *Taking Charge: State Action on School Reform in the 1980s* (Indianapolis: Hudson Institute).

DREIER, P. and KEATING, W. (1990) 'The limits of localism: progressive housing policies in Boston: 1984-1989', *Urban Affairs Quarterly*, 26(2), pp. 217–249.

GREENSTONE, J. and PETERSON, P. (1973) *Race and Authority in Urban Politics: Community Participation and the War on Poverty* (New York: Russell Sage).

GRUBB, N. (1982) 'The flight to the suburbs of population and employment', *Journal of Urban Economics*, 10(3), pp. 348–367.

HAMILTON, B. (1983) 'Is the property tax a benefit tax?', in G. Zodrow (ed.) *Local Provision of Public Services: The Tiebout Model After Twenty-five Years* (New York: Academic), pp. 85–107.

HIRSCHMAN, A. (1986) *Rival Views of Market Society* (New York: Viking).

IANNACCONE, L. and LUTZ, F. (1970) *Politics, Power and Policy: The Governing of Local School Districts* (Columbus: Charles Merrill).

KEARNEY, C. and KIM, T. (1990) 'Fiscal impacts and redistributive effects of the new federalism on Michigan school districts', *Educational Evaluation and Policy Analysis*, 12(4), pp. 375–387.

KERCHNER, C., KOPPICH, J., KING, B. and WEERES, J. (1990) 'This could be the start of something big', paper presented at the University Council for Educational Administration, Pittsburgh, PA.

LOWI, T. (1969) *The end of Liberalism* (New York: W. W. Norton).

LUTZ, F. and IANNACCONE, L. (eds) (1978) *Public Participation in Local School Districts: The Dissatisfaction Theory of Democracy* (Lexington: Lexington Press).

MARWELL, G., OLIVER, P., and PRAHL, A. (1988) 'Social networks and collective action: a theory of critical mass III', *American Journal of Sociology*, 94(3), pp. 502–534.

MCCONNELL, G. (1966) *Private Power and American Government* (New York: Vintage).

MICHAELSEN, J. (1980) 'A theory of decision-making in the public schools: a public choice approach', Institute For Research on Educational Finance and Governance, Project No. 80-A4, pp. 1–54.

MOE, T. (1984) 'The new economics of organizations', *American Journal of Political Science*, 28(4), pp. 739–777.

MOORE, D. P. and DAVENPORT, S. (1990) 'School choice: the new improved sorting machine', in W. Boyd and H. Walberg (eds) *Choice in Education: Potential and Problems* (Berkeley: McCutchan), pp. 187–223.

OLIVER, P., MARWELL, G., and TEIXEIRA, R. (1985) 'A theory of critical mass I: interdependence, group heterogeneity, and the production of collective action', *American Journal of Sociology*, 91(3), pp. 1–34.

OLIVER, P. and MARWELL, G. (1988) 'The paradox of group size in collective action: a theory of critical mass II', *American Sociological Review*, 53(2), pp. 1–8.

OLSON, M. (1965) *The Logic of Collective Action* (Cambridge: Harvard University Press).

PETERSON, P. (1981) *City Limits* (Chicago, University of Chicago Press).

SANDERS, H. and STONE, C. (1987) 'Developmental policies reconsidered', *Urban Affairs Quarterly*, 22(3), pp. 521–539.

SCHNEIDER, M. (1989) *The Competitive City: The Political Economy of Suburbia* (Pittsburgh: University of Pittsburgh Press).

SCHNEIDER, M. and JI, B. (1990) 'The political economy of intergovernmental grant seeking: targeting and suburbs', *American Journal of Political Science*, 34(2), pp. 408–420.

SHARP, E. (1984) 'Citizen-demand making in the urban context', *American Journal of Political Science*, 28(4), pp. 654–670.

STAHURA, J. (1988) 'Changing patterns of suburban racial composition: 1970–80', *Urban Affairs Quarterly*, 23(3), pp. 448–460.

TEAFORD, J. (1990) *The Rough Road to Renaissance: Urban Revitalization in America, 1940–1985* (Baltimore: Johns Hopkins).

TIEBOUT, C. (1956) 'A pure theory of local expenditures', *Journal of Political Economy*, 64(4), pp. 416–424.

TULLOCK, G. (1959) 'Some problems of majority voting', *Journal of Political Economy*, 67(4), pp. 541–579.

VOGEL, M. (1979) 'Fiscal and distributive impacts of grants consolidation', in C. Kearney and E. VanderPutten (eds) *Grants Consolidation* (Washington, DC: Institute for Educational Leadership), pp. 95–112.

WEERES, J. (1988) 'Economic choice and the dissolution of community', in W. Boyd and C. Kerchner (eds) *The Politics of Excellence and Choice in Education* (London: Falmer), pp. 117–130.

WILLIAMSON, O. (1975) *Markets and Hierarchies*, (New York: Free Press).

WONG, K. (1988) 'Economic constraints and political choice in urban policymaking', *American Journal of Political Science*, 32(1), pp. 1–18.

WONG, K. and PETERSON, P. (1986) 'Urban responses to federal program flexibility: politics of community development block grant', *Urban Affairs Quarterly*, 21(3), pp. 293–309.

ZEIGLER, L., and JENNINGS, M. (1974) *Governing American Schools* (North Scituate: Duxbury Press).

POLITICS OF EDUCATION ASSOCIATION YEARBOOK 1991, 71–86

PART 2: THE POLITICAL CONDITION OF URBAN SCHOOLS

5 *Leadership turnover and business mobilization: the changing political ecology of urban school systems*

Barbara L. Jackson and James G. Cibulka

This chapter addresses evidence of leadership turnover in urban school systems and explains this leadership problem as emanating from the changing political ecology of urban school systems. The average tenure of urban superintendents is now 2·5 years, coupled with a shortage of applicants for vacant superintendencies, indicating a crisis of legitimacy for many urban school systems. Demands for racial representativeness on school boards and among superintendents led to more African-Americans in these positions, but responsiveness to these demands did not check still other demands for improved quality. The evolution from racial equity (integration and representativeness) to quality is reviewed. Most recently, business leaders have mobilized to demand improved quality. An analysis of events in Detroit, Atlanta and Milwaukee illustrates the difficulty these school systems have had managing these cumulative political demands.

Introduction

Recently the governance of urban school systems has become a national issue.[1] The large number of vacancies among urban school superintendents in 1991 (in 15 cities at one point) appeared to signal a crisis of governance.

In this chapter we examine the nature and extent of this leadership 'problem' and explain its origins. We shall argue that the problem of leadership instability is an indication of a larger legitimacy crisis in urban schools created by a changing political ecology surrounding urban school systems. By political ecology, we refer to the political environment surrounding urban schools, consisting of the evolving demography of their student bodies and the changing character of political demands placed on them by various mobilized interest groups and superordinate governments. In recent decades urban school systems have been presented with successive and now cumulative demands for increased equity (in the form of both integration and representativeness) and excellence (or quality), generated both by local and national pressures. The principal reason for this shift in political ecology is the reassertion of business influence, not only through national influences, but through specific mobilization at the local level.

We lay out this general line of analysis at the start, followed by several case studies to illustrate these common dynamics in the several cities, despite some factual variations in the cities. Finally, we conclude with some thoughts on the implications of this changing political ecology for the future legitimacy and effectiveness of urban school systems.

Superintendent turnover as a leadership problem

How severe is the leadership instability in urban school systems? According to the Council of Great City Schools (1990), the average tenure of urban superintendents is now only 2·5 years, thus contributing to the political instability of these systems. Table 1 indicates

0268–0939/91 $3.00

Table 1. Recency of superintendent turnover among Council of Great City Schools member districts 1980–1991

Year appointed	*Number of superintendents still in same position in 1991*
1991	13*
1990	12
1989	4
1988	2
1987	1
1986	4
1985	1
1984	4
1982	2
1980	2

Source: Council of Great City Schools data and newspaper reports.
*Four of these are acting superintendents. Among the total of 45 districts, no information was available for three.

recent trends in turnover among superintendents of Council of Great City Schools (CGSC) membership. The following number of school systems appointed new superintendents in the last 3 years: four in 1989; 12 in 1990; 13 in 1991 (as of the publication date). Only a small number of superintendents have been in their positions for more than a few years.

While turnover is a great problem, it is not present in every city, nor has it grown worse than previously in all cities. Consider the data in table 2, which present data from the nation's 50 largest school systems back to 1977 (the earliest date for which systematic data were available). In 60% of the districts, the tenure of the current superintendent exceeds that of his or her predecessor. In those school systems the average tenure of the current superintendent is 6·8 years. In the remaining 40% of the school systems the current superintendent has been in the post fewer years (on average 2·95) compared with a predecessor. It is possible, of course, that with the passage of more time, their tenure may match or exceed the predecessor. When current superintendents are excluded from the analysis and instead the immediate past superintendent's tenure is compared with his or her predecessor, largely the same pattern occurs: two-thirds served longer than their predecessors. Apparently, the problem of leadership turnover in large cities has been around for a long time.[2]

Table 2. Superintendent tenure in the 50 largest school systems 1977–1990

	School systems where superintendent tenure has increased or remained same	*decreased*
	60% (29)	40% (19)
Average tenure of incumbent*	6.8 years	2.95 years

Source: Educational Directories, Inc. (1977–1990) *Patterson's American Education* (Mount Prospect, IL).
Note: Data were missing on two districts.
* Tenure for all incumbents is 4.47 years.

What aggravates the current problem is the demand for African-American superintendents. School boards and recruitment firms have complained of too few candidates. Because of this shortage, some of the same persons who were fired in one city have filled a vacancy in others, creating a 'musical chair' phenomenon. In sum, both the large number of recently appointed superintendents as well as the shortage of qualified applicants point to a national problem in our urban school systems, even though the frequency of turnover may not be increasing in all cities.

From race to excellence: a new challenge to legitimacy

Immediately after the Second World War urban school systems were for the most part well regarded and viewed as examples of sound management and innovative practice. To be sure, they had inherited many deferred problems from the Depression years, particularly in facilities and programme cutbacks. Chicago did experience a governance scandal in 1946, as did other cities from time to time, but these were noteworthy as an exception to the national pattern. For the most part urban school systems became preoccupied with the problems of building schools to accommodate the baby boom.

Racial equity

Educational quality, then, was not an issue because excellence was still associated with urban schools in this period. However, the changing racial composition of cities and urban school systems was a major challenge to this post-Second World War consensus. So too was the legal and political challenge to racial segregation represented by *Brown* v. *Board of Education* (347 US 483, 1954). By 1967 11 of the nation's 60 largest school districts had a majority African-American student body. In the ensuing two decades, by 1986, white enrolments constituted the minority in over half of these districts (Orfield and Monfort 1988). These figures reflected white flight, in-migration of other students of colour such as Hispanics, higher birth rates among non-white groups, and an overall decline in student enrolments in most systems beginning in the early 1970s. Table 3 indicates the racial composition of selected big-city school systems. In none of the cities were white pupils any longer in the majority. Ten of the 14 had predominantly African-American enrolments, and several others had Latino or Asian enrolments which exceeded a quarter of the student body.

The racial issues associated with demographic changes constituted a major challenge to the legitimacy of urban school systems. The civil rights movement raised demands not only for desegregation of public services but also for improved African-American representation in those institutions. Nearly all urban school systems had protracted battles over desegregation, leading to desegregation plans typically imposed by the federal courts. Among the Council of Great City Schools (CGCS) districts, 39% adopted desegregation plans in the 1970s, and another 34% in the 1980s.

Success in reducing racial isolation has been mixed at best (Orfield and Monfort 1988), for a variety of reasons. African-Americans, for example, became increasingly disillusioned with integration by the late 1960s. Consequently, political demands for further desegregation of students and faculty subsided. As city pupils have become principally children of colour, and in the face of continued political obstacles to the adoption of metropolitan desegregation plans, public demands for reform have turned elsewhere.

Table 3. Racial composition of selected urban school systems (1988)

City	*Percentage student enrolment by race* White	African-American	Latino	Asian
Atlanta	6.9	91.7	0.7	0.8
Baltimore	18.5	80.3	0.3	0.6
Boston	24.2	47.9	19.0	8.4
Chicago	12.1	58.8	26.1	2.9
Cincinnati	38.2	60.7	0.2	0.8
Detroit	8.5	88.5	2.1	0.7
Los Angeles	16.1	17.1	60.2	6.4
Memphis	20.9	79.1	0.0	0.0
New Orleans	7.8	87.4	1.8	3.1
New York	19.9	38.4	34.3	7.3
Philadelphia	23.5	63.2	9.3	3.9
St Louis	21.7	77.1	0.2	0.9
San Francisco	14.7	19.4	18.7	34.2
Washington	3.5	91.1	4.3	1.1

Source: The Council of The Great City Schools (1990) *The Condition of Education in the Great City Schools* (Washington, DC).

The second emphasis in demands for racial equity, as stated above, was greater racial representativeness among public officials. By the late 1960s and early 1970s these demands within urban school systems had broadened to include many groups and became a generalized demand for improved representativeness on schools boards. African-Americans, Hispanics, Asians and even traditional white ethnic groups favoured area or neighbourhood representation or seats unofficially designated for their groups. In some cities demands for community control of schools were made, with particular urgency by some African-American leaders. Urban school systems responded to these political demands for representativeness, typically by reducing white dominance of urban school boards. Some cities changed the size or selection process for their board, and a small number politically decentralized to create multiple boards. By 1990, only 38% of the school districts who are members of the Council of Great City Schools (1990) continued to elect all their members at large, while 42% elected members entirely from districts or wards, a significant shift from earlier years. In 1991 Boston, by state law, changed from a 13-member elected board to a seven-member board to be appointed by the mayor.

The data in table 4 suggest that progress has been made in most cities in making school boards more representative of African-Americans. Among the CGCS member districts, slightly under half (49%) had achieved representativeness, defined here as constituting a majority of African-American members or achieving African-American membership which is within ten percentage points of equalling the percentage of African-American students.

The demand for African-American superintendents was part of this quest for greater representativeness, frequently following increases in African-American representation on the boards themselves. Table 4 shows that in 1990 49% of the cities had a racially representative school board and 51% an African-American superintendent. (Several more had Hispanic superintendents.) Over half of the school boards with appropriate African-American representation also had African-American superintendents, while only 37% of the boards which were unrepresentative of African-Americans did (not reported in table 4).

Table 4. African-American representation on urban school boards and among urban superintendents (1990), Council of Great City Schools (CGCS) districts

Percent of cities	*School board representativeness**	*African-American superintendent*
Yes	49% (19)	51% (20)**
No	51% (20)	49% (19)

Source: Council of The Great City Schools (1990) *The Condition of Education in the Great City Schools* (Washington, DC); Joint Center for Political and Economic Studies (1987), *Roster of Black Elected Officials* (Washington, DC).

Note: Data were unavailable for appointed boards.

*Representativeness is defined as having an African-American majority on the board of achieving an African-American membership which is within 10 percentage points of the percent African-American students. No data were available for Hispanics.

**In addition, three school systems have Hispanic superintendents.

Of course, since many cities do not have a majority African-American student body, a school board representative of African-Americans would not necessarily be expected to appoint an African-American superintendent, even if we accept the assumptions of this socially descriptive approach to superintendent recruitment. Table 5 indicates the trends among 13 cities with majority African-American enrolments. Cities with racially representative school boards are more likely to have an African-American superintendent (46%) than those which do not have representative boards, although African-American superintendents have been hired in some systems without representative school boards.

These data indicate that considerable progress has been made toward recruitment of African-American members to school boards and to superintendencies. The issue now has become moot in a number of cities where African-American control appears assured. At the same time, looking at the matter from the national perspective, representativeness is far from accomplished. Many cities have an unrepresentative school board and/or superintendent, and in other cities this achievement could be reversed. Therefore, it is quite rational for reformers to argue that representativeness remains an important equity goal by which urban school system performance should be judged.

Table 5. African-American superintendents and racial representativeness in 13 cities with majority African-American enrolments (1990), Council of The Great City Schools (CGCS)

Superintendent is African-American	*School board is racially representative**	
	Yes	*No*
Yes	46% (6)	23% (3)
No	8% (1)	23% (3)

Source: Council of The Great City Schools (1990) *The Condition of Education in the Great City Schools* (Washington, DC); Joint Center for Political and Economic Studies (1987) *Black Elected Officials: A National Roster*, 17th ed; (Washington, DC).

*See table 4 for the definition of representativeness.

Educational quality

Public demands for greater accountability in our public schools and restoration of quality or excellence began to surface in the 1950s during the *Sputnik* scare. In the 1960s an accountability movement began to build, and by the 1970s many state legislatures had instituted state-level reforms aimed at improving quality in our public schools, such as minimum competency testing (Leight 1973).

In the 1980s, as is well known, concern over educational quality or excellence supplanted traditional equity goals such as desegregation and representativeness as the primary concern of reformers. This is merely the latest stage in these escalating demands for excellence from the *Sputnik* era to the present. Business interest groups usually have been among those pressing for quality. Recently, however, business leaders have mobilized a near crusade to reform the public schools and have pressed for reforms at every level, using their organizational structures and influence nationally, at the state level and in local communities.

Initially the reform movement, and business mobilization on this issue, appeared to bypass urban school systems. The Council of Great City Schools Report *Results in the Making* (1987) documented this disinterest and offered recommendations related to urban schools. However, anticipated labour force shortages caused business leaders in the 1980s to demand improved educational quality for students who traditionally have under-performed and even failed, large numbers of whom are concentrated in central cities.

This demand for quality represents the second major challenge to the legitimacy of urban school systems since the Second World War. Some (e.g. Brown *et al.* 1991) argue that urban school boards need to be less representative and more expert. Others rely on decentralizing strategies such as choice or site-based management. Indeed, a wide variety of reform nostrums are being advanced to improve quality in urban schools (Oakes 1987).

The implication of this twin press for greater equity (whether integration or representativeness) and also greater quality in our urban school systems has been to increase their political instability. The expectations and requirements posed by each set of demands, often pressed by different constituencies, sometimes even embraced simultaneously by the same constituencies, have severely tested the governance and performance capacity of these systems. The difficulty of managing these public expectations has contributed to membership turnover on urban boards of education and, in turn, superintendent turnover. The precise manner in which this occurs, particularly the timing and sequence of events, varies depending on the size and political strength of the African-American community (and other allies) as well as the organizational strength and assertiveness of the local business elites and their allies.

In order to illustrate these trends, we have selected three cities, Detroit, Atlanta and Milwaukee. All three have experienced the twin press of expanded equity (both integration and representativeness) and quality discussed above.

Detroit

African-Americans have been part of Detroit since before the Civil War. By 1940, they constituted approximately 10% of the central city population, living in a concentrated area euphemistically called 'Paradise Valley' an area of dilapidated housing, high unemployment and low income. The 1943 riot occurred in this area. An expanding African-American population and a long standing African-American middle class pressed for improved housing, access to neighbourhoods for homes, employment and public services, and encountered both overt and subtle discrimination. As was true in most cities prior to the 1960s, political action was primarily through coalitions with liberal whites and labour leaders, and only African-American candidates 'acceptable' to whites gained public office (Darden *et al.* 1987).[3]

By 1960 the African-American population in the Detroit public schools constituted about 50% of the estimated 300,000 student enrolment, but only one school board member was African-American. Some protests had been made against policies judged to be discriminatory with the solutions sought through integration. In 1964 a liberal coalition elected four new board members to the seven-member at-large board, giving a pro-integration majority to the board but not an African-American majority. Despite their hiring an aggressive integrationist as superintendent, Norman Drachler, dissatisfaction with the schools grew among both white conservatives and African-American activists. While the new board was devising its integrationist policies, the 1967 riot erupted, followed in the next year by the death of Martin Luther King and the emergence of the counter-force of black power. But the racially liberal board persisted and proposed to desegregate 12 high schools. This action resulted in 1970 in a successful recall of the pro-integrationist board organized by white constituents. The Governor appointed four replacement members (two African-American and two white), and the new board repealed its earlier integration policy.

Many African-American leaders continued to argue for more radical community control. The Michigan legislature, under the leadership of an African-American state legislator, Coleman Young (who later became Mayor of Detroit), attempted to strike a compromise by passing a decentralization law in 1969. The reform, which began in 1971, abolished the seven-member elected at large school board and established a 13-member board and eight decentralized regions, each with a separate regional board that had power to appoint a regional superintendent. The president of each regional board sat on the central board, which continued to have five members elected at large. All were elected for 4-year terms, although regional members served only as long as they remained in that leadership capacity on their respective regional boards. The first election brought only three African-American members (one at large), a smaller percentage than there had been on the last seven-member board.

Without waiting to see how the new structure would respond to the issue of equity or quality, the NAACP filed the first northern court case charging racial discrimination in the schools. In 1971 Stephen J. Roth of the District court found that *de jure* segregation did exist due to federal, state and local government action, including that of the school board, along with real estate firms and lending institutions. Roth concluded that a metropolitan remedy was required. (*Bradley* v. *Milliken* 338 F. Supp. 582, 1971.) However, on appeal from a further decision by the Circuit Court, the United States Supreme Court rejected Roth's finding that suburban school districts could be implicated without further evidence, thus scuttling a metropolitan remedy (*Milliken* v. *Bradley* 418 US 717, 1974). The extensive remedy later fashioned by the District Court focused on improving educational quality.[4]

According to Arthur Jefferson, who became the first African-American superintendent during this period, the plan was a mixed blessing; while it helped institute many educational changes, it also took away the flexibility often needed to respond to the changing needs of the school system. Thus, the 'city-only' desegregation plan may have made possible more quality but did not address the equity or integration issue.

This new regional governance system, with the combination of at-large and regional board members, eventually increased representativeness for African-Americans. It made possible the appointment in 1975 of Arthur Jefferson Jr. who before becoming superintendent had been a former teacher and regional superintendent. During Jefferson's early tenure, progress was made towards improving student achievement based in large part on the programmes stipulated in the court order. Federal funds were available at this time, and constituent support for the fiscally independent school system remained strong enough that local millage taxes were passed.

As the years passed, however, problems accumulated due to the changing student population; total enrolments plummeted, the white population left in increasing numbers, and the percentage of poverty pupils mounted. Whereas in 1967, 58% of the student body was African-American, this reached 79% in 1976 and 89% in 1986.

Dissatisfaction with the perceived inadequacies of the governance arrangement became so pronounced that in 1982 the regional boards were abolished. Decentralization had always been viewed with suspicion by whites who, despite their declining numbers in the city, viewed regionalization as a step toward African-American control of the city. The reform had never been popular with the Detroit Federation of Teachers, who had a vivid recollection of the 1968 struggle in New York City over decentralization. Even Arthur Jefferson, once he was superintendent of the entire school system, found the regional structure too unpredictable and unwieldy. Consequently, the new central board was reduced from 13 to 11 members, with four at-large seats and the remaining elected from newly designated districts, all for four-year staggered terms.

African-Americans have become a dominant force under this new centralized arrangement. Although white enclaves of the city preserved some representation through the district seats, the fact that the city and the school system were majority African-American made representativeness a less compelling issue than it had been previously.

Despite this increased representativeness, there were continuing concerns about the quality of education afforded Detroit schoolchildren. Business elites, along with municipal leaders, had been preoccupied with the economic redevelopment of Detroit for several decades. The commercial disinvestment of the city had begun in the 1950s and accelerated after the 1967 riots. Much urban renewal effort such as construction of the Renaissance Center focused on downtown Detroit, but city officials also gave great attention to compensating for the drastic loss of Detroit's manufacturing base and, in particular, the decline of its dominant industry, auto manufacture. While aspects of urban renewal, particularly public housing and neighbourhood development, were intensely conflictual, the city's African-American Mayor Coleman Young, elected in 1973, pursued policies largely compatible with the city's white business establishment, symbolized by its central spokesman, Henry Ford II. Indeed, Coleman governed with the help of the liberal-labour coalition as well as the city's African-American majority. He has continued to resist metropolitan solutions, however, for fear of losing his largely African-American majority in the city itself.

It was not until the 1980s that the city's schools came to be seen as a central prong in an economic redevelopment strategy. To be sure, they had been sources of intense racial conflict as neighbourhood redevelopment battles were fought. It was the national attention to the human capital-building potential of schools, and their importance in new international economic order, which encouraged local elites to give greater attention to the schools. By 1985 school officials could point to improved test scores in some grades and some subjects. Still, by the late 1980s the schools were perceived as beset by major problems of low achievement, by unacceptable violence and, to compound matters, by a financial deficit. (Financial problems, it should be noted, were not new to Detroit school officials. In 1972 the system was bankrupt, but the Michigan legislature had done little more than patch up the funding system.)

In 1987 the Detroit Strategic Planning Project was launched, largely as a result of the business community. The schools were a central part of the proposed plans. The Chamber of Commerce, which had not been active during most of Jefferson's tenure, joined others in calling for a change in school board membership. They supported a new group, HOPE, which won election in 1988. Jefferson lost his support on the board and resigned in 1989 after a 13-year tenure. While this new board was more representative of business interests, it also was more broadly representative than its predecessor and included whites, middle-class African-Americans, labour and neighbourhood representatives. During this same election citizens expressed their confidence in the school system by passing two costly tax proposals to pay off an operating deficit and provide new revenues.

The board prevailed on John Porter,the recently retired president of Eastern Michigan University and former state superintendent, to accept a 2-year tenure as interim superintendent. Porter developed a Quality Education Plan which included student achievement goals. He signed a Compact with the Chamber of Commerce to inaugurate a new partnership between the schools and the business community. Porter was succeeded as superintendent in May 1991 by Deborah McGriff, an African-American educator who previously served as Milwaukee's deputy superintendent.

In Detroit, then, over a period of several decades there was a gradual shift from issues of equity, exemplified by integration and representativeness, to quality. Throughout the 1960s and 1970s those favouring racial integration or representativeness assumed, and sometimes argued explicitly, that quality would improve as a result of such reforms. The failure of these reforms to realize this promise, coupled with a changing national climate – one which simultaneously abandoned equity and shifted public attention toward productivity – resulted in a new school board and superintendent and a new agenda for Detroit's schools. The dilemma of how to achieve equity and excellence is yet to be resolved.

Atlanta

Like other American cities, Atlanta has experienced out-migrations of middle-class residents, both white and African-American, to surrounding suburbs.[5] Yet unlike many other cities such as Detroit, Atlanta has retained a thriving downtown and a strong commercial base. Over a period of several decades the city's economic and political elites transformed Atlanta into the economic and cultural capital of the South.

Since before the Civil War, African-Americans have constituted a major population group in Atlanta. Black-owned businesses, historically Black colleges, strong churches and other African-American institutions created an influential African-American upper middle class dating back many generations. The city's white social and political elite developed coalitions with this African-American leadership even prior to the civil rights movement. By 1974 Atlanta had an African-American mayor, Maynard Jackson, who reached out to business elites while at the same time bargaining for important perquisites for African-American Atlantans. Jackson's successor, Andrew Young, continued to ally his regime with downtown business elites.

Atlanta's public schools were, of course, racially segregated by law. Historically, one or two prominent African-American educators served on the school board, but the school system remained under the control of white lawyers and others representing white business elites. Despite the 1974 *Brown* decision, Atlanta's first steps to increase integration did not occur until 1961 (Jackson 1978). As the system turned increasingly African-American (by 1967 it was 59% African-American), whites fled. Enrolments plummeted after 1967, reflecting this out-migration, and the school system became increasingly African-American. By 1973, when a desegregation plan was finally agreed on, the school system was over 81% African-American, making large-scale integration impractical. Accordingly, the Atlanta Compromise, as it came to be known, was the agreement entered into by the Federal court in *Calhoun* v. *Cook* (487 F 2nd. 680, 1974). While business elites feared the economic consequences of racial turmoil, African-Americans feared the impact of widespread busing, given the few number of white students still remaining in the school system. The settlement had as a central feature a guarantee that African-Americans would have 50% of the administrative posts reserved for them, including the appointment of an African-American superintendent; a pupil assignment plan; staff desegregation plan; and other provisions. Accordingly, Alonzo Crim was appointed superintendent under the plan in 1973.

Given the historic political strength of the African-American community in Atlanta, it might be asked why they did not muster the political capital to force integration rather accept a plan which focused almost entirely on improvements in quality and in representativeness. One tentative answer to this question is that African-American influence in the school system, given the history of *de jure* segregation, lagged behind African-American influence in other institutions, including city government. By the time a plan could be agreed on, whites had fled and African-American enthusiasm for integration was declining.

During Crim's tenure as superintendent, then, improving the quality of Atlanta's schools was his mandate. The city's white leadership never abandoned the school board, even though African-American representation on the board increased and the school board was led by a prominent African-American, Benjamin Mays, who was the former president of Morehouse College and is now deceased.

The city's business elites, while still predominantly white, maintained influence by a strategy of shared governance. This emphasis on growth and progress, so characteristic of Atlanta's self-image, also prevented business leaders from abandoning the school system. While the school system had become one serving predominantly poor African-Americans, civic elites never lost sight of the need to improve the quality of the school system in order to sell northern industry on relocating to Atlanta and to attract financial capital for further redevelopment.

Through much of Crim's tenure as superintendent, these politics of consensus provided an effective foundation for governance. According to Crim, during his tenure, finances were not a problem. He enjoyed ready access to local political leadership, the governor, and the state department of education. As part of his platform of progress, he reached out to the business community and to local colleges to form partnerships. Indeed, some schools such as the Mays High School acquired national recognition for excellence. Enrolments continued to decline, however, and student achievement did not improve to the degree anticipated.

Yet as Orfield and Peskin (1988) have argued, these positive findings must be placed in a larger political and economic context, which they link to the Compromise of 1973. That policy settlement accepted 'racial and economic separation as a starting point for program development' and thus made it inevitable that the 'underlying economic and racial stratification of the Atlanta region is reflected in its schools' (Orfield and Peskin 1988: 52).

In 1988, at the end of 15 years as superintendent, Crim retired. After the retirement of Benjamin Mays as school board president, conflicts erupted on the board itself and affected Crim's support. The board (consisting of six African-Americans and three whites) was split on the selection of Crim's successor but finally agreed on Jerome Harris, who had served as a community superintendent in a predominantly African-American district of Brooklyn, New York. Harris's plans to address the educational needs of the predominantly African-American school population met with disagreement on the board. His leadership style, which differed markedly from Crim's low-key approach, also provoked opposition, and he was asked to leave before he had completed two years of his contract. The board then turned to an insider, Lester Butts, a former high school principal and central administrator, who has sought to implement many of Harris's plans.

The leadership of the board was assumed by a leader of the white business establishment, Joseph Martin, who had been on the board since 1977. Martin is head of Atlanta Progress, Inc., the vehicle for central city redevelopment efforts.

In Atlanta, then, representativeness overshadowed integration as a social goal, and this approach had made 'quality improvement' a primary policy objective for a decade and a half. By 1988, however, the Compromise of 1973 which had symbolized this quality thrust no longer seemed sufficient to many on the school board and to those in the broader community. What ensued was a period of leadership instability as the board struggled to recapture the politics of consensus which carried Atlanta through racial change but which has yet to produce the improvements in quality which business leaders and others believe are necessary.

Milwaukee

Milwaukee presents an important demographic contrast to Atlanta and Detroit, because the size of its African-American population has never approached a majority.[6] According to the 1990 census Milwaukee's African-American population was merely 30% and its total non-white population only 37%. On the other hand, despite a slight (1·3%) decline in the city's population over the last decade, its minority population has continued to grow both in absolute numbers and as a percentage of the total city population. Indeed, during the 1980s it was one of the few northern cities to experience a sizeable growth (30%) in its African-American population.

Further, the percentage of African-American and minority school enrolments have steadily exceeded the minority population in the city. By the mid-1980s Milwaukee was a majority non-white school district. While whites continued to flee the school system in the 1970s and 1980s for suburban and private school systems, very few minorities moved to the suburbs. Milwaukee has the most segregated suburbs of any major metropolitan area in the nation. As a result, many African-American (and other non-white) middle-class persons continue to send their children to the city's public schools and to remain vitally concerned about the school system's well-being.

Racial issues did not begin to shape school board politics in a significant way until the 1960s. Most of Milwaukee's African-American population migrated to the city from the South or from other northern cities after the Second World War and, despite a tripling of the African-American population in the 1950s, African-American electoral and organizational strength in the city was quite negligible. During the 1960s African-Americans succeeded in electing one or two members to Milwaukee's then 15-member school board (its size was reduced in the late 1970s and district representation increased to improve representativeness), but a racially conservative majority on the board prevailed until 1976. They blocked efforts by an African-American attorney, Lloyd Barbee, and other community leaders to desegregate the schools. Indeed, even in 1970 African-Americans continued to be bused from overcrowded inner-city schools but were kept 'intact' in the receiving schools, i.e., segregated from white pupils. In 1976 school officials finally lost a desegregation lawsuit (*Amos* v. *Board of School Directors of the City of Milwaukee*, 408 F. Supp. 765; E.D Wis. 1976) which had been in federal court for over a decade.

By this time, of course, the civil rights movement in the nation had long since crested, as had enthusiasm for desegregation among African-Americans. Nevertheless, Milwaukee implemented a highly successful desegregation plan relying on magnet and specialty schools and much greater busing of African-Americans than whites. The enviable public relations skills of Superintendent Lee McMurrin helped establish this policy and fend it off from critics for over a decade. He and the school board successfully resisted efforts by African-American activist Howard Fuller to establish an all-black district within the city. The Milwaukee school board took the offensive against its suburbs and state officials by filing a lawsuit in federal court in 1986, arguing that they had acted so as to increase the racial isolation of city school pupils, in part because of their unwillingness to participate in a voluntary student exchange programme (Chapter 220) established at the time of the federal court order.

This lawsuit galvanized suburban and state officials to argue that Milwaukee's problems were those of mismanagement, not racial isolation or resources. Indeed, Superintendents McMurrin was warned quietly that if the school board did not desist from its lawsuit plans, a study would be conducted. The state delivered on this threat by creating a Governor's Commission, which published a voluminous study on the disparities in quality between city and suburban schools that assiduously avoided references to the racial aspects of the problem or to the need for additional resources. The report also ignored the important changes in Milwaukee's manufacturing economy which dramatically reduced job opportunities and quality of life for African-Americans and other persons of colour living in Milwaukee's central city. Few government or private sector policies addresses this larger problem surrounding the schools.

Nevertheless, this Study Commission on the Quality of Education in the Metropolitan Milwaukee Area Schools (1985), symbolized more than any other set of events the new demands for improved quality which would confront the School Board and McMurrin's successors, beginning in the late 1980s. While a voluntary student-exchange agreement was extracted from the suburbs and from the State of Wisconsin growing out of its metropolitan desegregation lawsuit, the school board failed to achieve what some board members had hoped for, a metropolitan redistricting plan.

By the time McMurrin left in 1988 complaints had mounted that he was doing little to address underachievement and the high dropout rate. Test scores were declining, with wide gaps between minority and white students. High-school attendance rates were dropping, and suspension rates increasing, particularly for African-American males. McMurrin's successor, Robert Peterkin, was recruited from Cambridge, MA, to be the city's first African-American superintendent. Peterkin's policies, while not abandoning racial integration, focused on improved representativeness and improved quality. Six administrative regions were created with community superintendents, the majority of whom were African-American or Hispanic. Peterkin announced ambitious plans to decentralize operations, restructure the curriculum and refocus the student selection system to improve failing schools.

After a short two-year tenure, however, Peterkin announced his resignation to accept a position at Harvard, thus assuring that his entire reform agenda remained incomplete. This unleashed unprecedented public criticism of the Milwaukee school system's management, most dramatically epitomized by Governor Tommy Thompson's proposal (later scuttled by the State Legislature) to break the Milwaukee school district into smaller systems no larger than 25,000 students each.

Several members favoured Peterkin's heir apparent, Deputy Superintendent Deborah McGriff, as superintendent. However, a divided school board could not agree on a successor. Milwaukee's business leaders stepped into this leadership vacuum. For some years the business community had begun to take a more active interest in the schools of the region. They had created the Greater Milwaukee Trust to encourage tutoring of inner city children and to offer financial guarantees for college to needy youngsters. Business leaders had worked with board members to hire the McKenzie Group, a well-known consulting firm, in April 1988 to consider regional decentralization, and had pressed this proposal on Peterkin when he was hired. In 1991 they openly solicited and sponsored Attorney Paul Lucy in his successful campaign for a seat on the Milwaukee Board of School Directors.

Thus, it was consistent with this new activist posture for business leaders in early 1991 to successfully lobby state legislators for special legislation making Howard Fuller eligible to be the next superintendent. Fuller, a former African-American community activist, had gone on to be appointed to a cabinet post in the administration of Governor Tony Earl during the early 1980s, to be an associate dean at the Milwaukee Area Technical College, and Milwaukee County's Director of Social Services. He had gained a doctorate in education at Marquette University but lacked the necessary licensure qualifications to be a superintendent. After the State Legislature made Fuller qualified, the Milwaukee Board of School Directors acquiesced to this pressure spearheaded by the city's business elite by appointing Fuller as Milwaukee's second African-American superintendent. Fuller promptly eliminated the regional offices created by his predecessor. Within two months of his appointment, he proclaimed that the school system was failing and outlined an ambitious plan to reward successful schools, penalize or close failing ones, decentralize decision making to the school level, and expand educational choices for parents.

In Milwaukee, too, the demands for racial equity and representativeness gave way to steadily escalating demands for improved quality. Concern over racial integration and racial representativeness were never abandoned, to be sure, but the expectations for both of the last two superintendents, in addition to their being African-Americans, have focused primarily on the restoration of educational quality.

So serious was this concern about quality in the State Legislature that African-American State Representative Polly Williams garnered support for the nation's first educational choice plan involving private schools. The plan, while targeted on only a small area of the city and only capable of serving a small number of low-income children, symbolized the depth of the legitimacy crisis which afflicted Milwaukee's public schools in a city otherwise reputed for governmental stability.

Conclusion

The leadership instability which we have observed in America's urban school systems has been explained as a function of a changing political ecology affecting these school systems.

Despite the differences in the local economies and political traditions of Detroit, Atlanta and Milwaukee, demands for racial equity have been overshadowed by concerns for educational quality. This does not mean that the struggle for racial equity has disappeared, however. While efforts for further racial desegregation are no longer a serious policy consideration in any of these cities, not even in Milwaukee, racial representativeness is an expectation which influences staffing and other decisions in all three cities. Therefore, these systems ae being asked to attend to *both* dimensions simultaneously.

These systems typify a pattern in many cities across the nation: the inability to manage growing demands for excellence, resulting in leadership turnover and problems of superintendent recruitment. In all three cities, the political coalitions which made possible the appointment of African-American superintendents were eclipsed by new ones demanding quality without demanding the abandonment of representativeness.

As we have pointed out, demands for greater accountability and quality are not new. What was new beginning in the 1980s was a new activism by business leaders, who have forged new support and coalitions in each city. Business involvement previously had occurred through programme support strategies such as business–school partnerships. This approach was not abandoned, as exemplified by new efforts to set up tutoring and college guarantees. What did change was the re-emergence of business interest in school governance and a willingness to lobby state and local politicians and the media to win support for business priorities in the schools. Business leaders have strengthened their representation on the school boards of all three cities, even in Atlanta, where the approach to shared governance dated back many decades.

The fact that similar developments occurred in all three cities despite the differences in local economies (Atlanta's growth profile as contrasted with the decline of manufacturing economies in Detroit and Milwaukee), is an indication of how much national forces have intruded on the local politics of urban education in American cities. Politicians and reformers who have tried for decades to make urban schools more accountable now have a potent new argument, that of international economic competition. Further, with labour shortages imminent, business cannot afford to abandon public education. Just as business leaders in Atlanta never lost sight of how that city's public schools could contribute to the growth of Atlanta's economy *vis-à-vis* the nation, now business leaders there and elsewhere see the international economic dimensions of this issue and how it must, from their perspective, drive reform.

It has ordinarily been assumed that state policy makers have been the principal architects of this national agenda, as they have increased mandates on local school districts in order to improve performance and 'competitiveness'. Yet the political role of business leaders, acting not only through state policy, but also locally, has been an important political shift as well.

It is yet to be seen how effectively urban school systems will be able to manage this newest layer of political demands. The administrative structures and many of the programmes of these school systems still reflect the 'politics of equity' which reshaped them in the 1960s and 1970s, often through state and federal policies and court decisions. While next to none of this has been dismantled, these systems now confront demands to improve student achievement and attendance, reduce the dropout rate, retool their curricula for employment, increase advanced placement and other college-oriented opportunities, and the list goes on. The financial capacity to address these problems remains debatable at best, generally much less than in surrounding suburbs with far less ambitious demands being placed on school officials. Indeed, the racial and ethnic diversity of urban school systems has increased, as Hispanic and Asian enrolments grow (frequently more rapidly than African-American enrolments), and new immigrant groups demand costly services.

What will the next stage be in the evolution of this changing political ecology? Boston has moved to an appointed school board. Chicago has created local school councils. Another governance option continues to be a serious possibility in Milwaukee, where Governor Tommy Thompson proposed to break up the school system into smaller school systems not to exceed 25,000 pupils each. While this proposal did not pass the state legislature in 1991, it may reappear in the future unless educational quality in the Milwaukee school system improves dramatically. Still another possibility is schools located around workplaces, which presumably would guarantee increased business influence in the name of excellence.

Nowhere is the dilemma of achieving both equity and excellence more clearly drawn than in our cities. The political turbulence these systems are experiencing reflects unresolved racial and economic stratification in American society, often expressed as demands to protect equity or excellence. Urban school systems now are populated primarily or entirely by children of colour, while many of the business leaders leading demands for excellence are white. Consequently, equity and excellence can become ideological labels which are sometimes seen by protagonists as being necessarily in conflict rather than compatible. Yet African-American superintendents are expected to achieve both equity and excellence and are held responsible accordingly.

Business leaders have come to understand that urban schools cannot be abandoned. This has reshaped the political ecology of urban schools in the 1980s and early 1990s. What has not emerged is a clear and compelling strategy for their renewal.

Notes

1. Both authors contributed equally to this chapter.
2. The same pattern is apparent for mayoral turnover. We examined mayoral turnover in the comparable municipal governments for the nation's 50 largest school districts. (Data were drawn from the International City Management Association, *The Municipal Yearbook*, Washington, DC for the years 1977 to 1990.) If immediate past mayors' terms of office are compared with their predecessors, two-thirds served longer than their predecessors. The cities with more rapid mayoral turnover were not necessarily those with quicker superintendent turnover. Thus, there is no special turnover problem in school governments, as compared with cities.
3. The historical data for this section were taken from Darden *et al.* (1987) as well as interview data with school officials and community leaders.
4. For details on the court case and remedy, see Hain, E. (1978) 'Sealing off the city: School desegregation in Detroit', in H. J. Koloder and J. J. Fishman (eds) *Limits of Justice: The Court's Role in School Desegregation* (Washington, DC: Ballinger Press), pp. 223–308.
5. Data in this section are drawn from Atlanta Public Schools Forum 1990, 1991, Jackson 1978, Orfield and Peskin 1988, and Plank and Turner 1991, as well as from interview data with school officials and community leaders.
6. Data in this section are drawn from the documentary files of the Milwaukee Public Schools, newspaper accounts, interviews with school officials and community leaders, as well as James Cibulka's work as a participant observer in events from 1972 to the present.

References

ATLANTA, PUBLIC SCHOOLS FORUM (1990, 1991) Atlanta, GA, Atlanta Public Schools, October and April.

BROWN, O. S., PETERKIN, R. W. and FINKELSTEIN, L. B. (1991) 'Urban CEOs: Untangling the governance knot', *Education Week*, 13 March 1991.

COUNCIL OF GREAT CITY SCHOOLS (1990) *The Condition of Education in the Great City Schools: A Ten Year Statistical Profile 1980–1990* (Washington, DC: The Council of The Great City Schools).

COUNCIL OF GREAT CITY SCHOOLS (1987) *Results in the Making* (Washington, DC: The Council of The Great City Schools).

DARDEN, J. T., HILL, R. C., THOMAS, J. and THOMAS, R. (1987) *Detroit: Race and Uneven Development* (Philadelphia: Temple University Press).

GRANT, W. R. (1971) 'Community control vs. integration: The case of Detroit', *The Public Interest*, Summer, pp. 62–79.

HAIN, E. (1978) 'Sealing off the city: School desegregation in Detroit', in H. J. Kolodner and J. J. Fishman (eds) *Limits of Justice: The Court's Role in School Desegregation* (Washington, DC: Ballinger Press), pp. 223–308.

JACKSON, B. L. (1978) 'Desegregation: Atlanta style', *Theory into Practice*, 17, pp. 43–53.

LEIGHT, R. L. (ed.) (1973) *Philosophers Speak on Accountability in Education* (Danville, IL: Interstate Publishers).

OAKES, J. (1987) 'Improving inner-city schools: Current directions in urban district reform', New Brunswick, NJ, Center for Policy Research on Education. Unpublished report.

ORFIELD, G. and MONFORT, F. (1988) *Racial Change and Desegregation in Large School Districts: Trends through the 1986–87 School Year* (Alexandria, VA: National School Boards Association).

ORFIELD, G. and PESKIN, L. (1988) 'Metropolitan high schools: Income, race, and inequality', in D. C. Mitchell and M. E. Goertz (eds) *Education Politics for the New Century* (Philadelphia: Falmer Press), pp. 27–53.

PLANK, D. N. and TURNER, M. (1991) 'Contrasting patterns in black politics: Atlanta and Memphis, 1965–1985', *The Journal of Negro Education*, 60, pp. 203–218.

STUDY COMMISSION ON THE QUALITY OF EDUCATION IN THE METROPOLITAN MILWAUKEE AREA SCHOOLS (1985) *Study Reports*, Vols 1–10 (Madison, WI). Unpublished report.

POLITICS OF EDUCATION ASSOCIATION YEARBOOK 1991, 87–103

6 *Urban schools as organizations: political perspectives*

Robert L. Crowson and William Lowe Boyd

Reformed at the turn of the century toward top-down, centralized administration, city school systems are frequently being reorganized today toward a bottom-up, decentralized construction. The most radical of these is Chicago. But Chicago, in a condition shared widely throughout the USA, is a city school system experiencing serious budgetary and infrastructure decline – a condition tending anew toward organizational centralization. Such political forces may not mesh well – as a new politics of adaptive realignment at the grassroots encounters renewed strength in an 'old politics' of bureaucratic centralization. Largely unstudied and unknown at this time are the effects on the internal politics of the organization in city schooling – a politics that may adapt in some unforeseen way to new battles between top-down and bottom-up.

In mid-April 1991, the *Chicago Sun-Times* began a week-long, headlined examination of facilities deterioration and disrepair throughout Chicago's public schools. The reports were complete with full-page pictures of falling plaster, rotted wood, disintegrating walls, broken glass, water-damaged ceilings and floors, electrical, plumbing and heating failures, filthy workspaces, and badly weathered, open-to-the-elements windows. It was concluded that the decided majority of Chicago's 600 schools 'are in ruins' (*Chicago Sun-Times* 14 April 1991). The newspaper investigation went on to claim that the lack of maintenance, and now ruination, of the Chicago schools is the product of 'decades of political and economic compromises that put labor peace, teacher wages and lower taxes ahead of student safety, day-to-day repairs and an environment conducive to learning' (*Chicago Sun-Times* 14 April 1991: 1).

Specifically, the argument in the Chicago case is that the city's scramble for money to balance budgets, especially to provide pay rises for teachers (following nine strikes between 1969 and 1987), has resulted in years of slashed repair dollars and the deferment of all maintenance beyond that needed for 'emergencies'. Noted the reporters, it's a city 'where unions have a strong voice, buildings don't go on strike, and children don't fight back' (*Chicago Sun-Times* 15 April 1991: 1). However, amid such 'ruination' and in the midst of a decentralizing reform movement, with power-to-the-people dimensions, Chicago's communities and Local School Councils were also found by reporters to be moving increasingly toward some fight-back attitudes. Observed one high school principal: 'School reform has opened up the can. It brought the community in' (*Chicago Sun-Times* 14 April 1991: 14).

As an example of a reopened 'can', Chicago is by no means alone. The facilities-repair crunch is equally severe in New York, Detroit and Los Angeles, and indeed in nearly every large-city school system in the nation. The poignancy of the facilities crisis, furthermore, is that it is just the tip of a system-deterioration iceberg for city schools. Whether the community is 'in' (and 'fighting back') or not, concerns about the quality of city schooling have never been greater. From reading achievement to job preparation, from dropout prevention to student health and personal safety provisions, from declining parental involvement and neighbourhood decay to a general malaise within the professional workforce, from questions of school-site leadership to worries about the superintendency – the urban school system in most of its settings appears to be '*in extremis*'. In this vein, the condition of the physical facilities for education in such cities as Chicago constitutes the least of its complex problems. Indeed, in late April, the plight of the Chicago schools continued to be major headline news for the city's papers, but the focus by now was on a projected $300 million shortfall in operating funds for the schools for the upcoming 1991–92 school year (*Chicago Tribune* 21 April 1991).

Although just a part (and perhaps even a lesser part) of the larger malaise, the facilities and budget-shortfall issues can be drawn on for two introductory insights into the 'politics of the organization' in urban schooling. First, the rob Peter to pay Paul flavour of deferred maintenance exemplifies a continuing, distinctive politics of decline management in urban schooling. Second, such issues as the facilities maintenance crisis and its full-blown exposé represent a changing politics of the organization in city schooling – from insulation, cover-up and accommodation to a new, reform-pressured politics of organizational modification and adaptation in the face of environmental change. This chapter outlines, and draws some implications from, each of these perspectives. It should be noted, however, that from our facilities-deterioration example on, we lean heavily on Chicago as a key example of big-city school system problems. While Chicago's radical decentralization reform is atypical, the city nevertheless does typify much of the large-city system experience.

The continuing politics of organizational decline

In 1979, at a time of widening concern over apparent growth in the power of teachers', unions, Grimshaw argued that a condition of 'union rule' had captured the politics of large-city schooling. Again, Chicago was the instructive case. Machine-rule government of turn of the century vintage has been replaced in most cities by reform-minded and management-autonomy-minded government. But, urban education politics has now evolved, claimed Grimshaw (1979) into an unprecedented control of schooling by its unionized public employees. A transition from machine to reform government had effectively transferred politician and citizen influence into managerial control; now, union rule, says Grimshaw (1979: 2) is taking the further step of separating the governance of education from *both* management *and* citizenry into the hands of a union leadership. This leadership is 'elected solely by the union's membership' and 'accountable only to the membership'.

By the mid-1980s, it seemed quite clear that the politics and management of large-urban schooling was far from the condition of union domination forecast by Grimshaw in 1979. To be sure, as Kerchner's (1986) analyses have indicated, there are some discernible effects of unionization on the organizational structures of city schools and on teachers' work. Indeed, there is evidence that teaching under the union contract has 'become more preplanned and structured', that discharging teachers has been made more difficult, that teachers' options for voicing dissatisfactions (versus quietly leaving) have much increased, and that principals now tend to be more negotiative with teachers than demanding of obedience to managerial authority (Kerchner 1986).

Nevertheless, union 'rule', in the near-monopoly sense of Grimshaw's (1979) analysis, has not developed. Presciently, the author warned of one constraint on union rule which in fact did materialize (in Chicago) during the very year of his publication Grimshaw (1979: 150) observed: 'When the financial limits are reached, the union rules' fiscal limits are necessarily reached too'. In fact, Chicago reached its financial limits in 1979 in a dramatic bankruptcy, a superintendent's abrupt dismissal, and the state's imposition of a special 'Finance Authority' to oversee the budget of the public schools. As Kerchner (1986) has observed, 'unionization did not occur in social isolation' – and no isolation was certainly possible from such powerful countervailing forces as a taxpayer revolt; race politics; a spate of new state controls over local schooling; a widespread effort to address a *Nation at Risk*; and, most powerful of all, city decline and a further isolation/ghettoization of the urban poor (Wilson 1987). In short, neither machine rule nor reform rule nor union rule can long survive the consequences and the 'fallout' of an organization in deep crisis.

What has taken its place? In some earlier work (Boyd 1982, 1983), it was argued that politics and management under conditions of decline display differing characteristics from that which accompanies growth. Resource allocations tend to shift to a more redistributive politics, questions of equity and entitlement (and of course 'vested interests' and job 'property rights') assume increased saliency, and morale may plummet (as career-advancement opportunities and incentives dry up) (see Behn 1980, Bardach 1976, Levine 1978, Berman and McLaughlin 1978). Indeed, although not treated in our earlier analysis, indications are that even deteriorations in physical facilities (let alone salaries and operating budgets) can quite badly erode the morale (and consequently the performance) of an organization's personnel and its clientele.

There was a heyday of retrenchment in public schooling in the late 1970s, and some near-determined efforts to pare administrative staffs (with the interesting result that more teachers were dropped proportionately than administrators) (Tyack 1990). Although retrenchment is no longer a front-burner term, by no means is 'growth' its early-'90s' replacement. To be sure, there is not everywhere a uniform story of ever-deepening decline to be noted in city schooling. In fact, Judd and Parkinson (1990) argue that a heavy dose of 'urban regeneration' is now to be found in a number of the industrial cities of both North America and Western Europe – with, consequently, new creativity and regenerative leadership to be found in the public schools. Indeed, whether the surrounding urban economy is moving 'up' or remains 'down', there is to be observed in city schooling today an interesting outpouring of impressive creativity – from choice, to decentralization and local 'empowerment', to community-relations initiatives, to co-ordinated-services experiments, to new corporate linkages and job-training efforts. Whether growth has replaced decline, there has been at least the image in a number of cities (e.g., Pittsburgh, San Diego, Miami, Indianapolis, Milwaukee) of a public school system 'on the move' – with some energetic leadership at its helm.

Furthermore, there is seldom organizational decline without, simultaneously, pockets of mysterious growth. Morris *et al.* (1984) watched with amusement as a number of savvy principals 'worked' an out-of-control school system, adding considerably to resource flows to their schools during the cutbacks accompanying Chicago's deep financial crisis of 1979. Years later, despite predictions that no one would apply, there was an outpouring of applicants to replace each of the principals summarily fired by Local School Councils under Chicago's reform. In a system closing its paths toward career advancement, these perilous jobs represented growth and opportunity. Additionally, in any complex system there will always be programmes and services (often of the categorical-grant variety) that grow, or at least maintain stability, while other budgets flounder. Personnel in these offices can gain considerably in system-wide influence while decline reigns elsewhere. Indeed, the fragmentation of even the most reputedly centralized of city systems offers a veritable cornucopia of opportunities for growth amid decay (Meyer *et al.* 1987).

Nevertheless, we would argue that a politics of organizational decline continues to be a defining characteristic of urban schooling. State funding and local tax revenues currently reflect a nationwide economic downturn; large-urban districts continue either to fall in school population or to grow too rapidly in enrolment (as in Dallas or Los Angeles) beyond fiscal abilities to keep up; and, as indicated earlier, the infrastructure of most of the nation's cities (especially its school facilities) represents the ravages of long-deferred maintenance. At the heart of the politics and management of decline in urban schooling is a continued question of whither goest the organization's scarce resources; and why. Not surprisingly, the complexities and intricacies of urban school systems (phrased by Tyack [1990: 172] as decision-making structures that 'only a Rube Goldberg could understand, much less appreciate'), have not assisted a clear understanding of bureaucratic resource flows. The evidence is that as financial conditions worsen, even greater confusion and 'anarchy' seem to prevail in city decision making. Difficult to fathom at the best of times, municipal allocations seem even more unstructured under 'worsened' conditions (Morgan and Palmer 1988).

As an example of such confusion, a popularly reported finding by Sorrel and Cooper (as reported in Wechsler 1990), indicates a continued top-heavy distribution of resources in New York City (despite decentralization), with shockingly few dollars flowing directly to children down in their classrooms. However, this finding has produced claims of serious methodological shortcomings in the researchers' failure to track properly the myriad ways in which educational resources do in fact reach pupils and the complexity of accounting for this impact. Presumably, many school services (e.g., inservice) budgeted to the central office and some personnel of the itinerant service variety (e.g., special educators, reading experts, psychologists, social workers) might have been identified as upper-bureaucracy resources when in fact the services and workdays are spent in the schools. Not at all clear at any time is just what is a school-site resource and what is not. Indeed, it should be noted that analyses of top v. bottom-heavy can cut both ways. Before its own decentralizing reform, Chicago was well known for 'hiding' the salaries of many of its central office personnel in the budgets of the separate schools.

It is equally difficult to track any redistributional effects on city schools and their programmes under organizational decline. An array of forces, pulls, pressures and counter-pressures are to be found (Cibulka 1987). Economic constraints on the pursuit of the city's interests and its social responsibilities, as portrayed in Peterson's (1981) *City Limits*, are powerful determinants of the service-delivery mix. Indeed, the continued saliency and even poignancy of the city limit construct, at this time of an expanded interest in children's services, is disturbingly apparent in research by Littell and Wynn (1989) – who found wide disparities in the activities and services (school-based and otherwise) available to children in the inner-city v. suburban ring of metropolitan Chicago. Beyond the 'economic constraint' model, the politics and management of decline appears to be much affected by state and federal mandates, the political strengths of varying policy contenders, and degrees of administrative independence (Wong 1990). Indeed, on this latter point, it is especially instructive to note that under conditions of decline, organizational decisions tend to return to centralized authority and to executive control. In their study of US cities generally, Morgan and Palmer (1988: 72) note that '. . . the cutback process is isolated from external influences. Interest groups and even unionized employees generally have only a minimal effect on the outcome.' Wong (1990: 152) has also observed that retrenchment studies in numerous cities have found a centralizing tendency and 'the allocation of cutback decisions follows a centralized process'.

From this perspective, Cibulka (1987) found expenditure cuts in schooling in a sample of ten major cities to be carefully managed by central administrators to maintain 'employee justice' (i.e., fair working conditions and wages). Similarly, in a study of Chicago, Wong (1989) found central office personnel dominating a delicate balance, under conditions of urban decline, to emphasize a magnet-school approach to forestalling middle-class emigration from the city – while simultaneously avoiding charges of inequity and racism in any neglect of neighbourhood schools. This was accomplished by awarding the magnet schools considerable governance autonomy but no bonuses in school system resources. Indeed, concluded Wong (1989: 26): 'By subjecting choice programs to the same allocative rules based upon universalistic criteria, local officials are able to diffuse much controversy over distributive favoritism'.

In brief summary, we have suggested thus far that organizational politics in urban schooling continues to be, in many settings, a politics of organizational decline (or at least a continuing politics of serious resource inadequacy). Strangely, there is not a surfeit of research into the internal politics of retrenchment in urban school systems, including effects on employee and clientele morale, career socialization and the career ladder, and the influences of within-organization 'interests' on school district decision making. There appears to be some evidence, however, that bureaucratic decision rules, and a centralizing tendency in decision making, can increase in saliency during retrenchment – all part of a complex, hard to fathom, Rube Goldbergian arrangement of organizational structures and workroles. As resources are increasingly scarce but environmental pressures increase, a retreat to bureaucratic decision rules (central-office dominated) can become a near necessity – rules which protect 'employee justice' or balance district-wide seemingly incompatible goals (e.g., magnet schools and distributive equity). Bureaucratic decision rules are usually conveniently 'buried', writes Toulmin (1988), but if made public, then 'even more controversy can be generated'.

A new politics of adaptation and modification

Bureaucratic decision rules are usually associated with managerial centralization. However, city systems were never as rigidly bureaucratized, as fully 'top-down', or as superintendent's-office dominated as popularly believed. Indeed, a more careful terminology refers to a 'fragmented centralization' (Tyack 1990) in city schooling or, less elegantly, to the 'intrainstitutional disarticulation' (Grimshaw 1979) characteristic of school hierarchies.

Nevertheless, there is legitimacy to the image of urban schooling as effectively 'reformed' earlier in our century from ward-responsive and machine-politics roots into corporate models of pyramidal, removed from politics, one-best-system management. The over-bureaucratized school system has been a sufficiently accurate picture to spark decades of concern over responsiveness/accountability and an 'erosion of lay control' in urban education (Guthrie *et al.* 1975). The current reforms to decentralize, grassroots-level professionalize, or add 'choice' to city schooling are sufficiently innovative to suggest that changed insights into the organizational politics of urban education may be on the horizon.

In *The One Best System*, Tyack (1974: 146) quotes Wallace Sayre's (1958) observation that, like other organizations, the educational bureaucracy 'works persistently towards stabilizing its relationship to each of the other elements in its field of forces in ways that will maximize its own autonomous role'. In a 1981 review of the 'changing conception and practice of public school administration' (Boyd and Crowson 1981) we similarly argued that despite extraordinary pressures over the years (from the civil rights revolution to the effective schools movement), the American public schools have been remarkably successful at resisting fundamental organizational change. Indeed, Seymour Sarason (1990) still refers to the public schools as peculiarly 'intractable institutions'. In 1981, we also noted that the characteristics of public schools 'do not appear to foster adaptive behavior' (p. 331). Furthermore, we suggested that 'attempts at the institutional level to open up the school governance process to greater parental choice, citizen participation and influence seem generally to have been ineffective' (Boyd and Crowson, 1981: 358).

This argument was supported by a literature indicating that organizational maintenance tends to take precedence over goal attainment, that little connection exists between the activities of management and the core activities of student learning, that intense pressures at the organizational 'street level' make it only modestly responsive to the rest of the organization (while the rest of the organization nevertheless works to tighten its controls), and that many organizational rewards lead heavily toward employee self-interest over performance (Boyd and Crowson 1981). In further work (Boyd and Hartman 1988, Boyd 1991), the argument has been that fundamental institutional deficiencies (e.g., an ill-designed workplace, a reciprocity-oriented control system, a perverse structure of incentives) are major developmental obstacles to school improvement/reform.

By no means are these within-organization forces any less salient today to a full understanding of the organizational politics of city schooling. Nevertheless, there is another feature, another force, that must now be considered. Again, Chicago can be used as illustration and introduction. While Grimshaw's (1979) 'union rule' did not materialize, it is generally acknowledged that the far-reaching legislation to reform the Chicago Public Schools in 1988 (establishing a parental/community decentralization of school governance) was in large part an outgrowth of a 19-day teachers' strike in 1987 (Wong and Rollow 1990, Hess 1991). Wong and Rollow (1990: 4) observe:

> The strike was the third in six years, the longest Chicago had ever experienced, and perhaps the most futile. Outraged by their settlement, many teachers resigned from the union. The press accused both the BOE and the CTU for their 'stranglehold' on the system, and the gulf between parents and professional educators at the school level had never been wider.

Indeed, community perceptions of an intransigent, if not unduly powerful, teacher's union strengthened handily the arguments of the more 'radical' of Chicago's reformers – those arguing for the populist solution of majority parental/community control at the school site (Wong and Rollow 1990). Following reform, parent and community representatives together comprise eight of the 11 members of each Local School Council.

Like most changes, Chicago's school reform was imposed from the outside. It was a coercive imposition of some new organizational structures, growing out of a sense of loss of institutional legitimacy and a sense that in addition to its labour woes Chicago was inexcusably engaged in a 'failure to educate' and a good deal of administrative misdirection/mismanagement (Hess 1991). Coercion, amid the problem of legitimacy, is one of three mechanisms, note DiMaggio and Powell (1983) through which organizations engage in 'isomorphic' change. In 'The iron cage revisited', DiMaggio and Powell (1983: 149) define isomorphism as a constraining process wherein 'organizational characteristics are modified in the direction of increasing compatibility with environmental characteristics'. In short, new sets of environmental conditions can lead to a new politics of organizational modification and adaptation – an adaptation, moreover, wherein there is a push towards a sameness (a 'homogenization') of organizational structures within common environmental fields (DiMaggio and Powell 1983). As an example of such homogenization, DiMaggio and Powell (1983: 150) reference Milofsky's (1981) finding that neighbourhood organizations in many cities, despite their commitment to participatory democracy, found it necessary 'to develop organizational hierarchies in order to gain support from more hierarchically organized donor organizations'.

It might be pushing too far to suggest that an 'adaptive realignment' (Elmore 1990) is under way in city schooling. Tyack (1990: 179) warns that 'no coherent new model of governance' arose from the turbulence of the 1960s – except, if anything, an even more complex and bureaucratized organization of schooling. However, times can change. Raywid (1990: 152) points to today's widely held sentiment that the 'schools are no longer in accord with their political environments – that is, with the desires of the parents and the communities they presumably serve and with the political system whose procedural principles public institutions are obligated to reflect'. Both Wong and Rollow (1990) and Hess (1991), furthermore, comment on the extraordinary mobilization of parents and community activists that developed on behalf of the Chicago reforms. Amid his discussion of 'intractability', Sarason (1990: 156) goes on to predict that the boundaries between the community 'and the encapsulated school and its encapsulated classrooms . . . will become far more porous than heretofore'. And, with an ear close to practice, Louis and Miles (1990) have already developed an *evolutionary* or *adaptive* model of school improvement for the site-level practitioner, emphasizing (per a McLaughlin and Talbert review 1991: 28) 'vision and judgment rather than rules as bureaucratic procedures'.

It is by no means clear just what would best describe or characterize a newly adaptive politics of the organization in city schooling. With some continuing insights from DiMaggio and Powell (1983), however, we will make three beginning observations:.

1. *An adaptive entrepreneurial superintendency*: It is increasingly apparent that Williams *et al.* (1987: 119) are correct (when discussing the school-district superintendency) in noting that 'increasingly, the power to direct and control the school district's operations and planning is powerfully influenced by individuals and groups and agencies that reside outside the district office and the district itself'. Relatedly, there is reported to be a deep sense of crisis in the present state of the large-urban superintendency. Amid claims that the position of the school system CEO in the nation's cities is a virtually impossible job, cities across the country (from Boston, to Detroit, to Milwaukee, to Houston, to Tuscon) were reported in December of 1990 to be in varying stages of searches while finding fewer and fewer qualified candidates (Bradley 1990). Fired and/or resigning in record numbers, reports continue, the large-urban superintendent has been 'hammered' by a national dissatisfaction with city schooling, by the increasingly insurmountable challenges of central-city deterioration, and by a 'new politicization' of the urban educational environment (Bradley 1990).

Just days after Chicago's newspapers headlined a $300 million shortfall on the horizon for the public schools in 1991–92, a new headline (*Chicago Sun-Times* 26 April 1991) blared 'No Bailout'. The Mayor and the Governor both vowed that no help would be forthcoming from either city or state, and that Chicago's School Superintendent, Ted Kimbrough, was on his own to 'straighten the mess out'. Indeed, one day later (27 April), the Governor 'helpfully' suggested that the Chicago Board of Education must now 'face reality' and cancel 2 years of teacher pay rises that were yet to come under the union contract (*Chicago Sun-Times* 27 April 1991). DiMaggio and Powell (1983) note that amid these kinds of deep environmental uncertainties (and Chicago's situation was by no means unique nationally in mid-1991), organizations tend to model themselves on other organizations that are perceived as more legitimate or successful. Simultaneously, organizational leaders tend to propose 'innovations' to enhance their own and the organization's legitimacy. Thus, beyond the coercion of Chicago reform, the 'lighthouse' restructuring of a Dade County, a Louisville, a Hammond and a Rochester can quickly become the focus of wide national interest and much 'let's try it here' experimentation (Lewis 1989, David 1990). Furthermore, a number of large-city superintendents have been much in the news with creative (albeit often controversial) proposals for improvement – including schools for black males only (Milwaukee); 'satellite' or workplace schools in centres of adult employment (Miami and New York); exit requirements for high school students, as part of 'measurement-driven instruction' (Pittsburgh); school-distributed condoms for pupils (New York); and a mandated, extra 4 hours per week of tutorials for students in the bottom quartile on state tests (San Francisco).

In a role that does not sit comfortably within the history of the position – a position history that tends to prefer behind the scenes action to the front-page – city superintendents appear increasingly to be asked (against the grain of their own inclinations and training) to become that which is identified by Terry Moe (1980: 36–39) as 'political entrepreneur'. The political entrepreneur must serve simultaneous goals of organizational maintenance (often amid decline) *and* organizational formation, working ably as both administrator and political leader to adapt organizational survival more creatively to complicated political environments. In such fashion, Judd and Parkinson (1990) describe the saliency of an entrepreneurial leadership (exploiting resources, identifying opportunities, forming political coalitions) in determining the success of urban regeneration strategies among 12 cities in both Europe and North America. In a further elaboration of the concept, and an insight into the near-impossible job of today's urban superintendency, Glassman (1986: 116) has described the value of 'manufactured charisma' in organizational leadership – a charisma that maintains external resources and support, while it 'maintains internal order and distributes life needs' and simultaneously 'boosts morale of the individual and the group'. In short, even with the centralizing forces of decline, city superintendents are increasingly seeking a bit of new direction for the schools amid little stability in either internal or external supports.

2. A bottom-up realignment in city schooling: If the CEO is under pressure, it is our second observation that the primary focus of an adaptive realignment of urban educational organizations is now on their school-site grassroots. Whether the object of decentralization, restructuring, choice, or a press toward 'effectiveness', the individual school is increasingly being faced with uncharted waters of uncertain depth in its 'neighbourhood-based' politics of education (Summerfield 1971). From 'Comer-like' interventions, to 'Accelerated Schools,' to District Four in East Harlem, to an array of co-ordinated services experiments, to a new focus generally on parent involvement in schooling – city schools in locations throughout the nation are giving at least some evidence of changed perceptions in the school–community relationship.

By no means has solid evidence surfaced to indicate that the environment is winning the 'realignment' struggle. On the one hand, parent involvement in governance, a 'reaching out' to parents, and notions of a home–school partnership in learning may be making a bit of an effective headway in school-site politics (see Jackson and Cooper 1989, Murphy and Evertson 1990, Payne 1991). As a spin-off, there occasionally emerge 'new players' in city politics from school-site reforms (Kass 1990); and there are occasionally stories of new, community-sponsored innovations in school programmes (Seibel 1991). On the other hand, there are studies indicating no 'real' progress in the shared decision-making objectives of school decentralization/restructuring, no solid evidence of school organizational renewal or altered influence relationships, and little parental satisfaction with school restructuring that does not include a meaningful partnership in decision making (see Malen and Ogawa, 1990, Malen *et al.* 1990, Goldring and Shapira 1991).

The likelihood is that these positive and negative conclusions will continue to be true for some time in diverse urban settings. Indeed, Cibulka (1991) suggests that there will be wide variability in the responsiveness of individual schools to their immediate environments, and there will be differences in the conditions under which schools achieve a 'good match' with their environments. Theorizing from an 'ecological' perspective, Cibulka (1991) concludes (using three site-level studies of Chicago reform) that varying levels of citizen commitment to reform, in the strength of community organizational resources, and in the response-to-the-community skills of school leadership – will be reflected in differences in the political and organizational 'match' of school to community.

One might add to the above model a point made by DiMaggio and Powell (1983) that would be consistent with Tyack and Hansot (1982) in *Managers of Virtue*. The point is that a newly *normative* press upon urban school systems can derive from decentralizing/reorganizing forces and from the community grassroots – a press varying in its capacity to drive the organization toward altered institutional alignments at its boundaries. A number of Chicago's Local School Councils, for example, seized an immediate opportunity under reform to take such budget or policy initiatives as the adoption of school uniforms for pupils, a hiring of additional bilingual personnel, a strengthening of African-American studies in the school curriculum, a printing of curriculum guides for parents, the purchase of Spanish-language computer software, the hiring of a 'security monitor', and even (although opposed by the affected school principal) a purchase of caps and gowns for kindergarten graduation ceremonies. In such fashion, the tendency increasingly may be for individual schools in city environments to be modified normatively in the direction of a somewhat greater compatibility with neighbourhood traditions and values. This is a point captured well by Cibulka (1991: 37) in noting a need in today's understanding of the politics of urban education to 'place emphasis on school-specific organizational and environmental influences acting quite independently of institutional features'.

3. An internal realignment of top-down and bottom-up: If urban school systems are simultaneously engaged in adaptive realignments at both the organizational top and the bottom, it is our *third* observation that newly adaptive forces in the *internal* politics of the organizational hierarchy in city schooling may be unleashed as well. Behind this phenomenon are the aforementioned pressures toward a simultaneous centralization and fragmentation in city schooling – a phenomenon already recognized fully by Wong (1990) in *City Choices*. Relatedly, Meyer *et al.* (1987: 199) have discovered that increases in the complexity or the fragmentation of an organization's environment act paradoxically to 'expand the administrative burdens of an organization'.

A Chicago vignette will again be used to illustrate the key point. It was not long after the implementation of the city's decentralizing reform in 1989 that Local School Councils throughout Chicago discovered they had extremely limited access to their buildings. Building custodians and engineers were not under the direct supervision of site-level administrators or their governing councils, and union rules stipulated that a school 'engineer' (the highest paid maintenance category) must be present whenever a school is open, with regular work rules strictly limiting the opening and closing hours of the schools. Discovering that they were shut out of their schools for council meetings and for other weekend or evening activities, the LSCs raised a public outcry. Eventually, the citywide Board of Education responded by agreeing to overtime payments to school engineers for many of the school council meetings and agreeing to compensatory time off for other evening or weekend affairs.

One of the city's news reporters sampled pay records for custodial overtime for one two-week period, found added overtime payments of just under $440,000 citywide for the two weeks, and estimated a total overtime cost of $4.8 million for the year (Vander Weele 1991). With this overtime-payment pressure, and under severe financial stress generally, the school district administration was beginning to make noises (by mid-1991) about 'privatizing' custodial care for the schools – a move understandably opposed by the union leadership. Meanwhile, throughout the city system, local councils and local administrators continued to complain about restricted access to the schools, even with overtime, amid a growing interest in opening the neighbourhood buildings earlier each day, using them later, and employing them more effectively as community resources at weekends.

Thus, a retrenchment crisis found the district's general superintendent, with the citywide Board of Education, seeking some cost-cutting alternatives to service-delivery traditions (e.g., suggesting privatization), seeking possible changes in union work rules, and regretting an earlier agreement (under grassroots pressure) to a payment of overtime. In a larger plan to pare the budget, the superintendent proposed (in early May 1991) a closing of some 30 schools, an increase in average class size across the city, an end to extracurricular activities including sports, a 'reopening' of employee contracts, a shortening of the school year, a reduction in administrative staff, and yet another year of deferred facilities repair (Vander Weele 1991). Despite such budget cutting, each of the city's individual schools (described by Cibulka [1991] as 'semi-independent political entities') worked feverishly to keep its doors open, protect its programmes and extracurriculum, add staff, remodel its facilities and (for some) lengthen the school day and the school year.

How does this interplay of top-down *and* bottom-up in environmental adaptation affect the *internal* politics of the organization? There is, to begin with, no solid evidence that existing authority relations in city schooling have been much altered under reform/restructuring (Wong and Rollow 1990). By no means, for example, has it been established that 'organizational processes' (e.g., red tape, standard operating procedures, turf protection, communications failures, prevailing employee norms) as described by Rogers (1969) in New York City and Peterson (1976) in Chicago, have changed toward greater school-site responsiveness. Indeed, from the LaNoue and Smith (1973) study of 1960s-era decentralization to the Rogers and Chung (1983) revisit to 110 Livingston Street, there are no solid indications of new accommodations or a 'new politics' of central versus dispersed authority (see also, Crowson 1985). Studies of large organizations show often how deeply rooted are administrator selection mechanisms, information systems, training devices and normative pressures in support of an ongoing control structure (see Feldman and March 1981, McPherson *et al.* 1986, Crowson and Morris 1985). School principals in Chicago, under reform, continue to complain of a centralized personnel system mired in red tape, burdensome report-filing and record-keeping mechanisms, a categorical-grant distribution system busily recentralizing its authority, and an unresponsive central-office control of such important auxiliary services as pupil transportation and facilities repair.

Nevertheless, both Rogers and Chung (1983) earlier, and Cibulka (1991), more recently, find the indications of upward-flowing change in 'a dramatic transformation' of the building principal's role – particularly in a shift toward a 'community orientation'

(Rogers and Chung 1983), in place of the role of 'lightning rod' (Cibulka 1991) which deflects community pressure away from upper administration. Some preliminary observations from informal interviews with a sample of Chicago principals may provide a few insights into the possible nature of that transformation.[1] One change, as Chicago's principals see it themselves, is a much enhanced sense of organizational *feudalism*. Long known for a bit of 'creative insubordination' (Morris *et al.* 1984) and for 'playing the system' (Cibulka 1991) in the interest of their own schools, city principals are nevertheless also used to taking comfort in an essential sameness and in equal-treatment formulae between the schools. Now, the principals charge, the press upon each principal is to accentuate school differences, to out-resource neighbouring schools, and to work the system with even greater vigour. Individual bonds and friendships within the organizational hierarchy have increased in importance, as principals use central-office acquaintances as their 'ins' to increasingly scarce resources (see Leibenstein 1987). However, charge the principals, there is no longer a bonding *between* schools and between principals. Each school, now a fiefdom of its own, senses a competition with, and is therefore wary of other school 'units' within the system.

A second and related claim, from principals' self-reports, is a current loss of valued hierarchical *protections* for site-level administrators. While a traditional responsibility of the principal is to protect or buffer the upper organization from attack, the responsibility cuts both ways (Crowson and Morris 1990). Principals expect to be 'backed up' by their central administrators; furthermore, principals are adroit users of school system rules as buffers against turbulent environments while simultaneously bending the rules from time to time to accommodate those environments (Morris *et al.* 1984). Now, the claim is, the building principal is on his or her own, without protection – sensing heavily, in this limbo state, some personal and ethical dilemmas of administration. 'We have no dignity,' observes one principal. Similarly, notes another. 'I have no voice; you have to struggle to let them know where you stand and that you are a person.' 'Where's your authority base?', says a third, 'you're stuck in there as a scapegoat without the resources to do it'. 'It's hard not to just cave in', concludes a fourth.[2]

One quite conceivable outcome of all of this is an internal politics of the organization in urban schooling that is characterized by an isolated, even feudal, administration of the school site, in an increasingly unresponsive relationship with the central office. Thus, at one end, the central office seeks sufficient system-wide authority to legitimize its efforts toward retrenchment, undertake an innovation or two, and constrain the system toward improvement. In the middle, internal forces, as Firestone and Bader (1991) note, can affect heavily the external authority and legitimacy of the superintendent. At the bottom, differences between the schools in adaptive relationships with their separate communities place pressures on the hierarchical organization to support and legitimize differences between the schools (see Metz 1990). Adaptive realignments at the top, at the bottom, and internally are by no means necessarily complementary and complexity-reducing.

Conclusion

A grassroots restructuring of urban education alongside a from-the-top scramble for resource savings, indeed some resource 'miracles'; exciting experimentation alongside desperate efforts to keep the ship afloat; new adaptive alignments between schools and their separate communities, alongside a press upon the schools to conform to citywide expectations; an ongoing bureaucracy accompanied by a steady removal of bureaucratic protections/standardizations – these are among the defining characteristics of today's politics of the organization in urban education. Although 'radically reformed' Chicago is a unique case, (thus overly depended on and possibly misleading as an illustration in this analysis), it is nevertheless suggested that the centralization-adaptation issues discussed in this chapter merit a bit of consideration generally in a further understanding of urban school organizations.

With pressures as never before on their chief executive officers, large-urban school systems face extreme demands to improve, restructure, renew, rehabilitate, build and simultaneously retrench. The improve-the-schools command (e.g., from the business community, from the mayor, from the press) is typically targeted on the city superintendent and on a citywide board of education. Retrenchment, it has been discovered, has a centralizing effect on organizations. Under decline, demands rain down on the organization from the top – close facilities, eliminate programmes, shave services, pare personnel. By no means are such demands left unopposed by the grassroots (e.g., the superintendents' list of to-be-closed schools in Chicago stirred determined neighbourhood opposition); nevertheless the initiative and even the 'greater-good morality' in decision making lies with the CEO.

Retrenchment and other centralizing forces can carry a tightening of bureaucratic decision rules. Never as rigid as bureaucratic mythology implies, such tightening as does occur can place added constraints on site-level administrators trying to either 'work the system' to special neighbourhood advantage or alternatively to protect the neighbourhood from the system. One morning in mid-May 1991, a list of some 30 school buildings targeted for closing was reported in a *Chicago Sun-Times* exclusive. That morning a small number of principals had been attending a two-day urban retreat of educational administrators. Two of the principals learned over breakfast to their surprise that their schools had been targeted. They rushed off to the schools, knowing they would encounter anxious teachers, parents and students. One commented on leaving that her people would not believe she had received no advance warning of the closure. While an adaptive realignment of urban education is by no means limited to the school site, much of its burden (under restructuring-type reforms and improved community-relations experimentation) does fall on the schools. The expectation is, and indeed some early findings indicate (Cibulka 1991), that individual schools under such conditions will increase in variability – moving, with greater or lesser success, toward a better ecological 'match' with their immediate environments.

A from-the-ground-up adaptation, amid a simultaneous tightening of expectations and decision rules, can have an as yet insufficiently examined effect on the *internal* politics of the organization in urban schooling. This is a politics that Boyd and Crowson (1981) found just a decade ago to be remarkably adept at resisting adaptation, at serving the self-interests of school district personnel and at organizational maintenance above goal attainment. The politics of a new organizational feudalism and of a new 'problem' in bureaucratic protection are drawn from the self-reports of Chicago principals as just a couple of examples of adaptive realignments.

An additional vignette from Chicago can expand the point: a high school under consideration for closure had fallen to just hundreds in enrolment from a capacity of thousands. The interpretation among Chicago educators was that this recognizably good quality, college prep high school had held too steadfastly to a required curriculum of vocational courses alongside its college preparatory offerings. The school's somewhat burdensome course and graduation requirements protected a faculty with long tenure and recognized excellence in vocational education. Nevertheless, with increased options for high school choice in Chicago, student demand for this school had plummeted. By protecting its teachers from a changing environment, the school was now in danger of failing to adapt to its environment.

Filtering upward through the organization from such school-site adaptations or non-adaptations as this low-enrolment case, are changes in the powers of sub-units within the bureaucracy. A reduced emphasis on the vocational curriculum or foreign languages or social studies or music or special education can be reflected in a shifting political chessboard organization-wide. Indeed, it may be argued that many of the trappings of a 'monopoly control' (Peterson 1990) in urban public education are fast disappearing – in increased competition among the separate schools, a lessened uniformity generally in school board policies and a bottom-up fragmentation of the old established baronies of a central office.

On the other hand, it remains to be seen whether any 'adaptive realignments' (at the top or the bottom organizationally) can go far at all in overcoming the deep deficiencies of urban education (Boyd 1991). A pervasive disengagement of teachers and students from teaching and learning, a structure of incentives that discourages professionalism, a scratch-my-back reciprocity, and mutually beneficial accommodations of self-interests among groups and actors throughout the sytem – these, in combination with cultural discontinuities and serious how-to-do-it problems in the delivery of urban education, offer yet-limited hope of a 'better world' of city schooling in the near future. Indeed, concludes Peterson (1990: 75), of one point can we remain quite certain: ' . . . it would be difficult to concoct a politically viable system more inefficient and less equitable than the one found today in most central cities of the United States'.

To reiterate, it is within this old interplay between inefficiency and inequity that a 'new politics' of the urban school organization may be under way. There is a continuing battle between top-down and bottom-up – but possibly a new power and determination to the bottom-up, while by no means has the top-down (particularly under tight budgeting) lost full authority. Ever fragmented, even when centralized, city schooling finds itself engaged in a community and school-site adaptation and 'entrepreneuralism' while it simultaneously lives with enduring 'bureaucratic qualities' of control and leadership from the top (Crow 1991).

In short, urban school organizations may increasingly display a politics of environmental adaptation in two equally powerful, but quite separate, directions. Known in the past for either 'trustee'-like behaviour (Mann 1976), which interprets school rules to the community, or for small 'insubordinations' in fitting organizational rules to the special needs of the community (Morris *et al.* 1984) the city's site-level administrator may now be drawn back to 'the neighbourhood,' if not in the old ward-politics sense, at least in the locally 'cherished institooshun' (sic) sense conveyed by Chicago's turn-of-the-century humorist Mr Dooley. An isomorphic fit of school to community, and indeed a drive toward a 'match' of school to community, adds impetus toward a renewed neighbourhood-based politics of education – thriving on diversity, on local reponsiveness and on a special 'market centredness' to the city's more mobile and vocal clientele (Kerchner 1990). The schools will increasingly come to 'look like' (culturally, politically) their separate communities.

Meanwhile, a central office and a beleaguered CEO may find themselves wrapped for some time in the turmoil of a city in crisis, a budget offering less rather than more, an infrastructure 'in ruins', a public (and particularly employers) with lost faith in the common schools, and employee organizations which if not in control vow to 'give' no more. An environmental 'fit' for the top of the organization means recapturing a bit of lost leadership viability for the CEO and giving evidence that the school system is now an integral part of a city under 'regeneration' – with an organization of schooling that is newly efficient, newly innovative and effective, and continuedly equitable in responding to community needs. A key battleground, underinvestigated and little understood, in an adaptive realignment at both organizational top and bottom, however, will likely be the *internal* organization of the city school system. The internal organization is well known for its intractability; it is, unfortunately, unknown at this time for its capacity to move from incentives problems and deficiencies toward effectively assisting either top or bottom with an improvement of city schooling. It remains to be seen whether adaptive realignment at both the top and the bottom in city schooling will meet with meaningful organizational change in the middle.

Notes

1. The principal interviews occurred serendipitously as an outgrowth of the planning and implementation of an 'Urban Principals' Retreat' in Chicago during Spring 1991.
2. Interestingly, one astute principal observed that some protections for parents have also disappeared in Chicago's decentralizing reform. In the past, a 'wronged' parent could go over the head of a principal to an area superintendent or even to 'downtown'. Principals were wary of area superintendents 'looking into' any school–parent incident. Now, the response to parents from the upper administration is: contact your Local School Council. School Councils, however, are even more reluctant than administrators to 'look into' individual grievances.

References

BARDACH, E. (1976) 'Policy termination as a political process', *Policy Sciences*, 7 (2), pp. 123–131.

BEHEN, R. (1980) 'Leadership in an era of retrenchment', *Public Administration Review*, 40, pp. 603–604.

BERMAN, R. and MCLAUGHLIN, M.W. (1978) 'The management of decline', in S. Abramovitz and S. Rosenfeld (eds) *Declining Enrollment: The Challenge of the Coming Decade* (Washington, DC: National Institute of Education).

BOYD, W.L. (1982) 'The politics of declining enrollments and school closings', in N. Cambron-McCabe and A. Odden (eds) *The Changing Politics of School Finance* (Cambridge, MA: Ballinger.)

BOYD, W.L. (1983) 'Rethinking educational policy and management: political science and educational administration in the 1980's', *American Journal of Education*, November, pp. 1–29.

BOYD, W.L. (1991) 'What makes ghetto schools succeed or fail?', *Teachers College Record*, 92 (3), pp. 331–362.

BOYD, W.L. and CROWSON, R.L. (1981) 'The changing conception and practice of public school administration', in D.C. Berliner (ed.) *Review of Research in Education*, Vol. 9 (Washington, DC: American Educational Research Association) pp. 311–373.

BOYD, W.L. and HARTMAN, W. (1988) 'The politics of educational productivity', in D. Monk and J. Underwood (eds) *Microlevel School Finance: Issues and Implications for Policy* (Cambridge, MA: Ballinger).

BRADLEY, A. (1990) 'Rapid turnover in urban superintendencies prompts call for reforms in governance', *Education Week*, pp. 1, 34–35.

CIBULKA, J.G. (1987) 'Theories of education budgeting: lessons from the management of decline', *Educational Administration Quarterly*, 23 (1), pp. 7–40.

CIBULKA, J.G. (1991) 'Local school reform in Chicago speciality high schools: a ecological view', paper presented at the annual meeting of the American Educational Research Association, Chicago.

CROW, G.M. (1991) 'The principal in schools of choice: middle manager, entrepreneur, and symbol manager, paper presented at the annual meeting of the American Educational Research Association, Chicago.

CROWSON, R. L. (1985) Book review of D. Rogers and N. H. Chung, *110 Livingston Street Revisited*. Reviewed in *Educational Studies*, 16 (1), pp. 88–91.

CROWSON, R. L. and MORRIS, V. C. (1985) 'Administrative control in large-city school systems: a investigation in Chicago', *Educational Administration Quarterly*, 21 (4), pp. 51–70.

CROWSON, R. L. and MORRIS, V. C. (1990) 'The superintendency and school leadership' paper presented at the annual meeting of the American educational research association, Boston.

DAVID, J. L. (1990) 'Restructuring in progress: lessons from pioneering districts', in R. F. Elmore and Associates (eds) *Restructuring Schools: The Next Generation of Educational Reform* (San Francisco: Jossey-Bass), pp. 209–250.

DIMAGGIO, P. J. and POWELL, W. W. (1983) 'The iron cage revisited: institutional isomorphism and collective rationality in organizational fields', *American Sociological Review*, 48, pp. 147–160.

ELMORE, R. F. and ASSOCIATES (eds) (1990) *Restructuring Schools: The Next Generation of Educational Reform* (San Francisco: Jossey-Bass).

FELDMAN, M. S. and MARCH, J. G. (1981) 'Information in Organizations as signal and symbol', *Administrative Science Quarterly*, 26, pp. 171–186.

FIRESTONE, W. A. and BADER, B. D. (1991) (Spring), 'Professionalism or bureaucracy? ''Redesigning teaching''', *Educational Evaluation and Policy Analysis*, 13 (1), pp. 67–86.

GLASSMAN, R. M. (1986) 'Manufactured charisma and legitimacy', in R. M. Glassman and W. H. Swatos (eds) *Charisma, History and Structure* (New York: Greenwood Press), pp. 115–128.

GOLDRING, E. and SHAPIRA, R. (1991) 'Choice, empowerment and involvement: what satisfies parents?' paper presented at the annual meeting of the American Educational Research Association, Chicago.

GRIMSHAW, W. J. (1979) *Union Rule in Schools: Big-City Politics in Transformation* (Lexington, MA Lexington Books).

GUTHRIE, J. W., THOMASON, D. K., and CRAIG, P. A. (1975) 'The erosion of lay control', in *Public Testimony on Public Schools*, National Citizens Committee for Citizens in Education Commission on Educational Governance (Berkeley, CA: McCutchan), pp. 76–121.

HESS, G. A., Jr. (1991) *School Restructuring, Chicago Style* (Newbury Park, CA: Corwill Press).

JACKSON, B. L. and COOPER, B. S. (1989) 'Parent choice and empowerment: new roles for parents', *Urban Education*, 24 (3), pp. 263–286.

JUDD, D. and PARKINSON, M. (eds) (1990) *Leadership and Urban Regeneration: Cities in North America and Europe* (Newbury Park, CA: Sage).

KASS, J. (1990) 'New player emerges in big-city politics', *Chicago Tribune*.

KERCHNER, C. T. (1986) 'Union-made teaching: the effects of labour relations on teaching work', in E. Z. Rothkopf (ed.) *Review of Research in Education*, Vol 13 (Washington, DC: in American Educational Research Association), pp. 317–349.

KERCHNER, C. T. (1990) 'Bureaucratic entrepreneurship: the implications of choice for school administration', in S. Bacharach (ed) *Education Reform: Making Sense of it All*, (Boston: Allyn & Bacon).

LANOUE, G. R. and SMITH, B. L. R. (1973) *The Politics of School Decentralization* (Lexington: Lexington Books).

LEIBENSTEIN, H. (1987) *Inside the Firm: The Inefficiencies of Hierarchy* (Cambridge: Harvard University Press).

LEVINE, C. (1978) 'Organizational decline and cutback management', *Public Administration Review*, 38, pp. 316–325.

LEWIS, A. (1989) *Restructuring America's Schools* (Arlington, VA: American Association of School Administrators).

LITTELL, J. and WYNN, J. (1989) 'The availability and use of community resources for young adolescents in an inner-city and a suburban community', report of the Chapin Hall Center for Children at the University of Chicago.

LOUIS, K. S. and MILES, M. (1990) *Improving the Urban High School: What Works and Why* (New York: Teachers College Press).

MALEN, B. and OGAWA, R. (1990) 'Decentralizing and democratizing the public schools – a viable approach to reform?' in S. B. Bacharach (ed.) *Education Reform: Making Sense of It All* (Boston: Allyn & Bacon), pp. 103–119.

MALEN, B., OGAWA, R. and KRANZ, J. (1990) 'What do we know about school-based management? A case study of the literature – a call for research', in W. H. Clune and J. F. Witte (eds) *Choice and Control in American Education* Vol 2 (London: Falmer Press), pp. 289–342.

MANN, D. (1976) *The Politics of Administrative Representation* (Lexington: Lexington Books).

McLaughlin, M. W. and Talbert, J. E. (1991) 'School change: lessons from the field', review of K. S. Louis and M. B. Miles, *Improving the Urban High School: What Works and Why*, *Educational Researcher*, 20 (3), 28–29.

McPherson, R. B., Crowson, R. L., and Pitner, N. J. (1986) *Managing Uncertainty: Administrative Theory and Practice in Education* (Columbus, OH: Charles E. Merrill).

Metz, M. H. (1990) 'Real school: a universal drama mid disparate experiences', in D. E. Mitchell and M. E. Goertz (eds) *Education Politics for the New Century* (London: Falmer Press), pp. 75–91.

Meyer, J., Scott, W. R. and Strang, D. (1987) 'Centralization fragmentation, and school district complexity', *Administrative Science Quarterly*, 32 (2), pp. 186–201.

Milofsky, C. (1981) 'Structure and process in community self-help organizations', working paper No. 17. (New Haven: Yale Program on Non-Profit Organizations).

Moe, T. M. (1980) *The Organization of Interests* (Chicago: University of Chicago Press).

Morgan, D. R. and Palmer, W. J. Jr. (1988) 'Coping with fiscal stress: predicting the use of financial management practices among US cities', *Urban Affairs Quarterly*, 24 (1), pp. 69–86.

Morris, V. C., Crowson, R. L. Porter-Gehrie, C., and Hurwitz, E., Jr. (1984) *Principals in Action: The Reality of Managing Schools.* (Columbus: Charles E. Merrill).

Murphy, J. and Evertson, C. (1990) 'Restructuring the schools: capturing the Phenomena', unpublished paper, Nashville, Vanderbilt University, and the National Center for Educational Leadership.

O'Donnell, M. and Vander Weele, M. (1991) 'Cash pinch leads to schools' decay', *Chicago Sun-Times*, 1, pp. 14–16.

Payne, C. (1991), 'The Comer intervention model and school reform in Chicago: implications of two models of change', *Urban Education* 26 (1), pp. 8–24.

Peterson, P. E. (1976) *School Politics, Chicago Style* (Chicago: University of Chicago Press).

Peterson, P. E. (1981) *City Limits* (Chicago: University of Chicago Press).

Peterson, P. E. (1990) 'Monopoly and competition in American education', in W. H. Clune and J. F. Witte (eds) *Choice and Control in American Education*, Vol 1 (London: Falmer Press).

Raywid, M. A. (1990) 'Rethinking school governance', in R. F. Elmore and associates (eds) *Restructuring Schools: the Next Generation of Educational Reform* (San Francisco: Jossey-Bass), pp. 152–205.

Rogers, D. (1969) *110 Livingston Street* (New York: Vintage Books).

Rogers, D. and Chung, N. H. (1983) *110 Livingston Street Revisited: Decentralization in Action* (New York: New York University Press).

Seibel, T. (1991) 'Amundsen teaching gets down to earth', *Chicago Sun-Times*, 1, 20 April, p. 10.

Sarason, S. B. (1990) *The Predictable Failure of Educational Reform* (San Francisco: Jossey-Bass).

Sayre, W. S. (1958) 'Additional observations on the study of administration: a reply to ferment in the study of organization', *Teachers College Record*, 60, pp. 73–76.

Spielman, F. (1991) 'Cancel teacher raises – edgar', *Chicago Sun-Times*, 1, 27 April, p. 4.

Spielman, F. and Vander Weele, M. (1991) 'School bd. told: no bailout' *Chicago Sun-Times*, 5, 26 April.

Summerfield, H. L. (1971) *The Neighborhood-Based Politics of Education* (Columbus: Charles E. Merrill).

Thomas, K. M. (1991) 'Cuts loom for Chicago schools', *Chicago Tribune*, 1, 21 April, p. 9.

Toulmin, L. M. (1988) 'Equity as a decision rule in determining the distribution of urban public services', *Urban Affairs Quarterly*, 23 (3), pp. 389–413.

Tyack, D. B. (1974) *The One Best System* (Cambridge: Harvard University Press).

Tyack, D. (1990) 'Restructuring in historical perspective: tinkering toward utopia', *Teachers College Record*, 92 (2), pp. 170–191.

Tyack, D. and Hansot, E. (1982) *Managers of Virtue: Public School Leadership in America*, (New York: Basic Books).

Vander Weele, M. (1991) 'Schools face drastic cuts', *Chicago Sun-Times*, 1, 2 May, pp. 8–10.

Vander Weele, M. (1991) 'Schools feel ot pinch', *Chicago Sun-Times*, 1, 29 April, p. 4.

Vander Weele, M. and O'Donnell, M. (1991) 'Schools in ruins', *Chicago Sun-Times*, 1, 14 April, pp. 12–14.

Wechsler, D. (1990) 'Parkinson's Law 101', *Forbes*, pp. 53, 54, 56.

Williams, R. C., Moffett, K. L., and Newlin, B. (1987) 'The district role in school renewal', in J. I. Goodlad (ed.) *The Ecology of School Renewal*, Eighty-Siz Yearbook of the National Society for the Study of Education Part I. (Chicago: University of Chicago Press), pp. 118–151.

Wilson, W. J. (1987) *The Truly Disadvantaged: the Inner City, the Underclass, and Public Policy* (Chicago: University of Chicago Press).

Wong, K. K. (1989) 'Choice in public schools: their institutional functions and distributive consequences', paper presented at the annual meeting of the American Political Science Association, Atlanta.

WONG, K. K. (1990) *City Choices: Education and Housing* (Albany: The State University of New York (SUNY) Press).

WONG, K. K. and ROLLOW, S. (1990) 'A case study of the recent Chicago school reform, part I: the mobilization phase', *Administrator's Notebook*, 34 (5), pp. 1–6.

POLITICS OF EDUCATION ASSOCIATION YEARBOOK 1991, 105–121

7 *Urban politics and state school finance in the 1980s*[1]

Thomas B. Timar

This chapter examines the effects of the major policy and political trends in lower education during the 1980s. Specifically, it assesses the programmatic and fiscal effects of the Reagan administration's fiscal federalism, the excellence agenda and the emerging state activism on urban school districts. The focus is on California as an illustrative case study, as the state represents an inchoate national trend toward fiscal centralization. The chapter argues that centralization has created a new politics of school finance. Not only do schools compete for funding with higher education, health, welfare, criminal justice and transportation, but students also compete with teachers over categorical funding. The chapter concludes that policies of categorical funding have changed dramatically. While symbolically they are rooted in equity, in reality they represent a new political spoils system.

Introduction

In the early 1980s, educational policy took a sharp turn. From the mid-1960s, educational policy and social policy generally were synonymous with social justice. Policy makers focused on creating a more just society – one in which wealth, status, and political power were equitably distributed. An egalitarian wave washed over the nation, leaving high expectations for social transformation in its wake.

Social reformers turned principally, though not exclusively, to schools as the vehicle to drive American public institutions to a more just social order. In 1954, *Brown* v. *Board of Education* put schools squarely in the centre of social reform by declaring the provision of education as the most critical function of state and local government. The court underscored the centrality of schools in achieving this goal by suggesting that a child deprived of adequate schooling could not hope to succeed in life.

When the USA came out of the economic recession in the early 1980s, however, it did so with a renascent vision of a new national and international economic order. The USA had recently elected a conservative president who championed that vision to a public grown disaffected and impatient with government's seeming incapacity to forge the Great Society. Achieving economic stability and growth through a strong economy that could compete with the economies of Japan and Europe replaced social justice on the nation's policy agenda. In education, the spotlight turned on the instructional system of schools and their effectiveness in advancing the US's economic advantage in highly competitive international markets. Excellence, not access, dominated the educational reform agenda. The Reagan administration preached, and the public accepted, the idea that social justice derived from economic growth. A strong and healthy economy, unconstrained by regulatory baggage, was Reagan's answer to a brooding Jimmy Carter who wondered aloud about the nation's moral decay.

The new political discourse of the 1980s has led to two important shifts in educational policy. Consistent with the Reagan administration's ideological commitment to a generally reduced federal policy and fiscal role in areas traditionally the responsibility of

0268–0939/91 $3.00

state and local governments, many educational policy decisions made primarily in Washington devolved to state and local governments. A central theme of the Reagan administration was deregulation of education, the desire to provide greater local decision making consistent with local needs and preferences and, generally, to streamline educational policy implementation by stripping it of unnecessary baggage. The second policy shift embraced the 'excellence' movement. Attention focused on the serious decline in educational quality. *A Nation at Risk* opened the floodgates to a stream of reports that documented the decline in nearly every aspect of educational performance. Studies that compared the performance of American students with those in other industrialized countries found the performance of American students to be lagging behind even those in poor East European countries like Hungary. Educational excellence was generally defined by policy makers in terms of increased high school graduation requirements, accountability and testing, tightened teacher training, certification and credentialling requirements. Generally, achieving excellence in schools embodied more regulations, a more obvious state presence, and a spate of rules, regulations and programmes to fix the ailing parts of the educational system.

This chapter examines the changes that the new policy agenda engendered in urban intergovernmental relations and fiscal support for urban schools. The focus of this chapter is on the programmatic and fiscal effects of the new fiscal federalism, a new policy agenda, and emerging state activism on urban school districts. Specifically, this chapter addresses several questions. How did declining federal fiscal support affect the financing of urban schools? Did the excellence agenda shift funding priorities in states? Did states mirror federal policy in efforts to 'deregulate' schools? How comfortably did deregulation fit with increased state policy activism? Did the constituencies mobilized by the Great Society reforms fade away, or did they remain an important political force in educational decision making?

The new educational policy agenda legitimated new interests and mobilized new constituencies to promote them. The excellence agenda focused on improving schools. Accomplishing that necessitated increased financial support for teachers, administrators, technology and facilities. Consequently, attention shifted from equity to shoring up teacher salaries, staff development, curriculum and instructional support, and technology. How the political system resolved tensions between the old and new policy interests is of particular concern.

In addressing these questions, we focus principally on California as an illustrative case study. California mirrored the changes in federal education policy. Fiscal retrenchment, state deregulation, categorical programme consolidation and educational productivity dominated the state educational policy agenda in the early 1980s. Moreover, California is the first state to change from a locally funded school system, supported by property taxes, to a state-funded school system.[2] As other states come under court-ordered pressure to equalize their school finance systems, they may look to California as a model since it is one of the few states that has achieved a legally defensible school finance system.[3] What are not well understood, however, are the political dynamics of a shift to state financing of schools. While the beneficiaries of a locally financed school system were property-rich districts, the beneficiaries of a state-financed system are, hypothetically, districts that have access to policy makers in the state capitol and can influence state budget decisions. What effect has this change had on school finance?

Changing educational priorities

The commitment to a reduced federal presence in educational policy matters lay behind the early plans of the Reagan administration to dismantle the Education Department and to consolidate nearly thirty federal categorical programmes into a single block grant in education. The conviction that schooling is essentially a state and local matter, not a federal concern, is further emphasized in *A Nation at Risk*, the Reagan administration's education manifesto. 'State and local officials, including school board members, governors, and legislators, have the primary responsibility for financing and governing the schools', the task force says, 'and should incorporate the reforms we propose in their educational policies and fiscal planning' (The National Commission on Excellence 1983: 33).

In addition to emphasizing the shift in educational policy making and implementation to the state, *A Nation at Risk* focused attention on a new set of issues, summed as educational excellence. The idea of excellence became synonymous with the nation's capacity to survive the challenge of international economic competition. While the animating principle of federal and state education policies for the past two decades has been the protection of *individuals* at risk, the new educational agenda focused on a *nation* at risk. In its hyperbolic prose the commission warned 'if an unfriendly power had attempted to impose on America the mediocre educational performance that exists today, we might well have viewed it as an act of war.... We have, in fact, been committing an act of unthinking, unilateral disarmament' (The National Commission on Excellence 1983: 5).

Reports of declining educational quality and the deterioration of the structural elements of education came in a constant stream during the Reagan administration's first term. And surveys showed that the general public viewed declining student test scores, poor teacher training and preparation, and recurring problems with student discipline with mounting concern. Education mattered to the public, but schools were not doing very well. Critics of the educational system advocated various remedies to the ills of schooling: merit pay for teachers, minimum competency tests for prospective teachers, more rigorous and demanding curricula, longer school days and stiffer high school graduation standards. All were designed to build quality into the institution.

Also during the early years of the Reagan administration, urban problems were redefined. Urban crime, violence, the breakdown of the social fabric in inner cities dominated both national headlines and policy discussions. A national commitment to ameliorate the effects of poverty, structural unemployment, crime and substance abuse, however, gave way to punishment, increasing criminalization and a focus on individual, rather than collective, social responsibility. The educational icons of the Reagan years reflected the new attitude (Kirp 1989). Joe Clark, the baseball bat-wielding high school principal in Paterson, New Jersey, showed that authority, discipline and control, not liberal social policies would keep deviants from the schoolhouse door. Jaime Escalante illustrated that even poor *barrio* kids could do well if they just tried hard and had teachers who made them work hard. The Reagan administration's celebration of these two icons sent a message that urban educational problems did not need social policies for their resolution. They needed 'true grit' and hard work. These qualities, furthermore, had to be mobilized within communities, not by the federal government. Most importantly, money was not the issue.

Federal funding reflected the Reagan administration's philosophical shift. The level of federal expenditures for 1983–84 (the year the 'new fiscal federalism' was in place) for California was \$11·1 billion – a decrease of 6·6% from the previous year's level. Though the reductions tended to be across the board, health and welfare absorbed the largest cuts.

The reductions totalled $852 million – $621 million in unemployment insurance benefits and $202 million in support for the state's Medi-Cal programme. On the other hand, federal support increased for business, transportation and housing – from $774 million to $836 million as the administration targeted monies to Republican constituencies. Federal funding for education is illustrative. A $77 million increase did not go to K-12, but to the University of California's Department of Energy Laboratories for weapons (primarily Star Wars) research. In constant dollars the level of federal aid to California declined by 12·5% between 1974–75 and 1983–84. (Legislative Analyst 1983: 32).

While federal support for health and welfare decreased, so did funding for K-12. In 1974–75, federal education aid to California was $550·4 million (7·6% of total funding). Federal support peaked in 1980–81 at $1065 million (9·1% of total funding). From there it declined to $839·2 million in 1983–84 to 6·9% of total K-12 funding. In constant 1972–73 dollars federal support declined by slightly more than 20%. The changes in levels of federal support are even more dramatic when viewed from 1974–75 to 1980–81 (a 100% increase in current dollars and 38% increase in 1972–73 dollars) and from 1980–81 to 1983–84 (a decrease of 21% in current dollars and a decrease of 42% in 1972–73 dollars).

The Reagan administration proved, however, that they could have it all. They could cut spending in the early years and, thus, appeal to the fiscal conservatives. They could then increase spending and legitimately claim those increases as benefits of Reagan policies. Hence, from 1982–83 to 1989–90, total funding for education in the state increased by 111·3%, or 42·5% in constant dollars. At the same time, federal support increased from $963·2 million to $1763·9 million, an increase of 83%, or 30·4% in constant dollars.[4]

California responded to the initial decreases in federal funding in the early 1980s by increasing state support. Total funding for education increased in the state from $7210·5 million in 1974–75 to $13,532 million in 1983–84, an increase of $6321·5 million or 88%. State general fund support increased most significantly, by 255%, while support from property tax and property tax subventions declined due to the combined effects of Proposition 13 and the state's fiscal relief programme enacted by the legislature in 1979.[5] Funding per pupil between 1974–75 and 1983–84 in constant dollars for the same years was from $1290 to $1411, an increase of $121 per pupil or 9·4% (Legislative Analyst 1983: 914). Statewide, overall K-12 support increased in spite of federal fiscal retrenchment and significant local revenue rollbacks precipitated by Proposition 13 and fiscal relief measures enacted by the state.

A more dramatic change, however, occurred in California during the 1980s in the structure of school finance. Proposition 13 and the accompanying 'Gann limitation' on state spending introduced an extended period of fiscal retrenchment; restricted the use of property taxes as a revenue source; virtually shifted authority over local government financing to the state legislature, which forced schools to compete for funding with criminal justice, health and welfare, transportation and a host of other state programmes; along with *Serrano* for all practical purposes eliminated the capacity of local boards to determine school revenues; and required the state to pay for locally mandated programmes. Second, educational excellence – the reform of the 1980s – shifted funding priorities from poor and disadvantaged students to bolstering a sagging educational infrastructure. Moreover, the state's policy posture – that a rising tide raises all ships – dovetailed conveniently with increasing demands from teacher unions for an infusion of state money which could then be put on the bargaining table.

Though the fiscal impact of Proposition 13's 'rollback' provisions was significant, its initial impact was absorbed by a $15 billion state surplus. Hence, revenue shortfalls to local governments could be mitigated for several years. Policy makers hoped that they could fill in the revenue holes through the combined effects of inflation, various state and local revenue enhancements and modest programme reductions. However, the two measures established a race to generally reduce taxes and index incomes to inflation in order to limit personal income tax increases. Sensing an anti-tax mood among the state's voters, Democrats and Republicans competed to reduce taxes, which explains why California slipped from the ten highest spending states in education to the five lowest spending between 1978 and 1984.

The new politics of school finance

As the federal educational agenda shifted to deregulation of schools and improved performance, the state took a similar turn. The push to 'deregulate' schools, the desire to dismantle the regulatory framework that was used to enforce compliance with state and federal requirements, became a major issue during deliberations over the state's educational budget in 1979 following voter enactment of Proposition 13. Republicans would not agree to support the budget – a more significant budget than ever before due to the state fiscal relief provided to local school districts – unless the Democrats agreed to strip categorical programmes of their regulations. Since the Democrats lacked the two-thirds majority in the legislature to enact the budget without Republican votes, they agreed to include 'sunset' provisions in the school finance bill.[6] The compromise required the legislature to conduct a review of the state's 19 categorical programmes. If the legislature did not conduct the review, or if, after a review, the legislature did not act to extend a particular programme, all regulations pertaining to the programme would be terminated. However, the funds for the programmes would continue to flow to districts which had to use the funds in a manner consistent with the legislature's intentions in creating the programme.

In 1981, the legislature enacted a second 'long-term' school finance bill in as many years.[7] Much to the unhappiness of the Democratic leadership in the Assembly, a conference committee on the measure agreed to a statutory provision that would permit districts to consolidate several categorically funded programmes. The School-Based Program Coordination Act allows schools and school districts to co-ordinate one or more of 11 categorical programmes at the school site.[8] The measure allows schools to combine materials and staff funded by some or all of the various categorical programmes without requiring the resources from each programme to be used exclusively to provide services to students who are specifically identified as eligible for the programme. In order to participate, however, schools must establish a school-site council composed of parents, staff, and, if appropriate, students. The site council plans how co-ordinated resources will be used.[9]

The dabate over categorical funding continues. During the 1989 budget deliberations conservative Republicans in the state assembly proposed that all categorical funding be 'equalized'. They proposed taking $500 million from current programmes and using that to equalize funding among those districts which presently receive less than average in categorical support. Among others, they argued that the existing allocation formula for compensatory grants had not been revised in over 10 years and, therefore, did not accurately reflect need or eligibility. Indeed, the data show considerable variation among districts in per pupil funding for Gifted and Talented, Economic Impact Aid and others. In 1986–87, for example, one urban district received $162 per pupil in Economic Impact Aid per AFDC and LEP student, while another received $256. The Republicans prevailed in getting $180 million set aside in a 'supplemental' grant category which is allocated to districts. 'Need' is defined in terms of equalization. Those districts that receive the least categorical support are first in line for the supplemental equalization funds.

Efforts to deregulate notwithstanding, one of the more interesting phenomena over the past decade is the proliferation of categorically funded programmes. In 1980, when the legislature established an oversight committee to conduct the 'sunset review' of categorical programmes, there were 19 state-funded programmes. In 1990–91, there are over 70. They represent an array of programmes. Among the programmes aimed at improving teaching and administration are the Mentor Teacher Program, Professional Development Program, New Teacher Project, Regional Science Resource Center, Administrator Training and Evaluation Program, and Bilingual Teacher Training Program. Other programmes include pupil dropout prevention and recovery, tobacco use and prevention, and prenatal substance abuse prevention. The proliferation of categoricals is more dramatically illustrated by the change in relative levels of general versus categorical support. In 1979–80 categorical funding represented about 13% of total K-12 funding. In 1991–92, the ratio is projected to be just over 29%.[10]

Clearly, legislators are not philosophically adverse to categorical funding. The proliferation of categorical funding has several explanations. One attraction of categorical funding is that it targets money to special areas and keeps it off the bargaining table. An ongoing struggle in Sacramento during much of the 1980s was between a conservative governor and his legislative allies who wanted to target money to programmes rather than salaries and teacher unions and their allies in the legislature who want to increase base funding that could be used for salaries. On the one hand, there is considerable political pressure to increase funding for schools, but no unanimity on how additional monies should be spent. Teacher unions argue that increased educational quality comes from higher teacher salaries. Others argue that higher salaries will not lead to improvements in student achievement unless they are tied to specific programmes and policies. Categorical funding is attractive to politicians because it associates individual politicians with programme benefits. Not only can politicians embody their pet ideas about education in special programmes, but they can also build constituencies around categorical programmes. The penchant for categorical funding represents a trend toward single-issue politics that is manifested on the national level. It is easier to built political constituencies around single-issue politics than around consensus politics.

Who benefits from categorically funded programmes? As noted earlier, Proposition 13 created a state-funded educational system and simultaneously shifted funding for local governments to the state. As a result, education funding competes with a host of state and local programmes and agencies for fewer discretionary dollars.[11] More importantly, state centralization created a new politics of education. Now, urban districts compete with suburban districts for funding, while each side makes its case for special funding consideration. Urban districts argue for more funding to educate more diverse and more difficult to teach students. Suburban schools argue that they, too, need additional funding to offset increasing operating and wage costs. Simultaneously, teachers compete with students. The California Teachers Association (CTA) the state's strongest teacher lobby (and one of the state's largest political contributors) has pressured the legislature to fund either those programmes that support teachers or programmes that are readily converted to teacher salary increases. State funding of a longer school day and year enacted by California's reform legislation in 1984, for example, increased base funding for schools by roughly $450 million in the first year and by $680 million in 1991–92. While some lawmakers may argue that categorically funded programmes protect money for programmes because they keep it off the bargaining table, the facts may belie their beliefs. The dramatic rise in teacher salaries and benefits over the past ten years relative to increases in other K-12 categories suggests that they have done well by the new politics.

California illustrates how the excellence agenda has created a new politics of education. The 'old' politics was bounded by intergovernmental relations. Conflicts of interest were among levels of government – federal, state and local; between teachers and school boards; or between lay goups and professionals. While these conflicts still exist, the complexity of the conflicts has increased. Excellence has legitimated a host of new funding categories and constituencies to advocate for them. Longer school time is needed to bring California schools in line with those in Japan and Germany. New teacher salaries need to be increased in order to attract better qualified college graduates into teaching. Higher teacher salaries, mentor teacher programmes and the like, are justified for retaining highly qualified teachers. Specific funding for staff development – which grew in California from \$2·5 million in 1979 to over \$100 million by 1986 – administrator training and curriculum development are justified as investments in higher achievement and productivity.

The pattern of K-12 funding over the decade reveals interesting trends. Though policy shifted, it is clear that politics controlled spending priorities as much as did policy. The constituents for compensatory funding were mobilized during the 1970s. Though legitimacy for urban school finance policy waned as new policies were legitimated by the excellence agenda, political support for them did not. Moreover, the new policy agenda and the legitimation of new interests strained traditional political relationships. The California Teachers Association favoured funding strategies that could be converted into benefits for teachers. The union's strongest legislative allies were urban Democrats who were also strong supporters of compensatory programmes. The solution was to use categorical funds to target monies to politically mobilized urban districts, but to attach few strings to their expenditure. Desegregation aid, for example, was intended to help schools achieve racial balance within their districts. Initially, funds were used to offset the cost of bussing students. Since Californian voters approved an anti-bussing initiative, funds are used for general programme improvement. The proposed funding level for the 1991–92 school year is roughly \$515 million. Of that, \$455 million goes to four school districts: \$360 million to Los Angeles, \$44 million to San Diego, \$29 million to San Francisco, and \$22 million to San Jose. While the purpose of desegregation funds is to offset the cost of desegregating activities, there is no state policy guiding local expenditures. Since districts are not mandated to use funds in any particular way, how they chose to define 'desegregation' efforts is left to their discretion.

Trends in state educational funding in the 1980s

In spite of limits on tax growth and an approximately 15% decrease (in the initial year) in California's tax base caused by Proposition 13, over the long term schools did not suffer major losses. According to California's Legislative Analyst, total funding for schools per ADA will have increased by 11% – after adjusting for inflation – between 1982–83 and the proposed 1991–92 budget. The analyst describes the 11% increase as 'higher than the amount that would have been needed to keep pace with overall enrollment growth and inflation-driven cost increases since 1982–83' (Legislative Analyst 1991: 916). The analysis also assesses the sources of funding growth (and the areas where expenditures increased) and how districts spent those monies.

Table 1 shows the major areas of K-12 funding growth and the estimated amounts by

Table 1. K-12 Education major sources of funding growth 1982–83 to 1991–92 (in $ millions)

Major programme areas growing faster than enrolment plus inflation	*Actual 1982–83 funding* ($)	*Funding 'needed' 1991–92* ($)	*Funding proposed* 1991–92 ($)	*Funding in excess of 'need'*[a] *amount*	%
Revenue Limits	7825	14,886	15,708	822	5.50
(Longer school day/year)[b]			(680)	(680)	[c]
(Equalization)[b]			(416)	(416)	[c]
(Supplemental summer school)[b]			(79)	(79)	[c]
(Beginning teacher salaries)[b]			(30)	(30)	[c]
(Other)			(384)	(384)	
Lottery[b]			614	614	[c]
Local miscellaneous revenues[d]	871	1657	2228	571	34.5
Special education	702	1335	1835	500	37.4
School facilities: state debt service[b]			343	343	[a]
Desegregation	141	268	515	247	92
Supplemental grants[b]			185	185	[c]
Education mandates	24	45	186	141	310
State teachers retirement system	212	404	529	125	31
Proposition 98 set-aside[b]			100	100	[c]
Major programme areas growing slower than enrolment plus inflation					
Child development	249	473	406	−67	−14.2
Home-to-school transportation	262	498	344	−154	−31
School facilities: local debt service	450	856	303	−553	−64.6
Other programmes (balance)	1925	3663	3459	−204	−5.6
Total	12,661	24,086	26,755	2269	11.1

Source: Legislative Analyst: *Analysis of the 1991–92 Budget Bill*, p. 917.

[a] 'Need' is defined as the amount necessary to keep pace with growth in total average daily attendance and inflation, as measured by the GNP Deflator and Local Government Purchases.

[b] New state programmes enacted after 1982–83.

[c] Not a meaningful figure.

[d] Includes developer fees.

which their proposed 1991–92 funding levels exceed enrolment growth and inflation since 1982–83.

Table 1 shows that, of the $2·67 billion increase above enrolment growth and inflation, approximately $822 million is associated with funding for state enacted 'reforms' since 1982–83. Categories include incentive funding for increasing the length of the school day and year and for increasing beginning teachers' salaries; revenue limit equalization aid and funding for non-remedial summer school, the mentor teacher programme, 10th-grade counsellors, and staff development;[12] other legislatively enacted special programmes such as facilities construction and deferred maintenance and a supplemental grants programme (which is discussed more fully below); and voter-approved initiatives such as the state lottery and Proposition 98 which guarantees approximately 41% of state general revenues to K-12 and community colleges. The major increases in funding in excess of enrolment growth and inflation were programmes funded with local miscellaneous revenues which include developer fee-funded school facilities projects; special education; desegregation aid to reimburse school district costs for voluntary and court-ordered desegregation programmes; and education mandates which reimburse school districts for the costs of state-mandated local programmes. The areas where funding failed to keep pace with enrolment growth and inflation were state child development projects, home-to-school transportation aid and local debt service on school facilities bonds.

Local expenditures of increased state funds are shown in table 2. The table shows relative growth by object of expenditure of school districts from the local general fund – that is the fund which districts deposit unrestricted, block-grant revenues and accounts for over 85% of district spending. According to the Legislative Analyst, in 1988–89 (the most recent year for which expenditure data are available) school district general fund expenditures were 16% higher than inflation and growth since 1982–83. Over the same period, employee compensation expenditure grew to 15% higher than enrolment- and inflation-adjusted 'needs', accounting for \$1·9 billion (81%) of the \$2·3 billion in additional expenditures (Legislative Analyst: 918–19). Within the employment compensation category, the fastest growing components were teachers' salaries (14% above enrolment and inflation needs) and benefits (25% above enrolment and inflation needs).

Table 2. K-12 Education school district expenditure by growth, by object[a] local general fund 1982–83 to 1988–89 (in \$ millions)

Object of expenditure	*Actual 1982–83 expenditures* (\$)	*Expenditures 'needed'*[b] *1988–89*	*Actual expenditure 1988–89*	*Expenditure in excess of need' amount*	*%*
Employee compensation					
Teacher salaries	4520	6685	7604	919	13.8
Other certificated salaries	922	1363	1508	144	10.6
Classified salaries	1723	2548	2826	278	10.9
Subtotals, salaries	(7146)	(10,596)	(11,938)	(342)	(12.7)
Benefits	1424	2106	2624	519	24.6
Subtotals, employee compensation	(8588)	(12,701)	(14,562)	(1860)	(14.6)
Books and supplies	455	673	727	54	8.0
Other services	728	1077	1300	224	20.8
Capital outlay	151	223	384	161	72.3
Totals	(9921)	(14,674)	(16,973)	2299	15.7

[a]*Source*: Legislative Analyst: *Analysis of the 1991–92 Budget Bill* p. 917.
[b]'Need' is defined as the amount necessary to keep pace with growth in total average daily attendance and inflation as measured by the GNP Deflator for State and Local Government Purchases.

Redefining the politics of finance

If politics, not need, drives finance, what impact has that had on schools? If students do not benefit, who does? The pattern of school finance suggests a funding stream away from compensatory programmes which follows special needs students – vertical equity – to a diffused pattern of support that responds to political rather than equity concerns. Has the concept of 'municipal overburden' been abandoned? The issue presses particularly hard on a number of urban districts in California which enrol large numbers of immigrant children, many of whom speak little or no English and many of whom require additional educational services.

In order to assess differential state funding patterns, nine urban and ten suburban Californian school districts were selected for analysis.[23] The urban districts represent California's major 'impacted' urban areas and represent an urban coalition within the state legislature. The suburban districts form a ring beyond urban districts. Some districts, like Riverside and Anaheim, could be regarded as 'transitional' districts. The concentration of ethnic groups in the inner city areas has, over the 1980s, dispersed to nearby suburbs.[14] The analysis disaggregates funding for fiscal year 1986–87[15] by five major categories: Total Funding, General Apportionments, Federal Funding, Variable Costs, Special Purpose Categoricals, and Student Needs Categoricals. (See Appendix A for specific funding items in each category.) Table 3 shows the differences between the two types of districts. Urban districts receive, on average, over $400 more per pupils, roughly $10,000 more per classroom. The data show that the differences are in the categorical funds. General Apportionments comprise each district's 'revenue limit', or base allocation. The data show that there is little variation among urban districts in their base allocations (0·02 coefficient of variation). The data also reveal that suburban districts receive a significantly higher base allocation than the urban districts. The difference, however, is compensated by categorical funds. Variation in the level of categorical funding is significant not only between urban and suburban districts, but also among urban districts (0·41 coefficient of variation). For suburban districts the variation is attributable principally to transportation costs. For urban districts, the difference is due to large variation in funding for desegregation. Desegregation monies, as noted earlier, are used primarily for 'programme improvement'. As noted earlier, too, this category of funding has grown by 92% 'in excess of need' between 1982–83 and 1991–92 (265% in absolute levels).

The urban and suburban schools selected for analysis differ from one another in all respects. As table 3 illustrates, the two types of districts differ significantly in total funding, general apportionment, federal and categorical funding as well as concentrations of minority and limited-English proficiency students and those whose families receive AFDC. The category in which they differ least is in the Special Purpose Categoricals. Higher levels of categorical funding for urban districts are strongly associated with the percentage of minority students, students who are limited-English proficient and students whose families receive AFDC. Indeed, the funding category which shows the least difference between the two types of districts is the Special Purpose category. This is explained by the inclusion of items in the category that are aimed at improving educational quality such as federal Chapter 2, mentor teacher, maths and science teacher training, school improvement and so on. Similarly, federal funding reveals not only higher levels of funding to urban districts, but a fairly small coefficient of variation; that is, funds are fairly equally distributed among districts. On the other hand, funding to suburban districts varies more and reflects the non-targeted nature of the funding. Federal monies to urban districts are composed of Chapter 1, child nutrition, and similar funding targeted to special student populations. Suburban districts tend to benefit from Chapter 2 monies, which are not targeted to special student populations.

It is obvious that urban and suburban districts are quite different from one another, not only because of the students they serve, but also because of differences in categorical funding. While, on average, categorical funding comprises 13% of total funding to suburban districts, it comprises 26% of total funding to urban districts. Among both urban and suburban districts the range varies. Los Angeles receives 31% of its total funding through categoricals, while Sacramento receives 21%. Among suburban districts, 17% of Riverside's funding is in categorical dollars, while only 8% of Palos Verdes' funding is in categorical dollars.

Clearly, urban districts have greater concentrations of minority, limited-English speaking and AFDC students. It is not clear, however, to what extent such factors drive categorical funding to urban districts. The textbook view of school finance argues that urban districts get more money because of the types of students they serve. Hence, vertical equity justifies higher levels of funding as urban students require higher levels of educational services than their suburban counterparts. A competing argument to the rational school finance model is that finance in a centralized state system is driven by political clout, not by student need. Urban districts form a powerful voting block in the state legislature and also form the nucleus of the Democratic caucus in both the Senate and Assembly. Moreover, the leadership of both houses represent urban districts. According to the political argument, categorical funds are a convenient way to funnel money to political constituencies. Categorical funding, then, becomes a way of rewarding political allies, not student needs.

Table 3. Summary data for funding per ADA by categories and type of district 1986–87

Funding categories	*mean*	*Standard deviation*	*significance*	*Coefficient of variation*	*Range* ($)
Total funding					
Urban	$3792	$236	0.000	0.06	3521–4171
Suburban	$3376	$182		0.05	3197–3756
General apportionment					
Urban	$2716	$53	0.000	0.02	2833–2668
Suburban	$2858	$208		0.07	2680–3204
Total categorical					
Urban	$984	$184	0.000	0.19	748–1293
Suburban	$452	$97		0.21	261–565
Federal					
Urban	$296	$59	0.000	0.20	193–382
Suburban	$97	$37		0.38	32–163
Variable costs					
Urban	$417	$173	0.000	0.41	698–233
Suburban	$74	$52		0.71	18–169
Special purpose Categoricals					
Urban	$119	$34	0.062	0.29	97–208
Suburban	$94	$12		0.14	73–110
Student Needs Categoricals[a]					
Urban	$224	$80	0.002	0.36	111–362
Suburban	$66	$25		0.38	19–111
Minority students					
Urban	68%	15%	0.000	0.22	49–90
Suburban	26%	9%		0.35	18–38%
Limited English					
Urban	20%	7%	0.000	0.35	11–25%
Suburban	6%	3%		0.50	1–12%
AFDC					
Urban	29%	10%	0.000	0.34	14–42
Suburban	7%	4%		0.57	0.2–14

Source: California State Department of Education.

[a]One of the distincts received no Special Education funds. Instead funds go to the county.

[b]Two districts show '0'%, although one district does receive funds.

How important a role does politics play in determining levels of categorical funding? The answer to that question can be examined by the following causal model:

Categorical Funding = Need + Urbaneness

'Categorical Funding' represents various categorical funding streams (Federal, Variable Costs, Special Purpose, and Student Need). 'Need' is an interaction variable that comprises the product of the percentage of minority students enrolled in a district, the percentage of students whose families receive AFDC, and the percentage of limited-English proficient students enrolled. 'Urbaneness' is a dummy variable that represents the urban districts in the sample. While the size of the sample ($N = 19$) necessitates some caution in interpreting the results, they suggest interesting findings.

The results are shown in table 4. By disentangling the mutual effects of Need and Urbaneness ($r = 0\cdot78$), we can estimate the relative importance of each of those variables in determining levels of categorical funding. The findings show that Need is a mediating, but not significant, determinant of Total Categorical Funding, which ranges from $261 in

Table 4. Step-wise regression model of categorical funding, need and urbaneness

Funding categories	*Steps in regression*	*Independent Variables*[c] *Need*	*Urbaneness*	*Adjusted* $R^{2/b}$
Total categorical funding	Step 1	Pearson $r = 0\cdot73$ $Pr^2 = 0.20$ sig t $p <= 0.00$		0.52 sig f $p<0.00$
	Step 2	sig t $p< = 0.43$	Pearson $r = 0.88$ $Pr^2 = 0.74$ sig t $p<0.00$	0.77 sig f $p<0.00$
Federal funding	Step 1	Pearson $r = 0.88$ $Pr^2 = 0.71$ sig t $p<0.00$		0.78 sig f $p<0.00$
	Step 2	sig t $p<0.00$	Pearson $r = 0.91$ $Pr^2 = 0.76$ sig t $p<0.00$	0.90 sig f $p<0.00$
Variable costs	Step 1	Pearson $r = 0.62$ $Pr^2 = 0.09$ sig t $p<0.00$		0.32 sig f $p<0.00$
	Step 2	sig t $p<0.719$	Pearson $r = 0.82$ $Pr^2 = 0.71$ sig t $p<0.00$	0.64 sig f $p<0.00$
Student special needs	Step 1	Pearson $r = 0.86$ $Pr^2 = 0.49$ sig t $p<0.00$		0.73 sig f $p<0.00$
	Step 2	sig t $p<0.00$	Pearson $r = 0.82$ $Pr^2 = 0.64$ sig t $p<0.04$	0.78 sig f $p<0.00$
Special purpose	Step 1	Pearson $r = 0.35$ $Pr^2 = 0.01$ sig t $p<0.14$		0.07 sig f $p<0.14$
	Step 2	sig t $p<0.95$	Pearson $r = 0.47$ $Pr^2 = 0.33$ sig t $p<0.18$	0.12 sig f $p<0.14$

[a]Special Education funding is not included.
[b]The adjusted R^2 reported in order to compensate for sample size.
[c]Pr^2 is the partial correlation coefficient.

Palos Verdes to $1293 in Los Angeles. The effects can be further disaggregated by looking at the various categorical funding streams. The Variable Cost category includes major funding items like desegregation and urban impact aid and ranges from $18 per pupil in suburban Palos Verdes to $698 per pupil in Los Angeles. While Variable Costs represent the largest categorical funding source to district, its funding is completely unrelated to student need ($p < 0 \cdot 72$). On average, being an urban district in California is good for an additional $344 dollars.

On the other hand, two categorical funding streams – federal aid and student needs, which includes federal Chapter 1 monies – are significantly affected by Need. This conforms to expectations as we expect federal funding to be more sensitive to student needs as it is immune to local political pressures. It is more difficult to influence the allocation of Chapter 1 monies than state-funded categoricals. On the other hand, district Variable Costs, which includes school desegregation monies as well as Urban Impact Aid and various other categories to compensate variations in district costs, is determined almost entirely by Urbaneness. Need is relatively unimportant in determining levels of support.

As one might expect, the model does not explain the allocation of Special Purpose categoricals which include federal Chapter 2 monies, staff development, mentor teacher, instructional materials and the like. This category targets school improvement and mirrors funding patterns that have followed the 1980s school reform agenda. Suburban and urban districts receive roughly the same amounts per pupil. However, Special Purpose categoricals comprises a more significant level of funding for suburban schools (21% versus 12%) since their absolute level of categorical funding is lower. It is interesting to note that in spite of major state reform efforts in California, only a small portion of categorical funding is associated with reform. While categorical funding ranges from 14% of total funding in suburban districts to 26% in urban districts, categorical funds that are tied to various school improvement initiatives account for only about 3% of total funding in both types of disticts.

Conclusion

In spite of both state and federal fiscal entrenchment and a significant shift in educational policy that threatened to shift both attention and dollars away from the problems of urban school districts, urban districts in California have done well financially when compared with other districts in the state. Their success appears attributable, in large measure, to their capacity to benefit from centralization of the state's school finance system. Urban districts are better mobilized into coalitions and have more votes in the legislature than their suburban or rural counterparts. They are also better connected to the leadership in both houses of the legislature than are other districts. The finance and policy committees of both houses are dominated by representatives of urban districts. The Speaker of the Assembly, the President pro Tempore of the Senate, the Chair of the Assembly Ways and Means Committee and the Senate Appropriations Committee, as well as the Chair of the Assembly Education Committee represent urban districts. While the chair of the Senate Education Committee represents a non-urban district, his district has over the past ten years changed significantly in the increased number of Hispanic residents in the district.

The vehicle for the success of urban districts in maintaining funding in spite of retrenchment and changing policy priorities has been through the use of categorical funding. Over the past ten years, categorical funding has come to serve a multiplicity of purposes. It is a system of political patronage to urban school districts, particularly the politically well connected with strong, mobilized teacher unions. At the same time categorical funding, particularly federal funding, provides additional monies for special student needs. Finally, categorical funds are used, in a fairly modest way, to leverage school reforms. The multiplicity of purpose and competition among special interests has resulted in a fragmented and generally incoherent system of school finance.

Funding has become a power struggle among competing special interests. School reformers want school finance to leverage change. The teacher unions want higher salaries. While reformers push for reduced class sizes, particularly in high schools, unions prefer to see the money go into base funding. In trying to accommodate competing demands, the legislature has proliferated the number of categoricals, thereby giving something to everyone. What has been lost in the political struggle, however, has been a commitment to either equity or reform. Finance is only marginally connected with student need, and then mostly because of federal categorical funding. Consequently, we can surmise that there are districts with concentrations of minority, AFDC and LEP students that are not receiving their share of state funding. And in those districts which do receive high levels of categorical support it is difficult to know where the money goes.

While categorical finding has increased significantly over the past ten years, both in the number of funding categories and as a percentage of total funding, its capacity to drive significant school improvement is marginal at best. The implications for school reform are not encouraging. While equity has been converted into political spoils, instructional reform has hovered at the margins. Although programmes like the Mentor Teacher Program, Math and Teacher Science Training and the like are promoted in the press, funding for these programmes accounts for a tiny portion of total categorical funding, especially for urban districts. Hence, leveraging categorical monies for reform seems to pay few educational dividends. Choice as a reform strategy is also unlikely. Insofar as a choice system would depoliticize funding, it would likely be opposed by urban districts and teacher unions. It would be difficult to justify on a rational basis the disparities in categorical funding which presently exist. If student need and other categories of exceptional district cost were the basis for different levels of funding under a choice system, the urban districts would be the losers. Hence, any choice system that crosses district boundaries will no doubt be vigorously opposed by teacher unions.

One of the lessons from this chapter is that school finance centralization does not lead to a more equitable or rational system. This is an important consideration as states seek for alternatives to local, property tax-driven school finance schemes. While local funding may lead to inequities based on wealth, state funding may lead to inequities based on political power. While school finance decision making is at some level political, who gets what should not be determined by power politics. More importantly, the educational needs of students should not become vehicles for the political spoils of adults.

Notes

1. I wish to thank the Charles E. Culpeper Foundation and the Working Group on State Educational Policy, Brown University for their support for this study.
2. Hawaii has a state school system. However, it has always been so.
3. According to the Center for the Study of Educational Finance, the school finance systems of 19 states are currently being challenged in the courts. One of the difficulties with school finance systems that rely on local property taxes is that permanent equalization is nearly impossible to achieve due to changes in local property values. Consequently, full state assumption becomes a legally defensible

strategy. See 'School Finance Constitutional Litigation', Center for the Study of Educational Finance, Illinois State University.

4. On a student average daily attendance (ADA) basis, however, the increase is deflated somewhat by a 30% growth in state ADA.
5. Assembly Bill 8 (Chapter 282, Statutes of 1979). See Legislative Analyst, *Analysis of the Budget: 1983–84*, California State Legislature, p. 1275.
6. Assembly Bill 8.
7. Assembly Bill 777 (Chapter 1551, *Statutes of 1981*) replaced AB 8, which was enacted in the months following passage of Proposition 13.
8. The major programmes include Economic Impact Aid, Special Education, School Improvement Program, Miller-Unruh Reading Program, Gifted and Talented Education, Educational Technology, and Local Staff Development.
9. According to the Legislative Analyst, implementation of this provision is ambiguous. By 1985–86, the fourth full year of implementation of the School-Based Program Coordination Act, the State Department of Education (SDE) indicated that 372 schools in 129 districts combined some categorical education services using the act's provisions. This was a reduction of 140 schools (38%) and 62 districts (48%) from the previous year. The participation rate for 1985–86 is probably more accurate since districts had misreported their participation. Legislation in 1983 (Chapter 1270, Statutes of 1983) repealed requirements that school districts submit to SDE school-site plans for the implementation of school-based co-ordinated programmes. Instead, plans are reviewed and maintained by each local school district, and are reviewed by SDE only (1) during on-site visits and compliance reviews, which are conducted in each district every three years, and (2) where there is a complaint regarding any of the categorical programmes at a particular school. As a result of this change in the law, it has not been possible to obtain comprehensive, detailed information regarding the implementation of school-based co-ordinated programmes, or, consequently, the effects of school-based co-ordination on those children who are specifically eligible to receive supplementary educational services under the categorical programme that may be part of co-ordinated services. (Legislative Analyst 1990–91; 1144–5.)
10. In 1979–80 total support for K-12 education was $10·982 billion and categorical support was $1·407 billion. In 1991–92 general support is projected at roughly $26.8 billion. Of that $7·8 billion is in categorical support. See Legislative Analyst 1991–92, p. 910 and Legislative Analyst 1983–84, pp. 1276, 1299.
11. The combined effects of various voter initiatives has limited discretionary spending to roughly 30% of a nearly $60 billion budget. Over $40 billion of the state budget is controlled by various state constitutional initiatives like Proposition 98 which guarantees about 41% of the budget to K-12 and community colleges.
12. For a discussion of the specific reform measures see Timar, T. and Kirp, D., (1988) *Managing Educational Excellence* (Philadelphia: Falmer).
13. I am indebted to William Furry, Principal Consultant for the minority Ways and Means Committee, California State Legislature for supplying the data. The urban districts are San Francisco, Los Angeles, Sacramento, Long Beach, San Diego, Oakland, San Jose, Fresno and Stockton. The suburban districts are San Juan, Riverside, Anaheim, Tustin, Palos Verdes, Morgan Hill, Santa Rosa, Santa Barbara, Mt Diablo and Fremont.
14. See the *Los Angeles Times*, Metro Section, 6 May 1991, pp. 1–8.
15. Although the district fiscal data are nearly five years old, the same pattern persists today. If anything, categorical funding comprises an even larger share of district funds now than it did in 1986–87.

References

KIRP, D. (1989) 'Education: the Movie', *Mother Jones*, January, pp. 36–46.

LEGISLATIVE ANALYST (1983) *The 1983 Budget: Perspectives and Issues*, California State Legislature.

LEGISLATIVE ANALYST (1983) *Analysis of the Budget Bill: 1983–84*, California State Legislature.

LEGISLATIVE ANALYST (1986) *Analysis of the Budget Bill: 1986–87*, California State Legislature.

LEGISLATIVE ANALYST (1989) *Analysis of the Budget Bill: 1989–90*, California State Legislature.

LEGISLATIVE ANALYST (1991) *Analysis of the Budget Bill: 1991–92*, California State Legislature.

THE NATIONAL COMMISSION ON EXCELLENCE IN EDUCATION (1983) *A Nation at Risk: The Imperative for Educational Reform* (Washington, D.C.: US Department of Education).

Appendix A

Funding categories to local education agencies

General Apportionments

School apportionments: includes (a) Revenue limits, (b) Small school allowance and (c) Meals for needy
Summer school
1986–87 instructional time
County office revenue limit
State lottery, cash disbursement
Opportunity class expansion
State loan (if any)

Support in recognition of variable costs

Home to school transportation
School bus replacement
Court ordered desegregation
Voluntary desegregation
Child nutrition
Pregnant lactating minors
Child nutrition, federal
Year-round schools incentive school bus reconditioning
Small district transportation
Urban impact aid, unified districts
Urban impact aid, non-unified districts
Meade aid

Categorical programmes for special purposes

ECIA, Chapter 2 block grant
ECIA, Chapter 2 other grant
Tenth grade counselling
School improvement (K–6)
School improvement (7–12)
Specialized secondary schools
Intergenerational programmes
Maths and science teacher training
Driver training
Educational technology
Environmental education
Health and physical education
Instructional materials (K–8)
Instructional materials (9–12)
Administrative training and evaluation
Mentor teacher programme
Local staff development
Teacher instructional improvement grants
Bilingual teacher training

Teacher improvement
Youth suicide prevention
School law enforcement
Pilot project for administrative personnel

Categorical programmes for students with special needs

College admission test pilot
Foster youth services
Motivation programme planning
Dropout recovery planning
Motivation programme, outreach
Dropout recovery, outreach
Education clinics (dropout)
Droupout model programmes
Economic impact aid
Gifted and talented
Miller-Unruh reading
Native American Indian education
ECIA, Chapter 1 Compensatory
ECIA, Chapter Migrant
Reading/Maths demonstration project
Special education
Special education entitlement, federal
Special education instructional services, federal
Special educational preschool incentive, federal
Special education, deaf/blind centres, federal
Alternative special education
Transition programme for refugees
Emergency immigrant education

Vocational education

Regional occupation centres
Vocational student organizations
Federal job training partnership act
Peninsula academies
Project workability II
Vocational education, federal
Agricultural vocational education

Non-K/12 programmes

Apprentice programmes
Adult education
Adult education, federal
Adults in corrections
GAIN, JTPA, match

POLITICS OF EDUCATION ASSOCIATION YEARBOOK 1991, 123–135

8 *Political and financial support for school-based and child-centred reforms*

Richard A. King and C. Kent McGuire

This chapter concentrates on the nature and focus of education reform efforts in city school systems during the late 1980s and early 1990s. A thesis is developed that political, and closely related financial, support for continuing efforts to reform or restructure education depends on two primary factors. The degree of agreement about values and goals among stakeholders within and external to school systems appears to influence the likelihood of a given set of reforms. Adoption and implementation of reforms also depend on the level of intensity of action devoted by those groups. This framework is used to examine whether current reform activities in urban environments engender political and financial support that might be essential for future reform initiatives. The paper concludes that future reform initiatives will need to consider changes in the delivery of non-educational services to garner sufficient political support for meaningful education reform. Yet there must be agreement among values and interests of diverse agencies and sufficient intensity of action of all groups to bring about meaningful change.

Introduction

We are approaching a decade of efforts to reform and restructure public schools. Generally characterized as successive waves of reform, these movements have challenged policy makers and educators to question nearly all aspects of the delivery of education. The early 1980s were witness to a focus on academic content and higher standards. As the initial waves ebbed, the debate broadened to include governance and organizational structures of schools themselves and, very recently, societal mechanisms for providing many other children's services.

The politics of reform in the 1980s and early 1990s is by various accounts a case of competing ideas, interests and values (Elmore 1990, Sarason 1990). Within the schools, teachers and administrators have been interested in improved working conditions, professional recognition and additional resources. Accordingly, labour–management relations, particularly as they are formalized through collective bargaining processes, have become instrumental in the push for reform in work conditions. At the same time, this internal coalition of professionals may impede efforts to change schools structurally or grant parents choice among schools.

Outside the schools, governors, legislators and business groups have formed a coalition of sorts, assisting if not pressuring the education establishment to change. The driving interest for this coalition is productivity – substantially improving student performance with minimal additional monetary investment (Cohen 1988, 1990, Kearns 1988, Murnane 1988, Committee for Economic Development 1991). Establishing new goals and standards, using legislation to create experiments and fostering collaboration between the private sector and the schools are the vehicles used with regularity.

Periodically the interests of children, exemplified by the push for early childhood education, dropout prevention, and related policies for 'at risk' youth, emerge as a central theme of reform. However, the political coalition for the interests of children appears the least well developed, if it exists at all. And to the degree to which child-centred reforms

0268–0939/91 $3.00

would alter current delivery structures for multiple social services, the above internal and external coalitions may resist change.

Nowhere is the push for reform greater than in the cities. This is where too many students are failing or, rather, where the education system is not working for many youngsters. City school systems are often characterized as too large, bureaucratic and unable to engage in change from within (Sarason 1990). These large school systems are described as lacking essential political support to foster meaningful reform or restructure.

Prior chapters detail urban demography and pupil performance that pressure schools to change. Current literature gives attention to international events, domestic political and economic conditions, and schooling conditions that alter public attitudes toward education – all of which may *trigger* policy change (Guthrie and Koppich 1988, Underwood 1989). Substantially less attention falls on changes in political support for schools as a *result* of educational reforms, perhaps because cities are in various stages of implementing new policy directions. This chapter is about the nature of political support for education reform in the cities.

We develop the thesis that political, and closely related financial, support for continuing efforts to reform or restructure education and the delivery of children's services in cities depends on two primary factors. The degree of agreement about values and goals among stakeholders within and external to school systems appears to influence the likelihood of a given set of reforms to be adopted. Consensus is important, but successful adoption and implementation of reforms also depend on the level of intensity of action devoted by those groups. We suggest that this framework is helpful in examining whether reform activities in urban environments engender political and financial support essential for adoption and implementation of future, perhaps more meaningful, changes.

In the debate about the most effective form of reform and restructure, there is realization that 'symbolic' change, which results, for example, from applying new labels for traditional governance or decision-making processes, differs greatly from 'meaningful' changes in curriculum and instruction, roles of schools and their teachers and principals, accountability mechanisms and so on. There are at present few, if any, cities where such meaningful restructuring has been realized. But reform means many things. What is a reform in one school, district or state may be accepted practice in another; thus, the operational definition of any one reform depends on the setting and the analyst–observer (Jordan and McKeown 1990). Schlechty (1990: xvi) urges fundamental and radical reconstituting of schools, defining restructuring as 'altering systems of rules, roles, and relationships so that schools can serve existing purposes more effectively or serve new purposes altogether'.

We reflect on who is influencing reform, the varied approaches suggested for reforming and restructuring schools, and relationships between financial and political support as they relate to reform efforts. By understanding how different notions of reform might influence the politics, we think it is possible to speculate about the political and financial support essential for adoption and implementation of future initiatives, particularly those addressing collaborative delivery of children's services, in urban schools.

Political support: an interaction of value agreement and intensity of action

Given the many conflicting forces that shape urban schools, we contend that it is imperative to seek reforms that elicit agreement in value positions among internal and external groups. If groups then devote sufficient energy to adopt and implement such reforms, there is greater likelihood of effective change in school operations and of building a base for continued political support for future reforms.

The model presented in figure 1 suggests that the depth of agreement and the intensity of action for a particular reform largely determine whether political support is sufficient to ensure that it will be adopted, successfully implemented, and in turn generate continued support for this and future policy changes. The four quadrants illustrate possible interactions of the level of agreement and vitality of constituents' actions for a given reform. Optimum conditions exist in Quadrant I, which depicts a high–high interaction between agreement and intensity. In this situation, there is sufficient agreement about the need for and the nature of reform among relevant actors within and external to the school system, and these groups devote high energy to the agreed-on direction.

Figure 1. Dimensions of political support

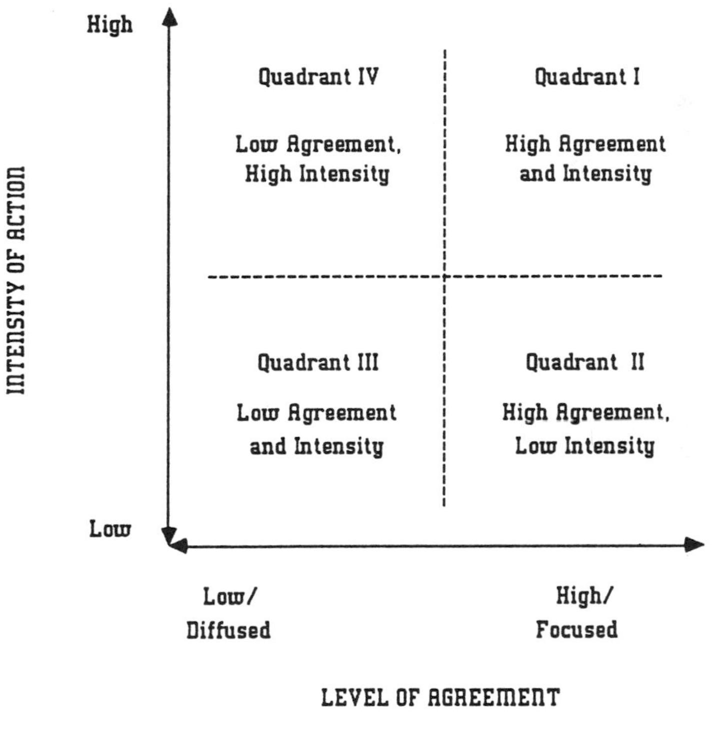

There is similar consensus among constituents as to the desired reform direction in Quadrant II, a depiction of a high–low interaction. There is insufficient action on the part of these groups, however, to ensure successful movement toward policy adoption. While there is likely to be much rhetoric regarding the need for a particular reform, there will not be successful adoption or implementation. Political support may indeed lead to policy adoption, but this support will likely not continue to ensure long-term success. The converse of this condition is illustrated in the low–high interaction of Quadrant III. Although there is high intensity of action, reforms fail to be achieved because constituents have diffused goals. A number of reforms may be enacted because of pressure brought by diverse internal and external groups, but the lack of sufficient agreement among constituents will likely lead to diffused political support built on competing interests and to ultimate failure of most of the reforms.

Quadrant IV presents the condition of low–low interaction between depth and vitality of political support. With a diffused focus among constituents, and with little interest in furthering reform agenda, it is unlikely that any reform will emerge. There will be dissatisfaction among groups leading to dissension within the school system and between schools and communities. There may be difficult management–labour relations, and the status quo will likely continue without state-level directives or other external pressure to force internal action. However, the lack of school and community commitment to changes does not bode well for meaningful or sustained reform.

The nature of reform proposals influences the level of agreement and intensity of action among constituents. An issue such as choice may unite insiders, including the school board and school personnel at all levels, against outsiders who must seek change through other policy mechanisms to satisfy their interests. On the other hand, proposals for shared governance or decision making may divide insiders, particularly district-level from school-based personnel, who are uncertain how respective interests will be served by altered decision structures. In either case, political support does not coalesce to ensure successful adoption of a given reform – despite the level of intensity which groups and individuals may devote to educational change.

The model suggests that the reform agenda in cities will best be realized if external and internal groups are able to reach consensus on the need for a particular set of reforms. This agreement is essential, but it must be accompanied by constituents devoting essential attention to reform adoption and implementation. In the next sections, we examine the diversity of stakeholders who influence urban school reform efforts and the many conversations and tactics that are associated with movements to reform and restructure schools. We then contend that changing the focus of reform from satisfying interests of professionals within schools to the needs of children, a direction that offers the greatest promise for meaningful change in conditions of urban youth, will require an immense commitment, in terms of value agreement and action, from affected constituents.

Stakeholders: those who influence urban school reforms

Decisions made through political processes require compromises among value preferences of diverse individuals and groups (Easton 1965). Without a meaningful give and take among differing value orientations, there may be little chance of effective reform. Many groups – internal and external to school systems – voice value preferences and interests in efforts to shape city schools.

Teachers and administrators who are responsible for educational programmes have clear interest in the shape of new structures and approaches (Rosow and Zager 1989). Labour–management relations are critical in the internal politics of adopting and implementing reforms. Differing value orientations are evident in recent experiences of Rochester, where the board and teachers had difficulty reaching agreement on performance-based pay (Bradley 1991b), and Denver, where the Governor stepped in to handle negotiations and shape school-based management after the failure of formal bargaining (Bradley 1991a).

School boards serve both as representatives of the local political/economic environment and as groups that directly influence internal relations between teachers and administrators. Interests and policies of local school boards invariably complicate efforts to reform schools, as do many decisions of district-level administrators (Timar 1989). Policies regarding personnel and budget, which are the most critical elements of organizational autonomy, have traditionally been made at the district level. Calendars and daily schedules, often standardized to accommodate bus schedules, and districtwide collective bargaining agreements also constrain school decision processes. We know that, for good reason, urban school boards and administrators have worked hard to control these aspects of school organization and operation. They have been pressured to do so by community groups and/or the courts in the name of educational equality (Ravitch 1983).

With entrenched but often conflicting interests of school boards and internal constituents, it is not surprising that reforms such as those recently instituted in Chicago to devolve district-level control over budget, curriculum and even personnel to parents and professionals, have come only when political forces outside the district brought pressure to bear on school policy makers. Nevertheless, groups comprising the external environment of the larger society, including businesses, the courts, and state and federal governments, also differ in interests and expectations for schools. They define conditions that may work to enlarge or constrain political and financial support of reform efforts. The rapid turnover of superintendents during the past year in urban districts undergoing massive reform, including Boston, Columbus, Charlotte–Mecklenburg, Detroit, Houston, Indianapolis, Memphis, Milwaukee, Tucson and Washington, is not surprising in this context. The pressure on these school systems is great, with demands for improved facilities, racial integration, fiscal austerity and higher student achievement all coming at the same time.

As much as external groups influence the nature of urban school reform in one way or another, their many interests and political relationships complicate the process of change. For instance, despite the growth of state legislative power, this potential centre of power has become widely dispersed. Interest groups have proliferated, and formal patterns of authority no longer prevail. Timar (1989) contends that the 'iron triangle' of educational politics, once including schools of education, state education departments, and NEA affiliates, yielded in recent years to more porous systems. It is difficult in today's complexity to find the centre of control over public schools in order to create a receptive policy environment for restructuring. It is no wonder that local restructuring efforts are so diverse and politically charged. Since a school's culture is derivative of the political cultures of states and districts in which it operates (Timar 1989, Timar and Kirp 1988), it is difficult to create coherence. Integrated responses to restructuring are tough when the environment is politically balkanized.

Value preferences expressed by parents, businesses, taxpayer groups, legislators, courts and other external groups differ from those represented by internal stakeholders. These external constituents' demands for reform reflect often contradictory value preferences of liberty, equality, fraternity, efficiency and economic growth (Swanson and King 1991). In contrast, Schlechty (1990) states that the variance in values and policy goals is much less among teachers and administrators. He concludes that internal support for reforms depends more on the degree to which proposals satisfy needs for positive recognition and affirmation, for intellectual and professional variety, for feeling that what one does makes a difference and that doing things differently will make a difference as well, and for affiliation and collegial support and interaction.

Reforms of the 1980s and 1990s are larger in scope and intensity than were earlier movements to alter educational goals and school structures. Greater public attention has been given to reform efforts, and, as suggested, the coalition of reform actors has broadened to include business representatives, politicians, and university faculty who are not directly involved in elementary/secondary education (Ginsberg and Wimpelberg 1987, Underwood 1989). The complexity of issues and personalities bring conflicting value preferences, thus lessening the likelihood of reaching easy consensus on reform agenda.

Conversations and tactics in school-based reform

Movements to reform and restructure America's schools represent a competition of ideas and philosophies about the schools, how they need to change and what tactics are most likely to produce the desired changes. The political dialogue associated with reform and restructuring clearly rests on differing values and interests of the previously discussed groups on the inside and on the periphery of the public schools.

First, there is the conversation that says that the schools are overregulated. They must be restructured so that decision making, and hence responsibility for performance, is closer to the school. According to reformers, school personnel are in the best position to decide how to use the resources at their disposal. Tactics related to this conversation would empower teachers (Carnegie Forum 1986, Holmes Group 1986) through school-site management and/or shared decision making. Moving the locus of decision authority to schools would yield more efficient uses of curriculum and instructional materials, with school personnel determining which services (such as testing or curriculum specialists) to purchase from the central district or other sources. School personnel would also identify appropriate teaching techniques and related staffing needs. Restructuring urban schools in this way would address values of concern to teachers, providing a larger role in defining and administering school policies, improving working conditions and recognizing teachers as professionals, and devolving greater authority over resources and curricula from central offices to schools (Hawley 1988, Schlechty 1990).

A second conversation, responding also to the overregulation theme, is about making schools more responsive to students and parents (Boyd and Kirchner 1988, Chubb and Moe 1990). The associated tactic is empowering families to exercise choice among schools, either within the public sector or between public and private schools. Greater choice is believed to be the lever needed to separate productive from less effective schools that are unable to attract sufficient clientele. Some argue that choice also includes a reward structure in schools that encourages professional educators to make decisions that are consistent with client preferences (Elmore 1986).

A third conversation explores whether the schools have lost sight of what they are to deliver in the way of information and skills. Part of the debate is over the difference between basic and 'higher-order' thinking skills. Many outside the schools hold both deep concern that the schools have failed youngsters by not giving the basics, and scepticism over whether schools that cannot teach the basics can deliver on their promise to impart higher-order cognitive skills. This conversation critiques how well professional educators use the existing knowledge base in education to conduct their work. If students were achieving at acceptable levels, graduating at acceptable rates and demonstrating competencies considered important in higher education or business environments, then there would be no need to reform or restructure. But, since only a small portion of high school graduates acquire the knowledge for today's work place, improved teaching is the central challenge before the public schools. The emphasis, continuing this line of reasoning, must be on changing things that influence the delivery of instruction or that are in some way associated with increased learning. The manner in which students are grouped for instruction, the way time is allocated and used during the school day, and the number and mix of personnel and other resources involved in instruction are all of concern (MacPhail-Wilcox and King 1986). There are any number of possible modifications to the way schools are organized and managed with the hope of producing better learning.

The objective, to enhance the institutional competence of schools, is often associated with the tactic of fostering the professional growth of teachers. By providing time and structures for school staff and students to pay attention to real problems and opportunities in schools, and by allowing school personnel, particularly teachers, to play a greater role in the day-to-day operation of schools, it is believed that better decisions will yield results in terms of student performance. To meet this objective, and satisfy the interests of teachers as professionals, a number of recent collective bargaining agreements have created opportunities for teachers to share in setting school policy, to assist in the evaluation and review of their peers, and to assume positions of leadership without having to leave teaching.

These conversations and tactics reveal conflicting ideas, interests and values among participants in the reform debate. Political support for any one reform will necessarily have to satisfy diverse groups' interests and needs. Initial waves of reform satisfied external groups' needs, particularly those of legislators and governors, to move quickly in visible ways. Groups within schools accepted increases in funds in the name of reform, often to satisfy needs unrelated to educational reforms. Proposals for improving working conditions and empowering professionals stand a better chance of satisfying internal needs for controlling resource decisions than they offer for meaningfully changing conditions of children. Similarly, current proposals for empowering families satisfy parent desires for choice, but fall short of meeting broader societal interests.

Hence, changes in ways schools make use of resources and in processes for involving professionals in decision making do not necessarily improve pupils' performance or their abilities to contribute positively to urban society. Many now argue for a more fundamental restructuring of educational services to be more inclusive of children's needs generally. The Carnegie Foundation for the Advancement of Teaching (1988) put it this way:

> America must confront, with urgency, the crisis in urban schools. Bold, aggressive action is needed now to avoid leaving a huge and growing segment of the nation's youth civically unprepared and economically unempowered. This nation must see the urban school crisis for what it is: a major failure of social policy, a piecemeal approach to a problem that requires a unified response. (p. xv)

Similarly, the urban study group of the National Association of State Boards of Education (1991) encourages schools to broaden their concerns for students' well-being:

> Educators have not traditionally considered non-academic concerns as their responsibility. But the Study Group believes that without better support for students' social, emotional and physical problems – and without working with families and neighborhoods as well as students – schools cannot help many students to graduate from high school or leave school adequately prepared for jobs or higher education. (p. 25)

Political support for child-centred services

We are persuaded by those who suggest that the strategies typically associated with restructuring the public schools must be linked with those associated with meeting the non-academic needs of children and youth. Children from turbulent home and community environments will not be active learners (Melaville and Blank 1991). The National Alliance of Business (1990) observes: '. . . while it is convenient to view the delivery of human services as a problem separate from the restructuring of education, the two are inextricably linked' (p. 59). Schools will need to develop strategies for managing their relationships with other institutions that serve children. Historically, this has been through accommodation (Elmore 1990) or improvisation, when what needs to occur is the development of strategic alliances with other youth-serving organizations.

Interagency collaboration for the provision of appropriate health, education and other social services (Wilson 1987, Murphy 1990, Kirst and McLaughlin 1990a, 1990b, Melaville and Blank 1991) offers a new paradigm for meeting needs of children and youth in urban environments. This final section examines political support for this reform direction, addressing several questions:

1. What constituent groups are likely to influence the direction of political support for altering current structures for service delivery?
2. Even if the goals of interagency collaboration can be agreed on, are current boundaries too impenetrable and are self-interests too entrenched to permit effective collaboration for children?
3. Is it possible to gain sufficient agreement among constituents for the value of child-centred strategies, and can there be sufficient intensity of action, to provide essential political support to adopt and implement drastic changes called for in governance and operations of agencies?

Expanded constituents and services

The constituents for restructuring societal agencies substantially expand the groups identified earlier with regard to school reform. Interagency collaboration involves school boards, teachers, and administrators internal to public schools as well as diverse public and private non-educational agencies, governing boards, local and state governments, families and children themselves. These groups widen the value preferences and interests to be satisfied in reform, complicating dramatically the process of building coalitions to gain sufficient agreement to move the reform agenda. Agreement over values, direction and focus must now be reached by a larger number of individuals and groups.

The need for improved services in cities requires diverse constituents to set aside differences and become advocates for children and youth. Hawley (1988) labels social programmes and preventive policies to address needs of prospective parents and preschool children as 'investment in children strategies'. He contends that families should assume advocacy roles in demanding appropriate services for their children from multiple public agencies, but '. . . when families are unable or lack the resources to make demands on the various institutions on which their children must depend, children's needs go unmet'. The family situation itself causes or contributes to special health, social and educational needs.

Kirst and McLaughlin (1990b) also question who is looking at all elements of children's lives: 'Few teachers, physicians, workers in the juvenile court system, social workers, or others focus on the interactive or interdependent nature of their contribution to the experience of youth. Instead, they look only at their own performance as members of particular agencies.' It might be concluded that few leaders or reformers are looking at all the elements of children's lives.

An initial question in advancing child-based reforms is whether there are realistic examples of the kind of restructuring associated with this strategy. There are a number of sites in which once-fragmented agencies are now collaborating, indicating that constituents are able to overcome barriers (Kirst and McLaughlin 1990b, Melaville and

Blank 1991). Many of these collaboratives introduce a new governance structure, and thus expand the capabilities of partnerships or co-operatives between schools and one or more independent agencies. For example, the Rochester Community School Program is one of four community school projects initiated by the New York State Board of Regents. Its steering committee, including the school principal, representatives from the Department of Social Services and a Neighborhood Center, the project co-ordinator and parents, oversees programmes for children and adults.

A broad coalition is evident in San Diego's New Beginnings initiative, which includes representatives of the school district, community college, city manager's office, housing and planning commissions, juvenile court, and County departments of health, probation and social services. A staff of Family Service Advocates, who work with families and students as case managers, is to be located at a centre in or adjacent to elementary schools. The Minneapolis Youth Coordinating Board, a creation of the municipal government and the 'vigorous commitment' of the mayor, includes 11 agencies to promote the integration and quality of services for all youth, not just those with special needs. The Ventura County Children's Demonstration Project co-ordinates mental health care for troubled youth. Initially created by the California State Assembly and subsequently duplicated in other counties, this pilot project's success depended on the involvement of influential community members and key agencies.

A partnership between the Concilio Hispano de Camabridge and local schools, the Ahora programme uses volunteers from Boston area colleges and universities to provide tutoring, mentoring, higher education and job counselling, leadership development, and recreational and cultural activities. A somewhat different arrangement is represented by the Ounce of Prevention Fund, which brokers and co-ordinates services for pre-teens, teen parents, and their families in a number of communities in Illinois. This fund is independent of service agencies and thus is 'free of suspicion of "special pleading," narrow institutional self-interest, or problem definitions, which are rooted in professionally prescribed domains' (Kirst and McLaughlin 1990b: 82).

The politics of collaboration

Given the emergence of these and other successful interagency collaboratives and other school-led attempts to service children comprehensively, what are the larger issues in policy and politics that must be addressed to see these reforms take place on a broader scale? Kirst and McLaughlin (1990b) note that the constituents involved in collaboratives have successfully reconceptualized the purposes of children's services and placed youth services in broader family, school and community contexts in which children live. We predict several additional issues – those related to institutional boundaries, agencies' willingness to collaborate, building their capacities, and the degree of agreement and action – that must be confronted directly to truly reform conditions for children and to create meaningful improvements in learning.

Institutional boundaries and professional self-interests: Collaboration means that once-impenetrable institutional boundaries and the personal interests of adults must give way to the conditions of children. Up to this point, reforms have largely focused on the working conditions of professionals. It is assumed that satisfying needs and interests of adults in schools makes a difference for children and youth. These changes may be necessary conditions for improving teaching, but they fall short of changing learning conditions of children whom they face daily. Similarly, until the mode of delivery of non-educational services is directed from a focus on agency and professional expertise, urban society (and hence urban schools) will not improve.

The politics of interagency collaboration demands governance changes and shifts from isolated, fragmented services. It demands that school boards, city councils, boards of mental health agencies, juvenile justice services, and so on, yield control of resources and personnel to meld their capabilities to develop integrated approaches to meet children's needs. What is needed is a fundamental shift in the philosophy, leadership and management of institutions at the local level (Cunningham 1989). Schools, observe Kirst and McLaughlin (1990b), are a primary cause of fragmentation.

It is not that school superintendents and other school officials are not committed to working collaboratively with public and private community agencies. Rather, a primary cause of the fragmented, even chaotic and duplicative array of services currently provided is the governance and finance structures supporting municipalities and other agencies. School districts, for instance, have their own tax bases and their own governing boards. The result is that '... metropolitan political separation is dysfunctional with respect to meeting the multiple needs of many students... and has weakened a potential coalition for children since educators rarely coordinate political strategy with other service providers' (Kirst and McLaughlin 1990b: 85–86). Schools are in a position to become the 'hub' of integration due to their locations in neighbourhoods and their daily contact with children. However, schools should not be responsible for a broad range of services, given their academic responsibilities and the danger of limiting other agencies' roles if they sense the schools have taken charge.

Increasing the appetite for collaboration: Commitment at the policy level notwithstanding, the will to collaborate must exist among the professionals and bureaucrats who work in schools and other youth-serving organizations. From the standpoint of the schools, if interagency collaboration does little but create extra work and draw time and resources away from existing activities, it cannot be expected to be embraced. Reformers will need to develop tactics that promote collaboration as a way for schools to focus more energetically on academics. This, after all, is their central purpose. From the standpoint of other youth-serving professionals, the question is whether collaboration enhances their overall capacity to deliver specialized services to more children. Unless these professionals see collaboration as a means toward more effective delivery of their services, they will continue to be disinterested in working with or through the schools. In short, there needs to be commitment among professionals and executives in education, health, protective services, and other agencies for effective development of truly integrated services.

Capacity building: Even where there is willingness to collaborate, there may not be the know-how. Arguably, this is something that comes with experience, but the fact that the people who must work together have different backgrounds and training and respond at present to different incentive structures is an issue. There might be a number of tactics to strengthen the opportunity for success in developing co-ordinated and integrated services. One is to focus specifically on training opportunities that cut across professional lines (Houle *et al.* 1987). In this way, professionals and mid-level managers get to know each other and develop a common understanding of how learning and other aspects of a child's experience or condition are related. This interprofessional interaction and training could serve as a vehicle for developing and working from a common information base on the needs of children. In addition, barriers to collaboration can be broken and plans for integrated service can be developed.

Agreement and action for interagency collaboration: Schools will need to be accessible and flexible for collaboration to work. Policy makers may need to rethink the role of schools in the production of education services (Kirst and McLaughlin 1990b) from that of 'deliverer' to that of 'broker' of a variety of resources associated with helping children and youth become more productive contributors to society. There may also be a real need to draw special conclusions from the existing examples of success in collaboration. For instance, labour leaders must observe that people do not lose their jobs due to collaborative service delivery. Professionals must find that their judgement is not undermined by collaboration. Political leaders must find that more children succeed in school and that costs do not mushroom. It must be someone's job to discover if these outcomes are possible and someone's job to communicate them effectively in the policy arena.

The model presented in figure 1 suggests that there must be sufficient agreement among values and interests of diverse agencies, and sufficient intensity of action of all groups, to bring meaningful change in the current fragmented-agency paradigm, such that governance and delivery structures focus on the child.

It is doubtful that school reform efforts, or changes in non-educational service delivery systems, during the past decade have created the conditions essential for building political support for interagency collaboration in all cities. With internal labour–management differences over proposals to alter teachers' work, and with differing value preferences among internal and external constituents inhibiting proposals for empowering parents to choose among schools, gaining support for reform that changes the role of urban schools to become a 'hub' of integrated social services seems unlikely.

School reform has been successful in many cities, however, and the political support generated may be sufficient to expand reform from the schools to other sectors. Moreover, the nature and scope of this agenda for co-ordinating and restructuring multiple societal agencies may itself mount political support even in cities that have not been successful in coalescing agreement on educational reform. Current attempts at co-ordination, if they are successful at making a difference for a few children, may generate their own political momentum, particularly in the midst of more popular reform initiatives that produce mediocre outcomes.

There will not be sufficient support for such fundamental restructuring of local governance on behalf of the interests of children and youth in all cities. It is realistic to expect that all schools view students as active parts of their families and their neighbourhoods. In fact, we argue that schools must be held accountable for forging real working partnerships with families and other community agencies to assure that all young people receive the personal support and services they need to achieve academically.

In time, many more cities will gravitate toward interagency collaboration as the public realizes that improvements in children's lives and learning, and thus in society's potential, are worth the sacrifice of agencies' identities, budgets and independence. We believe that a collaborative model will ultimately strengthen the capabilities of participating institutions, and that the political support generated for the needs of children will bring more of society's resources and status than occurs today through the competitive, fragmented service delivery approach.

References

Boyd, W. L. and Kerchner, C. T. (eds) (1988) *The Politics of Excellence and Choice in Education* (New York: Falmer Press).

BRADLEY, A. (1991a) 'Denver board, union await governor's contract proposal', *Education Week*, *X* (23), 27 February 1991, p. 5.

BRADLEY, A. (1991b) 'On third try, school board and teachers agree on two-year contract in Rochester', *Education Week*, *X* (32), 1 May 1991, p. 4.

CARNEGIE FORUM ON EDUCATION AND THE ECONOMY (1986) *A Nation Prepared: Teachers for the 21st Century* (Washington, DC: Carnegie Forum on Education and the Economy).

CARNEGIE FOUNDATION FOR THE ADVANCEMENT OF TEACHING (1988) *An Imperiled Generation: Saving Urban Schools* (Princeton, NJ: Princeton University Press).

CHUBB, J. E. and MOE, T. M. (1990) *Politics, Markets, and America's Schools* (Washington, DC: The Brookings Institution).

COHEN, M. (1988) *Restructuring the Education System: Agenda for the 1990s* (Washington, DC: Center for Policy Research, National Governors Association).

COHEN, M. (1990) 'Key issues confronting state policymakers', in R. F. Elmore (ed.) *Restructuring Schools: The Next Generation of Educational Reform* (San Francisco, CA: Jossey-Bass), pp. 251–288.

COMMITTEE FOR ECONOMIC DEVELOPMENT (1991) *The Unfinished Agenda: A New Vision for Child Development and Education* (New York: Author).

CUNNINGHAM, L. (1989) 'Reconstituting local government for well-being and education', The Paul B. Salmon Memorial Lecture, The American Association of School Administrators 1989 National Convention, Orlando, FL.

EASTON, D. A. (1965) *A Framework for Political Analysis* (Englewood Cliffs, NJ: Prentice Hall).

ELMORE, R. F. (1986) *Choice in Public Education* (East Lansing, MI: Center for Policy Research in Education, Michigan State University).

ELMORE, R. F. (1990) *Restructuring Schools: The Next Generation of Educational Reform* (San Francisco, CA: Jossey-Bass).

GINSBERG, R. and WIMPELBERG, R. K. (1987) 'Educational change by commission: attempting "trickle down reform" ', *Educational Evaluation and Policy Analysis*, 9 (4), pp. 344–360.

GUTHRIE, J. W. and KOPPICH, J. (1988) 'Exploring the political economy of national education reform', in W. L. Boyd and C. T. Kerchner (eds) *The Politics of Excellence and Choice in Education* (New York: Falmer Press), pp. 25–47.

HAWLEY, W. D. (1988) 'Missing pieces of the educational reform agenda: or, why the first and second waves may miss the boat', *Educational Administration Quarterly*, 24 (4), pp. 416–437.

HOLMES GROUP (1986) *Tomorrow's Teachers* (East Lansing, MI: Holmes Group).

HOULE, C. O., CYPHERT, F. and BOGGS, D. (1987) 'Education for the professions', *Theory into Practice*, 26 (2), pp. 87–93.

JORDAN, K. F. and MCKEOWN, M. P. (1990) 'State fiscal policy and education reform', in J. Murphy (ed.) *The Educational Reform Movement of the 1980s: Perspectives and Cases* (Berkeley, CA: McCutchan), pp. 97–120.

KEARNS, D. L. (1988) 'An education recovery plan for America', *Phi Delta Kappan*, 69 (8), pp. 565–570.

KIRST, M. W. and MCLAUGHLIN, M. (1990a) *Improving Policies for Children*, proceedings of the 1989 New York Education Policy Seminar, Special Report Number 29 (Albany, NY: The Nelson A. Rockefeller Institute of Government).

KIRST, M. W. and MCLAUGHLIN, M. (1990b) 'Rethinking policy for children: implications for educational administration', in B. Mitchell and L. V. Cunningham (eds) *Educational Leadership and Changing Contexts of Families, Communities, and Schools*, 89th Yearbook of the National Society for the Study of Education (Chicago, IL: University of Chicago Press), pp. 69–90.

MACPHAIL-WILCOX, B. and KING, R. A. (1986) 'Production functions revisited in the context of educational reform', *Journal of Education Finance*, 12, pp. 191–222.

MELAVILLE, A. I. and BLANK, M. J. (1991) *What It Takes: Structuring Interagency Partnerships to Connect Children and Families with Comprehensive Services* (Washington, DC: Education and Human Services Consortium, Institute for Educational Leadership).

MURNANE, R. (1988) 'Education and productivity of the workforce: looking ahead', in R. E. Litan, R. Z. Lawrence and C. Schultze (eds) *American Living Standards: Threats and Challenges* (Washington, DC: The Brookings Institution), pp. 215–245.

MURPHY, J. (1990) 'The educational reform movement of the 1980s: a comprehensive analysis', in J. Murphy (ed.) *The Educational Reform Movement of the 1980s: Perspectives and Cases* (Berkeley, CA: McCutchan), pp. 3–55.

NATIONAL ALLIANCE OF BUSINESS (1990) *The Business Roundtable Participation Guide: A Primer for Business on Education* (New York: The Business Roundtable).

NATIONAL ASSOCIATION OF STATE BOARDS OF EDUCATION (1991) *More than a Vision: Real Improvements in Urban Education* (Alexandria, VA: NASBE).

RAVITCH, D. (1983) *The Troubled Crusade: American Education 1945–1980* (New York: Basic Books).

ROSOW, J. M. and ZAGER, R. (1989) *Allies in Educational Reform: How Teachers, Unions, and Administrators Can Join Forces for Better Schools* (San Francisco, CA: Jossey-Bass).

SARASON, S. (1990) *The Predictable Failure of Educational Reform* (San Francisco: Jossey-Bass).

SCHLECHTY, P. C. (1990) *Schools for the Twenty-First Century: Leadership Imperatives for Educational Reform* (San Francisco: Jossey-Bass).

SWANSON, A. D. and KING, R. A. (1991) *School Finance: Its Economics and Politics* (New York: Longman).

TIMAR, T. (1989) 'The politics of school restructuring', *Phi Delta Kappan*, 71 (4), pp. 165–175.

TIMAR, T. B. and KIRP, D. L. (1988) *Managing Educational Excellence* (Philadelphia: Falmer Press).

UNDERWOOD, J. (1989) 'State legislative responses to educational reform literature', in L. S. Lotto and P. W. Thurston (eds) *Recent Advances in Educational Administration, Vol. I* (Greenwich, CT: JAI Press).

WILSON, W. (1987) *The Truly Disadvantaged: The Inner City, the Underclass, and Public Policy* (Chicago: University of Chicago Press).

POLITICS OF EDUCATION ASSOCIATION YEARBOOK 1991, 137–148

PART 3: URBAN SCHOOL RENEWAL AND IMPLEMENTATION STRATEGIES: POLITICAL IMPLICATIONS

9 *Urban school desegregation: from race to resources*

David Colton and Susan Uchitelle

Until the mid-1970s, the politics of urban school desegregation concentrated almost exclusively on the attainment of some form of racial balance. The racial balance paradigm became the focal point for desegregation planners and for local, state and national dispute about 'forced bussing'. However, in its 1977 *Milliken II* ruling, the Supreme Court added critical new elements to the urban school desegregation paradigm. By affirming a desegregation plan which included remedial education components in all-minority schools, and which required state participation in financing these components, *Milliken II* heralded a new era of urban school desegregation. Resource issues and school effectiveness issues joined racial balance issues in the crucible of desegregation politics. In this chapter, the post-*Milliken* politics of urban school desegregation are highlighted through examination of the St Louis and Kansas City cases. New goals, new issues, new alignments of interests and new political strategies are apparent, presenting new challenges to students of urban education policy and politics.

In 1990, 36 years after its *Brown* decision focused attention on segregation's harm to the hearts and minds of young children, the Supreme Court addressed a more arcane matter: could a court require Kansas City authorities to set aside state tax limitation statutes in order to levy taxes for new programmes and new schoolhouses in a desegregation plan (*Missouri* v. *Jenkins*, 110 S.Ct. 1651)? Four members of the Court protested that the Kansas City desegregation plan was extravagant, that desegregation planners had 'demonstrated little concern for . . . fiscal consequences', and that the plan strayed past the remediation of segregation and into redress of resource problems created by 'the ineptitude of educators or the indifference of the public' – matters beyond the reach of the Constitution. However, a narrow majority of the Court declined to review the Kansas City desegregation plan, and held that the district could be ordered to levy taxes to pay for the plan even if such taxation by-passed tax limitation statutes.

Jenkins manifested a major shift in the paradigm and the politics of urban school desegregation. The established paradigm centred on racial balance and techniques for achieving it (Foster 1973). Politics at the local level emphasized issues associated with student reassignment and bussing (Rubin 1972, Crain 1968). Nationally, the politics of desegregation were concentrated on Congressional and White House responses to the busing controversy (Vergon 1990). Resource questions, where they arose at all, rested on the assumption that desegregation added costs to the already stressed budgets of urban school districts. Civil rights advocates responded that costs were minor and that inflated claims about costs simply were pretexts masking opposition to integration (NAACP 1973). Policy researchers sought to moderate the argument by gathering data on actual costs and their determinants (Colton and Berg 1981).

In Kansas City and elsewhere, desegregation issues and politics took a different form in the 1980s. Civil rights plaintiffs aligned themselves with school defendants, helping to design costly remedial plans, and seeking court orders which tapped public funds previously unavailable. Armed by the courts with revenue-generating capability at both the local and state levels, and supported by their erstwhile adversaries in court, Kansas

0268–0939/91 \$3.00 © 1991 Taylor & Francis Ltd.

City school authorities turned a finding of unlawful segregation into an opportunity to finance a complete overhaul of their school system, despite the fact that thousands of African-American students remained in racially isolated schools. Similar events already had occurred in St Louis, where desegregation orders infused huge sums of new money into a city school system which continued to operate many predominantly African-American schools. By 1991 Kansas City and St Louis had tapped state and local revenue sources for more than one billion dollars for remedying segregation. Resource issues joined racial issues at the centre of urban school desegregation politics.

This chapter traces the transformation of issues of race into issues of resources in two cities in America's heartland, and it discusses the significance of this transformation for the politics of urban education. The pivotal case is St Louis. Initially conceptualized as a traditional student assignment problem, remedy planning in St Louis became infused with resource questions as the case progressed. In Kansas City, culminating in *Jenkins*, resource questions were paramount almost from the outset.

The Missouri setting

Before the Civil War, Missouri law barred the education of African-Americans. After the war, their education could be provided only in segregated schools. Following the 1954 *Brown* decision, state officials ceased enforcement of the segregation statutes, and local districts adopted 'neighbourhood school' policies which ostensibly were colourblind. Missouri won national acclaim for its apparent compliance with *Brown*. However, neither city nor state officials acted affirmatively to dismantle the vestiges of segregated education. Moreover, as the courts later would find, officials utilized a variety of techniques to sustain racial segregation in schools. Two decades after *Brown*, most African-American students in the St Louis and Kansas City metropolitcan areas still attended racially identifiable schools.

Early in the 1970s, civil rights advocates initiated legal proceedings attacking segregation. An Office of Civil Rights action in a St Louis suburb precipitated major school reorganization and improved racial balance in that district (Staff Report 1977). In Kansas City an administrative law judge found that the district had acted to maintain segregation (Missouri Advisory Committee 1981:22). The US Department of Justice brought suit against Missouri and three contiguous districts in suburban St Louis. One of them – the all-minority and impoverished Kinloch district – was surrounded by the predominantly white Berkeley and Ferguson districts. The District Court concluded that state and local actions and inactions had unlawfully created and sustained Kinloch's segregation; consolidation of the three districts was ordered (*US* v. *Missouri* 515 F.2d 1365).

The Kinloch ruling heartened advocates of interdistrict desegregation in St Louis and Kansas City, where predominantly African-American central city districts were surrounded by predominantly white suburban districts. In its 1974 '*Milliken I*' ruling (418 US 717) the Supreme Court had blocked the use of such a remedy in the Detroit area, inasmuch as the Detroit suburbs had not been shown to have contributed to Detroit's segregation. The Kinloch case held open the possibility that interdistrict student reassignment remedies might be ordered in St Louis. That possibility decisively shaped the pending St Louis case. Equally decisive was the 1977 '*Milliken II*' Supreme Court ruling (433 US 269) which affirmed a Detroit-only remedy including compensatory and remedial programmes in all-minority schools, and which ordered state payment of a portion of the programmes' costs.

St Louis

In 1972 a class action suit was filed against the St Louis Public Schools (SLPS) on behalf of Craton Liddell and other African-American students. Initially the suit took the standard form, alleging unlawful school segregation and requesting integration of the city's schools (*Liddell* v. *Caldwell*, 546 F.2d 768). The defendant SLPS insisted that school racial isolation was caused by factors beyond its control. In any event, SLPS asserted, a stable integration plan could not be accomplished without the inclusion of the suburbs.

Liability proceedings dragged on for seven years. Meanwhile, the St Louis schools, virtually paralysed by the lawsuit, continued a slide in quality which had begun decades earlier, leading eventually to a downgrade in the state's quality classification rating system. White flight to the suburbs and to non-public schools was substantial, leaving the city's schools populated predominantly by African-American students. Public opinion, fuelled by politicians' rhetoric, inveighed against forced busing, warned about white flight, blamed housing patterns for causing school racial isolation, and invoked *Milliken I* doctrine protecting the autonomy of suburban school districts.

However, SLPS and the State of Missouri were held liable for the segregated condition of the SLPS and were ordered to prepare remedial plans (*Adams* v. *US*, 620 F.2d 1277). An intra-city plan quickly was adopted and implemented. It required student reassignments which integrated the city's remaining all-white schools, authorized some magnet programmes, and established compensatory and remedial programmes in exclusively African-American schools. The costs of these programmes were to be split between the city and the state, as in *Milliken II*. Missouri's appeal was rebuffed (*Liddell* v. *St Louis*, 667 F.2d 643).

Public and official attention shifted to two other provisions of the court order. One required the development of a plan for a voluntary interdistrict student transfer programme permitting African-American SLPS students to attend suburban schools. The other required development of a plan for a single metropolitan district, for consideration if pending court hearings established interdistrict liability for segregation. These orders, as intended, inspired action in the political arena, leading to a court-approved Settlement Agreement in 1983 (*Liddell* v. *Missouri*, 731 F.2d 1294). Money was the key to the agreement.

The political process which led to the Settlement Agreement required meshing of group interests and legal standards (LaPierre 1987). One set of interests was represented by African-American plaintiffs. The original *Liddell* plaintiffs sought integrated schools, but also attached great importance to quality education. Schools attended solely by African-American students would be acceptable if they were quality schools; desegregation which was inattentive to quality was not the central goal of these plaintiffs (*St Louis Post-Dispatch*, 18 January 1976). Fearing that such sentiments would compromise its long-term desegregation strategy, the NAACP intervened in the case in 1976 and began laying the foundations for a trial which could lead to a metropolitan remedy embracing the suburban districts.

Suburban districts, another group, found some comfort in the *Milliken I* limitations on interdistrict remedies. Many suburban leaders urged stout legal resistance to any effort to involve the suburbs in solving St Louis's problem. However there was a worrisome history which involved pre-*Brown* transportation of suburban African-American students to St Louis's African-American schools, post-*Brown* resistance to school district reorganization initiatives and the recent imposition of an interdistrict remedy in the Kinloch case. If a voluntary settlement could be achieved, the expense and uncertain outcome of an interdistrict trial might be avoided.

SLPS, a defendant *vis-à-vis Liddell* and the NAACP, was a plaintiff *vis-à-vis* the suburban districts and Missouri. For SLPS, segregation was contextualized in a long-term decline in school quality, in lack of fiscal support from impoverished parents and alienated taxpayers, and in indifference or hostility at the state level. These problems could be ameliorated by the imposition of a metropolitan remedy, by a suitably financed interdistrict transfer plan, by court-ordered school improvements, or by combinations of these approaches.

Finally, there was the State of Missouri. State officials courted voter support by opposing bussing. Asserting its innocence, Missouri regularly appealed court orders and it limited its participation in the settlement negotiations, thereby missing the opportunity to moderate other participants' demands for state funds as a precondition for settlement.

The legal standards informing the settlement negotiations were enunciated by the Eighth Circuit Court of Appeals, which had its own agenda. It wanted the plaintiffs' rights effectuated without prolonged legal wrangling, consistent with constitutional commands (Heaney 1985). Two commands in the *Milliken* cases were of particular interest to the court:

1. Mandatory interdistrict remedies, the court acknowledged, 'seemingly' were deterred by *Milliken I*. However, the court felt that *Milliken I* standards were not insurmountable; hearings on the question of interdistrict liability were invited (*Adams* v. *US*, 620 F.2d 1277). Moreover, even without a prior finding of interdistrict liability, voluntary efforts could be encouraged; SLPS was directed to seek the co-operation of suburban districts in accepting minority transfers (*Liddell* v. *Caldwell*, 546 F.2d 768). In what proved to be a key statement on the matter, the court in 1982 declared that the state could be compelled to pay the costs of a voluntary interdistrict transfer plan (*Liddell* v. *St Louis*, 677 F.2d 626).
2. Before *Milliken II*, educational quality issues were deemed to be outside the Appeals Court's domain. For example, in 1976 the court observed that emphasis on quality 'fundamentally misapprehends the constitutional requirement . . . . The sole goal of *Brown* is to erase the effects of prior school segregation . . . [It] is the "equal opportunity", not the quality education which is germane to the constitutional concern' (*Liddell* v. *Caldwell*, 546 F.2d 768). After *Milliken II* the court adopted a more expansive view. Defendants were advised to include educational components in their proposed remedy (*Adams* v. *US*, 620 F.2d 1277). To the Appeals Court, the central meaning of *Milliken II* was that segregation's harm was inflicted not only on individual African-American students; the harm also was 'systemic' in nature, thus warranting system-wide educational improvements (*Liddell* v. *Missouri*, 731 F.2d 1294).

Within this evolving legal framework, the parties in the St Louis case came to the negotiating table, guided by a Special Master charged with seeking a comprehensive settlement of the case. On the eve of the inception of interdistrict liability hearings in early 1983, a Settlement Agreement was reached. Shortly thereafter, with minor adjustments, it received judicial assent (*Liddell* v. *Missouri*, 731 F.2d 1294).

The agreement was a classic political compromise. The suburban districts would be released from the threat of future imposition of a metropolitan remedy if they successfully implemented a voluntary interdistrict transfer plan. The African-American plaintiffs and SLPS would cease pressing interdistrict claims and would accept some predominantly African-American schools if their quality could be improved through the establishment of new magnet schools, a Quality Education Program, and capital improvements. The key to these trade-offs was state liability for the agreement's costs (LaPierre 1987:984). Resource issues had come to centre stage.

The Interdistrict Transfer Program

The Settlement Agreement projected the transfer of approximately 15,000 African-American students from St Louis to 16 suburban districts. Major fiscal incentives were required to make the plan palatable. For St Louis, 15,000 students represented more than one-quarter of the district's enrolment. Their transfer to the suburbs could adversely affect hundreds of the district's employees and its state revenues. Such a price would be unacceptable. For the suburbs, the addition of 15,000 transfers could require the employment of hundreds of additional teachers and possibly the construction of new classrooms; local taxpayers were unlikely to tax themselves to carry this burden.

To overcome these problems, the Settlement Agreement developed what amounted to a new state funding formula. It provided that the suburban districts would receive from the state the full cost of each transferring student's education, while SLPS would continue to receive one-half of its state aid for each student who transferred to another district. The aid could be used to improve the education and reduce class size for the students remaining in St Louis. Transportation for transfer students was to be fully funded by the state. The costs were high, totalling more than $41 million in incentive payments and $20 million in transportation payments in 1989–90 alone (Voluntary Interdistrict Coordinating Council 1990:32, 37).

To oversee and manage the interdistrict transfer plan, the agreement created a Voluntary Interdistrict Coordinating Council (VICC) to recruit students, assist in their placement, monitor their experience, provide staff development, trouble-shoot in the complex transportation programme and work with receiving districts to create conditions for the success of transferring students. Thus the Settlement Agreement spawned a new type of regional service district – accountable to the court, brokering a programme whose costs would be passed on to the state, and serving as advocate and agent for St Louis African-American parents represented through their attorneys.

Magnet schools

During the years when the St Louis case was moving toward settlement, magnet schools were popular desegregation tools. Unlike mandatory student reassignments, they coupled integration with quality improvements and voluntarism. Magnet schools were costly, inasmuch as they usually required programme enhancements, facility improvements and transportation. The Settlement Agreement required the state to meet these excess costs.

The Appeals Court acceded to Missouri's pleas that careful planning should precede investment in new magnet schools. A Magnet Review Committee was established to screen proposals for new magnet schools and to evaluate existing magnet schools. Seats on the committee were allocated: two to the city, two to the suburbs, one to a representative of the African-American plaintiffs and one to the state, which was to foot the bill.

The magnet school component of the remedial plan spawned a host of resource-related political and governance issues. For example, magnet schools created in the 1980 city-only plan operated under one set of funding orders; magnets created within the framework of the Settlement Agreement operated under a different funding arrangement. Bookkeeping nightmares ensued, eventuating in special studies, hearings, and ultimately a new decree establishing a 'system' of magnet schools in which overall enrolments rather than school-by-school enrolments would be calculated, and for which the state would be responsible for 71.5% of the costs and SLPS the rest (*Liddell* v. *St Louis*, 696 F. Supp. 444). Other issues – site selection, programme design, facility planning – regularly arose within the Magnet Review Committee, complicating and slowing its work.

Quality Education Program

In contrast to the interdistrict transfer programme and the magnet programme, which were designed to foster integration, the Quality Education Program (QEP) sought to improve the school experience of SLPS students not participating in the transfer or magnet programmes. System-wide QEP components specified in the Settlement Agreement included employment of additional teachers and counsellors; expanded library/media services; the restoration of art, music and physical education programmes sufficient to regain for SLPS the state's AAA classification; all-day kindergartens and preschool centres; and parent involvement programmes. Additional QEP components focused on the remaining predominantly African-American schools; these components included further reductions in class size, after-school and summer programmes and the creation of new Instructional Co-ordinator positions in each school.

In the proceedings leading to the Settlement Agreement there were few constraints on the design of QEP components, other than the imagination of the planners. In contrast to standard budget milieus, revenue limitations were not fixed; it simply was necessary to persuade the court that specific QEP components were related to remedying the residual effects of segregation. As one Appeals Court judge noted, in the negotiations leading to the Settlement Agreement 'none of [the parties] had any real incentive to prevent the others from piling their plates high with programs and funds that would benefit their school systems' – and for which the state must pay half the bill (731 F.2d 1294).

The bill was substantial, exceeding $20 million in 1986–87 alone. Its computation was a complex and controversial task, requiring judgment calls on matters such as staffing ratios and facility requirements, appropriate relationships between estimated and actual expenditures, and between pre-payments and reimbursement payments. Disputes were referred to a court-appointed Budget Review Committee which was to examine long-range and annual budgets and to bring unresolved disputes to the court for its decision (731 F.2d 1294).

Even this mechanism failed to contain the politics of budgeting. The magnitude and complexity of the QEP, the absence of definitive deadlines, divisions within the Committee and the availability of judicial appeal forums resulted in frequent delays in budget approval, impeding school operations. A pattern of QEP underspending by SLPS prompted questions about SLPS motives and efficacy, but these matters seemed beyond the reach of both the Committee and the court (Grady 1988).

Capital improvements

The Settlement Agreement called for a major capital improvement programme in St Louis. Two large problems ensued. The first required agreement on the nature and magnitude of the improvements that could be made in the name of desegregation. Conflicting estimates were prepared by the SLPS, an outside engineering firm, and the state. A special magistrate was directed to devise a standard against which to assess competing plans. Eventually the whole matter fell into the lap of the court, which was obliged to make determinations on enrolment projections, programme requirements, building capacities, renovation costs, and allocation of costs between desegregation and non-desegregation items. A cost of $114 million, to be split 50–50 between SLPS and Missouri, finally was approved in 1988. Once this matter was resolved, there was the problem of finding a way to cover the SLPS share of costs. Three bond issues were rejected by the voters. Faced with this dilemma, the court undertook a study of SLPS finances, and then directed SLPS to reorder its spending priorities. SLPS was ordered to place funds into a Capital Projects Fund; if the fund ran short of needs, the state was to make a loan. Thus the tax levy problem was by-passed (*Liddell* v. *St Louis*, 674 F. Supp. 687). The tax issue would be less tractable in Kansas City.

Summary: St Louis

Despite difficulties, the Settlement Agreement has been substantially implemented. By 1990 more than 12,000 minority students from SLPS attended suburban schools. Missouri pays the full cost of education and transportation for these transfer students. Magnet schools, largely funded by the state, have attracted hundreds of private school and suburban school students into the SLPS. Quality Education components, whose costs are split by SLPS and the state, have expanded educational services in both integrated and segregated SLPS schools. A major capital improvement programme is under way. In 1990 St Louis voters signalled their approval of all this by approving a bond issue, and by electing a slate of school board members advocating support of the Settlement Agreement. The state, after years of resistance, has begun discussions to bring the case to an end and, perhaps, to reduce its burden on the state treasury (*Education Week* 10 April 1991, 24 April 1991).

Kansas City

Like St Louis, the Kansas City School District (KCSD) by the late 1970s served a predominantly African-American student population exhibiting a high incidence of the educational problems associated with poverty and prejudice. Voter antipathy to school taxes was reflected in traditional programmes and decaying schoolhouses. Adjacent suburban districts were predominantly white and exhibited higher levels of support by taxpayers.

Metropolitan approaches to KCSD's woes were advocated. For example, one report described the area's use of metropolitan approaches to transportation, housing and environmental protection; a similar regional approach to education was urged as a solution to problems of school inefficiency, ineffectiveness and racial isolation (Bi-State Committee 1977). Official reaction was cool. Whatever the merits of metropolitanism, its intimate connection with issues of school integration made it politically unpalatable.

Hemmed in by uncooperative suburbs, rebuffed by local taxpayers, and receiving no succour from the state, the KCSD sought judicial relief. Claiming that it was economically injured by diminishing tax potential and by the increased costs of educating disadvantaged students, KCSD asserted that its injuries were caused by unlawful segregation resulting from intentional actions and inactions by Kansas and Missouri state officials, by suburban districts and by federal agencies. A regional remedy was warranted, according to the KCSD.

Most of this rather novel approach was rebuffed in court. KCSD was realigned as a defendant, whereupon it filed a cross-claim against the state defendants. The Kansas defendants were dismissed from the case. The federal defendants were found not culpable and suburban district responsibility was held to be insufficient to warrant an interdistrict remedy – a finding narrowly sustained by a bitterly divided Appeals Court (*Jenkins* v. *Missouri*, 807 F.2d 657). Eventually, KCSD and the state were found jointly liable for segregation in Kansas City schools.

Stymied in its effort to achieve a metropolitan remedy, KCSD developed a rationale for a remedy based on resources rather than on racial assignments. Turning the white flight thesis upside down, KCSD contended that whites had left the system because it was segregated. In order to attract them back to the system and thus to desegregate it, KCSD programmes and facilities should be measured against a metropolitan yardstick, i.e., the suburban schools to which the whites presumably had fled. Furthermore, KCSD contended, segregation caused a decline in minority student achievement. Thus, a remedy for segregation should encompass programmes known to enhance minority student achievement – even in segregated settings. Invoking Appeals Court language about the 'systemic' remedies employed in St Louis, KCSD argued that education components must be present throughout the KCSD rather than solely in all-minority schools.

Missouri, correctly sensing that these conceptions of remedy involved high price-tags, found itself arguing for lower standards. Programme quality, Missouri argued, should be measured against the state's classification system rather than against programmes in suburban schools. The state also found itself arguing for student reassignment within KCSD, in order to limit the numbers of students remaining in predominantly African-American schools which would qualify for more costly educational programme components.

The Appeals Court favoured the KCSD arguments, noting that 'the purpose of public schools in this state . . . is to furnish quality education to its students' (*Jenkins* v. *Missouri*, 593 F. Supp. 1485). KCSD prepared, and the courts substantially approved, a remedial plan requiring funds for reduced class size, employment of new programme specialists, large numbers of magnet schools, alternative schools, educational technology, tutoring, early childhood programmes and staff development programmes. By the second year of implementation, operating costs of the plan were calculated at $48 million, with 75% of this amount charged to the state (*Jenkins* v. *Missouri*, 639 F. Supp. 19).

Major attention was given to the task of upgrading the district's school facilities – a task estimated by KCSD officials to cost $260 million. State officials countered by proposing a $61 million renovation programme. The District Court rejected it as a 'patch and repair' strategy which failed to meet the standard of suburban comparability. Capital expenditures of $187 million were approved (*Jenkins* v. *Missouri*, 672 F. Supp. 400, 405).

As in St Louis, the court quickly found itself bogged down in fiscal issues. How should enrolment be projected? How many teachers would be needed, given projected changes in enrolments and teacher–student ratios? Which schools should be closed, renovated, rebuilt? Should salary projections be based on average salaries, entry-level salaries or suburban district salaries? To propose answers to such questions, and to provide forums for resolving disputes, court-sponsored advisory bodies were established and staffs were hired, independent of those already existing in KCSD, and responsive to different schedules and standards (*Jenkins* v. *Missouri*, 672 F. Supp. 400).

Significantly, the standard for resolving such issues was not racial integration. It was suburban comparability. Despite District Court admonitions that costs were to be considered in the fashioning of remedial plans, available evidence indicates that planners engaged in little cost–benefit analysis of available options. KCSD officials simply projected the costs deemed necessary to bring the city's schoolhouses and programmes up to metropolitan standards, relying on the court to order funding of whatever was constitutionally permissible.

Following court determination of permissible and impermissible expenditures under the remedial plan, it was nececessary to apportion the KCSD and state shares. Initially the court assigned the lion's share of costs to the state. Missouri appealed and won an order directing the District Court to reconsider in light of the *Milliken II* 50–50 split (*Jenkins* v. *Missouri*, 807 F.2d 657). After reconsideration, however, the District Court again declared the state responsible for the major share of the cost (*Jenkins* v. *Missouri*, 855 F.2d 1295).

Even with the major burden shifted to the state, KCSD was unable to find the funds to pay for its share. Judicial relief was sought. Rather than shifting more of the costs to the state, the District Court fashioned orders designed to enhance local revenues. KCSD was ordered to seek voter approval for a school tax increase. It failed. An effort to obtain legislative support also failed. Asserting that financial constraints should not impede the vindication of constitutional rights, the District Court then imposed an income tax surcharge on all residents and non-residents doing business within the KCSD. This approach was overturned on appeal (*Jenkins* v. *Missouri*, 855 F.2d 1295). KCSD then was ordered to sell $150 million in bonds. To retire these bonds and to generate revenues needed to operate court-approved programmes, an increase in local property taxes was ordered. The increase required setting aside state tax limitation statutes – the issue which precipitated the Supreme Court ruling cited at the beginning of this chapter.

Discussion

Resource considerations long have been key factors in school politics (Katzman 1971). In fact the architects of the pre-*Brown* legal assault on southern school segregation utilized a fiscally oriented strategy. Litigation ostensibly aimed at securing strict enforcement of the *Plessy* 'separate but equal' doctrine actually was intended to pressure policy makers to abandon separate education because of the costs of making it equal (Kluger 1976:136). However, when the Supreme Court took the high ground in *Brown*, ruling that segregation was inherently unlawful, fiscal issues faded away. Eradication of the vestiges of segregation seemed more a matter of resolve than of resources. Race-based student assignment became the focus of attention (Orfield 1978). The courts held that their task merely was to assure equal access to whatever resources were available.

However, resource issues resumed their historic centrality after the desegregation movement reached central city districts in northern and border states in the mid-1970s (Berg and Colton 1982). *Milliken II* linked race and resource issues. That linkage transformed the St Louis case and dominated the Kansas City case. New issues and new alignments of the parties were created. District-level budget making and budget management procedures were altered by the introduction of vast sums of money mediated by the courts. Desegregation-related community politics changed from the single-issue politics of busing to multiple-issue politics, including not only choice and quality education, but also issues of district management and control. The relationship between state and local education agencies was altered. The core issues of law shifted from racial balance to a convoluted mixture of race and resource questions.

St Louis and Kansas City are not the first or only urban districts where resource issues have become a central focus of segregation remedies. '*Milliken* remedies', i.e., compensatory and remedial programmes in all-minority schools, have been introduced in other desegregation plans. State co-payments for remedy costs now are required in several cities undergoing court-ordered desegregation.

The Missouri cases provide useful contexts for discerning the agenda of a post-*Milliken II* politics of urban school desegregation in which resource issues join racial issues in the political arena. First and foremost, the desegregation paradigm has changed. A generation of research on urban school desegregation had rested on a paradigm in which student assignment was the core of the matter. Implementation of *Brown* had been assessed by examining changes in measures of minority racial isolation and by correlating measures of isolation with variables such as achievement scores, attitudes and white flight. Community studies concentrated on the politics of reassignment and busing. State and federal policies were assessed in terms of their significance for the redress of racial isolation. The Missouri cases show that desegregation has acquired a second focus: resources and their acquisition and allocation. In both St Louis and Kansas City, fiscal issues have come to the fore, often driving issues of racial balance into the background. New issues and new goals have arisen, along with new relationships among interest groups. These changes require adjustment in the perceptual lenses which policy scientists bring to the task of understanding the politics of urban school desegregation.

The change of course raises questions about policy goals. If student reassignment occupies a less transcendent place in school desegregation politics, what is the significance for race relations? Does the nexus of race and resources offer more promise of uprooting racism, or less, than a focus on race alone?

The stuff of school politics – curriculum, budgeting, facility planning, programme development, taxes, salaries, public relations, student assignment, programme evaluation – customarily is managed through complex bureaucracies with lives of their own. Colton and Berg (1981) described the effects of assignment-oriented segregation remedies on these bureaucracies. The Missouri cases exhibit more extensive intrusion, replete with new agencies and administrators responsible to the court and hence to a judicial culture which is guided by an adversarial mode of decision making, which knows no annual cycles of work, which is insulated from local and state politics, and whose lodestone is the Constitution rather than conceptions of schooling. Resource issues deepen and broaden the interface between courts and urban schools. What are their modes of accommodation and conflict? From the perspective of schools and their clients, is the effect liberating or does the situation simply create more constraints on discretion? How is the experience of students and other stakeholders changed, when resource issues are associated with issues of race? What differences do resources make in urban settings? What are the real trade-offs between integrated education and compensatory programmes – particularly in terms of race relations?

The Missouri cases raise questions about the dynamics of school governance in a federal system. National housing policy, a turnabout on federal support for magnet schools, and changes in judicial philosophy affected the evolution and outcome of both the Kansas City and St Louis cases. Established state–local relations in Missouri were turned upside down when SLPS and KCSD cross-claimed against the state. The relative roles of the legislature, the judiciary, and the local taxpayers were significantly altered by developments in the Missouri cases. Analysis of the permanence and impact of these events warrants thoughtful and systematic scholarly attention.

Though judges might prefer to have us think otherwise, the law is not 'found'.

Parties in court venues may cloak their goals in legal language, but they function as interest groups competing for judicial acceptance of their particular version of the law's commands, especially when resources are at stake. The resources involved in the Missouri cases transformed the traditional roles of defendants and plaintiffs alike. Defeat on the liability issue permitted KCSD and SLPS to function as virtual plaintiffs, fashioning arguments intended to maximize their revenues rather than minimize their costs. Missouri, on the other hand, in a decade when most state governments were asserting responsibility for school reform, found itself arguing to minimize its responsibility, and to slow down rather than speed up the pace of change in schools. Minority plaintiffs in the Missouri cases were obliged to adjust their litigation strategies to reflect the new significance of resources. The play of political interests, intensified by the magnitude of the resources to be allocated, shaped the law as it was brought to bear on segregation in St Louis and Kansas City. Scholarly attention to judicial decision making on resource issues is warranted.

Finally there is the question of court disengagement. The Missouri cases have matured just as an earlier generation of cases, such as Oklahoma City's, are forcing questions about court disengagement from segregation cases. In the older cases, the attainment of unitary status centrally involved questions of racial isolation. However, in future years when *Milliken*-based cases come on for termination, the measure of success and the means for disengagement will be more difficult to discern. Must disengagement await the hoped-for return of white students to improved urban schools? If state-funded programmes are factors in success, would disengagement be predicated on their continuation? Can the 'temporary systems' created to manage desegregation resources be dismantled without returning urban schools to their inequitable and impoverished pasts? Will the courts seek a standard of resource equity which focuses on resource inputs, or on educational outputs? How should social researchers advise the courts on such issues?

Such questions lie at the heart of the new politics of urban school desegregation. Efforts to address them can make important contributions to both theoretical and practical understanding of contemporary urban school politics and education.

References

BERG, W. M. and COLTON, D. L. (1982) '*Brown* and the Distribution of School Resources', in D. Monti (ed.) *New Directions for Testing and Measurement: Impact of Desegregation* (San Francisco: Jossey-Bass).

BI-STATE COMMITTEE ON EDUCATION OF THE KANSAS AND MISSOURI ADVISORY COMMITTEE TO THE US COMMISSION ON CIVIL RIGHTS (1977) *Crisis and Opportunity: Education in Greater Kansas City* (Washington, DC: US Commission on Civil Rights).

COLTON, D. L. and BERG, W. M. (1981) *Budgeting for Desegregation in Large Cities*, St Louis, Washington University Center for the Study of Law in Education. Final Report, National Institute of Education Grant NIE-g-79-0106. ERIC Doc. 211 651.

CRAIN, R. L. (1968) *The Politics of School Desegregation* (Chicago: Aldine).

FOSTER, G. (1973) 'Desegregating urban schools: a review of techniques', *Harvard Educational Review*, 43, pp. 5–36.

GRADY, M. K. (1988) *Confronting the Presumption of Unconstitutionality: An Assessment of the Implementation of Milliken II Relief for the All-Black Schools of St Louis, Missouri* (Cambridge: Harvard Graduate School of Education).

HEANEY, G. (1985) 'Busing, timetables, goals, and ratios: touchstones of equal opportunity', *Minnesota Law Review*, 69, pp. 735–820.

KATZMAN, M. T. (1971) *The Political Economy of Urban Schools* (Cambridge: Harvard University Press).

KLUGER, R. (1976) *Simple Justice* (New York: Knopf).

LAPIERRE, D. (1987) 'Voluntary interdistrict school desegregation in St Louis: the special master's tale', *Wisconsin Law Review*, pp. 971–1040.

MISSOURI ADVISORY COMMITTEE, US COMMISSION ON CIVIL RIGHTS (1981) *School Desegregation in the St Louis and Kansas City Areas* (Washington, DC: US Commission on Civil Rights).

NAACP LEGAL DEFENSE FUND AND EDUCATION FUND (1973) 'It's not the distance, it's the niggers', in N. Mills (ed.) *The Great School Bus Controversy* (New York: Teachers College Press).

ORFIELD, G. (1978) *Must We Bus?* (Washington: Brookings).

RUBIN, L. (1972) *Busing and Backlash* (Berkeley: University of California).

STAFF REPORT (1977) *School Desegregation in Kirkwood, Missouri* (Washington, DC: US Commission on Civil Rights).

VERGON, C. B. (1990) 'School desegregation: lessons from three decades of experience', *Education and Urban Society*, 23 (1), pp. 22–49.

VOLUNTARY INTERDISTRICT COORDINATING COUNCIL (1990) *Seventh Report to the US District Court: Eastern District of Missouri* (St Louis, MO).

POLITICS OF EDUCATION ASSOCIATION YEARBOOK 1991, 149–165

10 School decentralization and empowerment

Rodney J. Reed

School results for children of poverty – those forced by that poverty to live in inner-city neighbourhoods – generally indicate educational failure at a much higher rate than is seen for students nurtured by wealthier school districts. This failure in school severely limits chances of social and economic upward mobility, which translates into a waste of human capital for the nation's business–industrial–political complex, and dashed hopes, dreams and self-esteem for the individual. Parents and concerned citizens from across socio-economic strata, long aware of the general inadequacy of schools in poor communities, have demanded improvement, often seeking it through legal and political means. Important strategies among the various federal, state and local school reform efforts to make schooling a meaningful process for all students, and particularly the minority poor, are decentralization and citizen/parent empowerment, the focus of this chapter. The movement to decentralize school governance – an effort to place control into the hands of the people being served – has gained momentum and exists in some form in most large-city school districts today. An extension of administrative decentralization, citizen/parent empowerment is seen as one of several factors, including teacher and administrator preparation, curriculum renewal, school financing, and school restructuring, vital in the improvement of schools. A look at the meaning and scope of decentralization, operationalized through citizen/parent empowerment, and its probable effectiveness in improving school outcomes indicates that, alone, it is insufficient to ensure positive academic and social performance in school.

It is fairly well established that students who attend schools located in poor communities generally experience school failure at higher rates than their counterparts in more advantaged geographical areas. Comparisons of standardized test scores, dropout rates, suspension and expulsion rates, assignments to classes for remediation and for the educable mentally retarded, representation in college prep tracks, and college-going rates are painful reminders of the ineffectiveness of schools in economically depressed communities (US Commission on Civil Rights 1971, Astin 1982, Steinberg *et al.* 1984, National Coalition of Advocates for Students 1985, Arias 1986, Ekstrom *et al.* 1986, National Education Association 1987, Research and Policy Committee of the Committee for Economic Development 1987, Commission on Minority Participation in Education and Life 1988, First and Carrera 1988, Wilson and Justiz 1988, Goodlad and Keating 1990, Quality Education for Minorities Project 1990). The failure of these schools to produce well-educated students is ultimately manifested in high unemployment rates, broken homes, teenage pregnancy, engagement in crime, a high risk of early death or lengthy incarceration, diminished hope and aspirations, and for many, condemnation to a cycle of poverty from which there is little prospect of escape (Wilson 1987, Wacquant and Wilson 1989). Moreover, the loss of human capital for a nation that, in the coming years, increasingly will require the skills and talents of all individuals has raised concerns in the nation's business–industrial–political complex (National Governors' Association 1986, Johnson 1987, Research and Policy Committee of the Committee for Economic Development 1987, Carnegie Council on Adolescent Development 1989).

For the children whose proverty forces them to live in ghetto or inner-city neighbourhoods, school failure significantly limits their chances of social and economic upward mobility. Even for those who survive in school, the education they receive is likely to be inadequate. Yet these children do not enter school as failures. For the most part, they are eager and able to learn until what they experience in the school convinces them that they cannot, or should not, succeed academically, socially or economically. The devastation and devaluation of the human spirit which occurs in this process is incalculable, and the loss to the skilled work-force of this growing cadre of individuals has become economically intolerable.

Ultimately, these conditions must be addressed comprehensively, through a multifaceted approach involving health services, housing services, employment training, employment opportunities, economic development, community enhancement, human and social services, and educational services. Effective educational services, or schooling, while only one aspect of what is needed, nevertheless represents what should be an indispensable front against the forces which perpetuate the destruction of the desire to achieve among young inner-city Americans.

Parents and concerned citizens inside and outside economically depressed communities, however, have long been aware of the inadequacies of the schools indigenous to those communities and the effects they have had on children. Individually and collectively they have raised their voices in protest and have turned to the courts for relief (*Brown* v. *Board of Education* 1954, 1955, *Green* v. *County School Board of New Kent County* 1968, *Swann* v. *Charlotte-Mecklenburg Board of Education* 1971, *Larry P.* v. *Wilson Riles* 1972, *San Antonio Independent School District* v. *Rodriguez* 1973, *Lau* v. *Nichols* 1974, *Milliken* v. *Bradley* (*Milliken II*) 1977) and have sought to influence the educational decision-making process through political means (Mitchell 1988, Wong and Rollow 1990a 1990b). They know first-hand that these schools fail to develop within students the skills and knowledge that will enable them to grow and develop educationally, that will enable them to climb above the devastation and despair with which they live, that will enable them to be productive and contributing members within a global social and economic order, and that will enable them to enjoy a life of personal satisfaction and fulfilment. It is not surprising, then, that the Commission on Minority Participation in Education and Life (1988) proclaimed:

> America is moving backward – not forward – in its efforts to achieve the full participation of minority citizens in the life and prosperity of the nation.
> In education, employment, income, health, longevity, and other basic measures of individual and social well-being, gaps persist – and in some cases are widening – between members of minority groups and the majority population. (p. 1)

The fundamental issue is whether or not the widening gap between the 'haves' and 'have nots' can be closed. Related to that issue is another: can the educational system develop the human resources necessary to sustain the economic and social growth of the nation? These human resources must be developed within the population of the minority poor who, in the past, have virtually been written off. Because birth rates within this population exceed that of more advantaged populations (Hodgkinson 1991), their numbers among school-age students alone make it imperative that we find ways to develop and nurture the range of talent that is to be discovered there, a task entrusted to the schools.

In some major urban school districts, more than 50% of minority students leave high school before graduation, with neither skills nor behaviour patterns suitable for employment (Hirano-Nakanishi 1984, Hahn, Danzberger and Lefkowitz 1987, Ford Foundation Project on Social Welfare and the American Future 1989, Hodgkinson 1989). Concomitantly, a serious shortage of technically competent and literate workers skilled in problem solving and creative thinking will exist in the coming years unless we can change the current pattern of school failure (Research and Policy Committee of the Committee for Economic Development 1987, Carnegie Council on Adolescent Development 1989). Like the greenhouse effect, the crisis of schooling for poor and minority students now belongs to the present rather than the future. The long-acknowledged imperative to make schools and schooling effective for all students – regardless of ethnicity, gender, national origin, or socio-economic status – can no longer be postponed.

Improving the quality of schooling for all in general and the education of the minority poor in particular has been the *raison d'être* of several federal, state and local intervention reforms or strategies. Included among these are compensatory education, Chapter I, English as a second language programmes, alternative school organizational patterns, accelerated schools, magnet schools, school-business and/or university partnerships, decentralization and parent empowerment. Whereas all of these initiatives are important, it is the latter two strategies which form the focus of this chapter. Discussed here are the meaning and scope of these interventions, some experiences in their implementation and finally, a look at whether such interventions or reforms will make a difference in the outcomes of schooling for those students trapped in the economically depressed areas of the nation. These discussions are prefaced by a brief focus on general, broad-based views which have been used to undergird previous and ongoing attempts to effect improved school results for inner-city and other economically poor students – often referred to as disadvantaged and at-risk students.

Conceptual frameworks of previous attempts to improve schooling for disadvantaged and at-risk students

It is important first to note the definitions of disadvantaged and at-risk students as used in this chapter. The term 'economically disadvantaged' is used to designate students whose socio-environmental life circumstances are potential obstacles to school success, educational achievement, and the acquisition of the skills and attitudes necessary for employment and career and occupational advancement. By definition this population of students is heterogeneous with respect to race, national origin and gender. It is homogeneous in two dimensions: school failure and a disproportionate number of the poor. The term 'at-risk' is used to designate students whose profile suggests that they are likely to experience school failure and to drop out of school. Included within this population are pregnant teenage students, youth in single parent families and youth who are frequently the recipients of school punishment.

Four concepts have guided most previous attempts to improve school performance of disadvantaged and at-risk students: student deficits, student differences, effects of schools or effective schooling and early childhood education. A selective review of the literature in these areas illuminates the basic tenets which underlie each concept, assesses the effectiveness of the interventions derived from them and summarizes the criticisms they have generated.

Cultural deficit model

Past views of the disadvantaged have sought to blame the victim for school failure. In the 1960s, the argument was made that urban poor minority students experienced school failure because they were culturally deprived. This argument hypothesized that poor children were at a disadvantage because their culture did not provide the white middle-class experiences common to the student populations for whom the schools had been successful (Gordon and Wilkerson 1966, Bloom *et al.* 1965, McCone Commission 1965, Olsen 1965, Passow 1963). The minority child's cognitive capacity for school work was, it was argued, impaired because of deficits in the culture of the family as reflected in the lack of books, amenities and other forms of enrichment. Acting on this theory, schools, aided by federal funds, invested in programmes of remediation designed to provide culturally enriched activities such as trips to concerts and museums, compensatory education and Head Start programmes. Proponents of this approach defined cultural differences as deficiencies, and failed to recognize that poor, urban minority children and their families indeed have a culture. Not surprisingly, the cultural deficit concept was soundly criticized and eventually abandoned as a viable concept (Gay 1975, Ogbu 1978, Zigler and Anderson 1979, Hale 1980, Jones 1983).

Cultural differences model

An alternative thesis to this cultural deficit theory held that the failure of the schools to recognize and build on the cultural differences and strengths of minority students inevitably led to poor social and academic performance. For example, Labov (1970, 1972) and Johnson (n.d.) have written convincingly about the complexity of the language usage of African-American students in economically depressed communities and how teachers neither understood nor valued the language which grew out of the culture and family experiences of these students. In recognizing that all distinct social groups in America are bicultural, Boykin (1986) argues that African-American students face a triple quandary: they must negotiate concurrently the mainstream experience, the minority experience and the minority cultural experience. This dilemma is expected to exist for other minority groups as well.

Schools traditionally value mainstream experiences which derive fundamentally from Euro-American culture and treat any other cultural orientation as interior. Children in schools are often thought to devalue their own culture and to emulate Euro-American traditions (Bowles and Gintis 1976, Boykin 1986, Carnoy 1974, Ogbu 1978). Although there is considerable support for the idea that schools need to build on cultural differences, there is little understanding of how to bring cultural values into the classroom in a meaningful way (Gay 1975, Hale 1980). Whereas numerous studies have detailed the cultural strengths of African-American children (Banks 1981, Boykin 1986, Epps 1974, Johnson n.d.) and other minority children (Matute-Bianchi 1986, Ramirez and Castaneda 1974), little work has been done to assess the efficacy of multicultural education (Sleeter and Grant 1987). In part, this may account for the apparent failure to implement widely effective multicultural education programmes in the schools. However, other factors such as the lack of teacher knowledge about minority student cultures that are different from their own and a lack of will and commitment on the part of the school officials to incorporate multicultural education into the school curriculum must be considered.

Effective schools model

The effective schools research of Weber (1971), Brookover and Lezotte (1977), Rutter (1978), Edmonds and Frederickson (1979), and Edmonds (1979a, 1979b) demonstrates that schools for the urban poor can be effective. This research refutes the notion advanced by Coleman *et al.* (1966), Jencks *et al.* (1972), and Mosteller and Moynihan (1972) that familial characteristics are more important for student performance than are school effects.

Effective schools have been characterized as those in which there is strong and committed instructional leadership, clear goals, a school climate conducive to teaching and learning, close monitoring of student progress and high teacher expectations for student performance (Edmonds 1979a, Lightfoot 1983). Other scholars have affirmed these basic characteristics (Purkey and Smith 1983, Rossmiller 1987), and by 1983, more than 850 school districts located in 25 states had implemented effective school projects (Miles *et al.* 1983).

Although the effective schools formulation is intuitively compelling and important in calling attention to salient aspects of school practice, it remains theoretically and methodologically limited. Most studies on effective schools have been based on questionnaires, interviews and averaged student achievement outcome measures which have varied across studies and have usually been standardized or criterion-referenced test scores in computational skills or reading (Brookover *et al.* 1979, Purkey and Smith 1983, Good and Weinstein 1986, Zirkel and Greenwood 1986). In addition, as Stedman (1987) notes, the presence of the frequently used effective schools factors does not always signal successful school performance. Other criticisms of the effective schools research focus on the inconsistency or lack of agreement among researchers regarding the definition of an effective school (Brookover *et al.* 1979, Purkey and Smith 1983, Rowan 1985, Stedman 1987, Zirkel and Greenwood 1986); inappropriate comparison between extremely effective and ineffective schools (Purkey and Smith 1983, Rosenholtz 1985); the fact that longitudinal studies designed to establish causation between school or classroom variables and student performance are virtually non-existent (Rosenholtz 1985, Good and Weinstein 1986, Zirkel and Greenwood 1986); and the failure to establish the relative importance of school effectiveness variables (Rosenholtz 1985, Good and Weinstein 1986).

The effective schools research also comes under attack because most of the studies have been conducted at the elementary level and the generalizability of the findings is limited (Rosenholtz 1985, Good and Weinstein 1986); because of the lack of clarity or clear definitions of the effectiveness variables, e.g., a strong principal (Brookover *et al.* 1979, Zirkel and Greenwood 1986); and because of a lack of specificity regarding the length of time a school must display effectiveness or ineffectiveness to be included in either camp (Brookover *et al.* 1979, Good and Weinstein 1986, Purkey and Smith 1983, Zirkel and Greenwood 1986).

Although the criticisms of the effective schools research are well founded, they do not invalidate the notion that some inner-city schools are more effective than others in teaching economically disadvantaged students. Rather, the criticisms indicate a need to sharpen the focus of the research strategies used to examine effective schools so that scholars, school officials and policy makers can have more confidence in the research findings and their generalizability.

Early childhood education

At the heart of the early childhood education movement is the notion that early intervention in a child's life will lead to a solid base for later learning, strong self-esteem, and enthusiasm about school (Cahan 1989). As early as 1880, kindergarten was seen as an extension of the ideal home, with teachers assuming the role of surrogate mothers (Grubb

1987). The nursery school movement of the 1920s was based on the idea that professional teachers could enrich the learning experiences of even the most advantaged middle-class children. More recently, early childhood education and child care programmes have been strongly advocated for economically disadvantaged and at-risk children (Children's Defense Fund 1989, American Association of School Board Administrators and the National School Boards Association 1991). The longitudinal study of 123 children in the Perry Preschool Program revealed significantly improved high school graduation and employment rates for economically disadvantaged children who went through the programme, contributing to the present consensus that quality preschool education is a productive intervention (Berrueta-Clement *et al.* 1984).

In the past 20 years, the administration of early childhood education programmes for economically disadvantaged and at-risk students has shifted from federal to state governments. In 1988, 28 states funded, or were committed to fund, prekindergarten or parent education programmes (Warger 1988). In 1989, 30 states had funded early childhood education programmes (Trachtman 1991). However, since the decline in federal funding for Head Start, the commitment of public funds has been inadequate to serve even a narrowly defined eligible population. Consequently, the majority of economically disadvantaged and at-risk students begin formal schooling without the benefit of preschool education. The national Head Start project, for example, serves only one in five eligible children (Day 1988, Weikart 1989, Trachtman 1991), and it is estimated that fewer than 40% of 4-year-old children from families with incomes less that $10,000 are enrolled in preschool programmes (Children's Defense Fund 1989). Yet research evidence supports the efficacy of such programmes, not only in preparing children for kindergarten and first grade, but also for success in the later school years (Berrueta-Clement *et al.* 1984, Weikart 1989, Richardson 1990).

Summary

Previous attempts to improve the school performance of economically disadvantaged students have focused primarily on what were defined as the students' deficits and on school factors though to ensure effectiveness. It was taken almost as a given that the students' lack of exposure to middle-class values and activities and their use of non-standard language patterns (whether as members of a ghetto subculture with its own language usage or as immigrants with a primary language other than English) constituted inadequacies for meeting school demands and standards. The approaches used previously to improve educational outcomes for disadvantaged and at-risk students failed to give credence to their considerable and frequently unrecognized strengths and those of their parents, community members and school staff (Levin 1986). Parents, for example, manifest commitment and determination to serve as positive influences for their children. Many poor students begin eager to learn and to achieve, having a sense of collectivity and group-centred ethos. And some teachers are highly motivated and desire to improve their effectiveness in teaching disadvantaged students (Reed 1988).

The success of previous approaches has been limited for three basic reasons. First, many of the interventions were predicated on the notion of student deficits which, according to proponents such as Hunt (1969), Kagan (1973), and Denenberg (1970), did not provide a readiness and motivation for learning and intellectual development. Yet, it is clear that students may have different cognitive styles and adaptive propensities – including strong oral traditions of communicative competence, non-literate memory processes, implicit informal learning strategies, as well as broad extended-family systems of support – along with a number of other strengths which can be used to ensure school success.

Second, some of the interventions were isolated and singular. Such approaches usually fail to acknowledge the multiplicity and interrelationships of school community, family, classroom and individual factors which impinge on learning and school achievement, and they fail to address those interrelationships adequately.

Third, earlier interventions failed because they did not address both the heterogeneity of the disadvantaged population and the complex nature of the problems. Solutions to the challenges presented by a particular economically disadvantaged or at-risk group must be specific to that population and include a range of services and programmes both inside and outside the formal school setting. Schooling problems are not generally isolated abnormalities that can be solved simply through the addition of school-site resources (Sarason 1971). Although individual schools have important effects, they are part of a larger formal and non-formal educational system. Hence, school central office functions and decisions pertaining to school-site resource allocations, are inextricably comingled with the school and community environment and the expectations transmitted therein, school leadership, teacher quality, curriculum and instructional practices, classroom groupings, and school organizational and governance patterns. School reform must therefore be viewed as programmes of institutional or system change.

Both in-school and out-of-school elements and the interactions between them are important in shaping students' social development and academic performance (Reed 1975). There are, of course, out-of-school factors which schools can only attempt to counteract, such as historical and societal conditions which have constrained economic and social mobility to the point of creating what Ogbu (1978, 1986) defines as a caste system. When employment opportunities are proscribed by ethnicity, motivation to achieve becomes problematic. Nonetheless, there are significant school factors which can and must be addressed if schools are to become effective for all students.

At a fundamental level, schools must recognize that children from poor backgrounds are not characterized by cognitive deficits. They may, as Ginsburg (1986) posits, develop intellectual adaptations to their environment that are distinctive and different from those of non-poor children; however, they possess cognitive strengths and styles which research must confirm and on which schools can build effective programmes.

Schools must also recognize that the insistent question is not whether economically disadvantaged and at-risk students can learn, but rather how their aspirations for learning and achievement can be built on, raised or sustained. It is within this context that the press for decentralization and parent empowerment has been perpetrated, and these are the themes to which we now turn.

Decentralization: a shifting paradigm

The move from ward school boards to centralized city boards in the late 1800s represents a shift in power from neighbourhoods, many of which were working class, to more professionally oriented citizens; from broad-based representation and involvement in schools to a concentration of power in the hands of a few (Cronin 1973). Efforts to return the control of schools to the people, to the neighbourhoods, did not occur in any meaningful fashion until the 1960s primarily because of the push by minority parents and concerned citizens for high-quality integrated schools, particularly in New York City (Fantini 1970, Lopate *et al.* 1970).

In part, the move from ward or neighbourhood boards to single, centralized city school boards coincided with the growth in the size of cities and the greater demands placed on neighbourhood boards. This movement was also fuelled by calls for greater operational efficiency (Cronin 1973). It must also be recognized that since education is a function of the state, centralized boards were authorized to serve as local school district governing bodies within state law. Local school boards, therefore, as agencies of the state, are subject to administration and fiscal controls imposed by the state, to which they must adhere. The power of the centralized board has been tenaciously guarded and has been shared, in most instances, only when state legislative action has authorized it. The decentralization movement was thus an effort to share control, to dismantle centralized control either through administrative arrangements or the establishment of neighbourhood or community boards. More recently, decentralization has been advocated through school-based management schemes (Pierce 1977, Clune and White 1988).

The demand for decentralization is aptly illustrated by the events in the New York schools during the 1960s. Frustrated over the quality of schools in their neighbourhoods, African-American parents and leaders pushed for control of the schools as a political means to achieve improved educational outcomes (Fantini 1970). This struggle of New York neighbourhood parents and citizens to control the schools, and thus make them more responsive to their needs, set the stage for school boycotts and a series of teacher strikes over the issue of teacher and administrator selection and transfer (Fuchs 1966, Cronin 1973, Reed 1973, Schiff 1976).

In spite of the resistance of teachers and administrators to the legitimate demands of parents and leaders to improve the quality of schooling by assuming more direct control over the selection of teachers and administrators and the curriculum, the seeds of decentralization and community control had been planted. They were nourished by the democratic tradition of participation, the belief that decisions made closer to the client were more realistic and more responsive to local needs than those made from greater distances by individuals whose agendas and vested interests may have been different. They were also fed by the actions and support of study commissions funded by the Ford Foundation and subsequently legitimized by state legislative enactments.

It is instructive to note the title of the 1967 report of the New York City Mayor's Advisory Panel on decentralization which was chaired by Ford Foundation President McGeorge Bundy: 'Reconnection for Learning'. This report states, in its preamble, the basis for its recommendations to decentralize the New York City schools:

> In order to . . .
>
> - increase community awareness and participation in the development of educational policy closely related to the diverse needs and aspirations of the city's population,
> - open new channels and incentives to educational innovation and excellence,
> - achieve greater flexibility in the administration of the schools,
> - afford the children, parents, teachers, other educators, and the city at large a single school system that combines the advantages of big-city education with the opportunities of the finest small-city and suburban educational systems, and
> - strengthen the individual school as an urban institution that enhances a sense of community and encourages close coordination and cooperation with other governmental and private efforts to advance the well-being of children and others,

- all with the central purpose of advancing the educational achievement and opportunities of the children in the public schools of New York City. (Mayor's Advisory Panel on Decentralization of the New York City Schools, McGeorge Bundy, Chairman, 1969: xiii)

The Bundy report then goes on to recommend a plan for reorganizing the New York City schools in '... from thirty to no more than sixty Community School Districts... ranging in size from about 12,000 to 40,000 pupils...' (Section 3). These districts were to be 'largely autonomous', governed by boards of education both selected by parents and appointed by the mayor. A central education agency and a superintendent of schools would retain control over citywide educational policies and provide specified centralized services.

As might have been anticipated, the Bundy plan was criticized by community leaders concerned about its effect on school integration and the power of the mayor to appoint community board members. A revised New York Board of Regents bill, which called for 15 large districts, brought about the ire of teachers and administrators who were concerned with the power of community boards to transfer them from neighbourhood schools. Their concern was effectively highlighted by an action of one local board, that of Ocean Hill-Brownsville, which sent termination notices to six administrators and 13 teachers and referred them to the central board for reassignment. That action precipitated the New York teacher strikes of 1968 and ultimately resulted in a new compromise plan developed by the governor's office, calling for 30 to 33 community districts (32 were certified). While these districts could have elected local boards with control over elementary and middle schools and selected community superintendents, a central board and a citywide schools chancellor were to retain much of the power and control over all of the schools and exclusive control over the high schools. Local boards could, however, recommend budgets; select textbooks, subject to the approval of the chancellor; and administer a school repair and maintenance budget of as much as $250,000 (Cronin 1973, Fantini and Gittell 1973).

The threat to teacher and administrator due process and the sanctity of tenure were major rallying calls for teacher resistance to the desire and demands of local citizens to assume greater control of the schools and have them become more responsive to the educational needs of their communities. In reality, over time, 'some of these local boards have become patronage mills, fraught with political infighting' (Celis 1991: 14), and there is little evidence that overall school quality improved or that student achievement was enhanced (Schiff 1976). Nevertheless, the movement toward decentralized school districts gained momentum, and most large city school districts now have some form of administrative decentralization – the dispersion of central services to smaller administrative units (Ornstein 1980).

Empowerment: the Chicago experiment

Participation and citizen influence through decentralization as a means of effecting change and fostering reform, or of maintaining the status quo, remain important concepts in America (Bastian *et al.* 1986). The recognition by elected officials, business and corporate executives, professionals and parents that the quality of education, as measured by achievement outcomes and international comparisons, in many schools (particularly those serving poor communities) is inadequate has led to more vocal cries for involvement in the schools by citizens outside the education profession. Concern with the quality of education now reverberates from the lips of President Bush (1991), the National Governors' Association (1986), and the American Association of School Administrators and the National School Boards Association (1991). Since the issuance of the National Commission on Excellence in Education report *A Nation At Risk: The Imperative for Education Reform* (1983), literally hundreds of reform reports and school critiques have been written and disseminated. The message is clear: schools must improve and become more accountable; students must achieve at higher levels in the traditional areas of maths, science, English, history and geography. How this improvement should occur varies, of course, by advocacy group, although state-imposed curricular standards and state and national testing programmes will no doubt influence the content of what is taught. In Chicago, however, decentralization through community control is viewed as the engine that will drive the school improvement train.

The Chicago school district has embarked on one of the most far-reaching school reform efforts in the nation – the establishment of school councils with defined administrative and budgeting powers for each of the district's 540 schools. The plan calls for a central 15-member board of education and a superintendent authorized to carry out the central administrative functions of collective bargaining, systemwide personnel policy formulation and operations, and the management of district funds (Wong and Rollow 1990a, 1990b). Local school councils are composed of ten elected members (six who have children in the school; two community residents without children in the school, two teachers at the school; and the school principal, who has no vote in the principal-selection process). These local school councils have the responsibility of hiring the principal and negotiating a four-year contract, developing the school's educational goals, approving the school's budget, approving the school's curriculum and a plan to raise academic achievement, and making recommendations regarding faculty selection and teaching materials (Wilkerson 1991). The net effect of these responsibilities presumably will make teachers and principals more accountable to the local school council (Wong and Rollow 1990b).

The Chicago school reform plan appears to rest on two assumptions posited earlier by Katz (1971: 129): (1) that political change must precede educational change, and (2) the expectation that political change (community control) will foster pedagogical reform – children will receive a better education. There is yet another assumption embedded in the move to decentralize and toward community board or citizen empowerment, and that is one expressed 20 years ago by Rhody A. McCoy who, at the time, was district superintendent of the Ocean Hill-Brownsville district in Brooklyn, New York, an economically poor district whose actions to terminate and reassign teachers and administrators led to the New York teacher strikes of 1968. McCoy wrote, 'Community control means community growth and development, and the school is the hub of this growth' (1970: 171).

Whether, in the long run, the empowerment of citizens to become directly involved in the governance of the local school will ensure educational improvement and community growth and development remains to be confirmed. Before assessing this aspect, we first turn our attention to school site decentralization as a vehicle for school reform and improvement.

Decentralization: realistic expectations for school improvement?

Whereas a compelling case can be made to involve parents and citizens in the educational process (Comer 1980, Bastian *et al.* 1986, Henderson 1987), there are barriers to participation which may be difficult to overcome. For example, in many cases, because of the struggle to fulfil basic human needs, parents may not have the time to participate on local school boards or they may not have the means to provide home supervision to enable them to become actively involved in school governance.

On another level, tension is fostered when lay persons participate in the decision-making process in areas normally thought to be within the purview of professionals, e.g., what is taught. Educators, through professional associations, have advanced the cause of teacher professionalism considerably. One of the characteristics of a profession is that its members become intimately conversant with an identifiable body of knowledge that guides their decisions and actions. Presumably, lay individuals outside the profession are not as well prepared educationally in this regard, and thus are not viewed as being qualified to make decisions requiring professional judgement.

It is also the case that the influence and requirements imposed on schools by outside agencies and institutions (Cohen 1990) can be significant obstacles to local school governance. Curriculum requirements are influenced and mandated by state boards of education, by college entrance requirements, by standardized and competency testing programmes, by high school graduation standards and, increasingly, by the skills and knowledge articulated by the business community as requirements for its future work-force. Equally important, local community school boards do not have taxing authority to raise funds sufficient to operate schools. Because they are dependent on authorized budget allocations from centralized boards, they may be constrained in their ability to implement programmes or strategies that require sustained and substantial new funds. Notwithstanding these obstacles, it is unlikely that school improvement will occur without the meaningful involvement of parents (Comer 1980, 1986).

Participation of parents who traditionally have been excluded from school governance functions is in itself a reform of significant magnitude. Through such meaningful participation, it is not unrealistic to expect that the chasm of alienation that has existed between school personnel and parents in poor communities can be lessened. But as a panacea for bringing about improved school performance, school site decentralization must be viewed as only one component of a much broader array of interventions, including teacher and administrator preparation, curriculum renewal, school financing and school restructuring.

It must be acknowledged that there frequently is but one unifying characteristic in economically poor communities – poverty. Thus, clear agreement on educational goals, what should be taught, how it should be taught and who should teach it – all of which have implications for who should be hired as teachers and as principals – is unlikely given the diverse experiential and educational backgrounds of individuals within these communities. Moreover, it may be unrealistic to expect newly elected local boards to have the experience necessary to ensure that resource allocations are consistent with desired outcomes. Furthermore, the same differing human propensities for power and influence that exist in other groups will surely be present in these boards. In fact, previous results from administrative decentralization at the regional level (e.g., in New York and Detroit) suggest that the problems of decentralization at the school-site level through local school boards may be similar.

It is revealing to note a recent *New York Times* article regarding the Chicago decentralization plan which states:

> What began as a revolution born of hope and desperation has become a tug-of-war for many of the local school councils as they struggle against a resistant central office, intransigent principals, factional fighting on the councils themselves and major setbacks that have put into question their very place in the school system. (Wilkerson 1991: 1)

The article goes on to point out the overly political dimensions of the Chicago experience and that school councils have spent much of their time dealing with the system and little on school achievement: 'Indeed, student test scores have stagnated since decentralization went into effect, and the dropout rate has risen from 40 per cent before the councils took office to 46 per cent last year' (Wilkerson 1991: 1). Quoting Gary Orfield, professor of political science at the University of Chicago, the article then goes on to state:

> There is enough divisiveness that now bitterness is beginning to be directed at the councils as much as at the bureaucracy. The councils are becoming part of the status quo. Anybody that's around gets blamed for the catastrophe. (Wilkerson 1991: 14)

The authorization of school-site decentralization in Chicago by the Illinois state legislature may have been a political solution for school accountability, but as an educational initiative to address pressing problems related to school performance, it may be an inadequate move (Schiff 1976, Wohlstetter and McCurdy 1991).

Community development

Can schools alone make the desert bloom? Can good schools play a pivotal role in transforming communities, as suggested by McCoy? Whereas good schools are clearly necessary in all communities, the level of economic deprivation to be found in inner-city communities requires, if there is to be a positive difference, a massive infusion of money for health care and housing development, meaningful employment opportunities (which are virtually non-existent), and a general infrastructure that would assist student and parental aspirations to be realized. Unfortunately, there is little on the horizon to suggest that such changes will occur in the near future. Thus, schooling in such communities represents a way out for students, rather than an agency for community development. Yet, as a part of a larger socio-economic system, good schools are important for long-term community growth and development.

Conclusion

Herbert George Wells wrote, in *The Outline of History* (1920), 'Human history becomes more and more a race between education and catastrophy' (p. 594). Education must become effective for the many students, disproportionately minority and poor, who experience failure in the nation's schools. This population increasingly will be relied on for the nation's future work-force, its economic sustenance, and its leadership. If we are unable to improve educational outcomes and win the educational race for all, then we may indeed be heading for the catastrophe Wells observes.

School decentralization, local control of schools, citizen empowerment and choice schemes as discussed elsewhere in this volume, individually or collectively, are insufficient to reform schools in ways which will bring positive results for all students. At a fundamental level, very serious and penetrating discussions must focus on the purposes of schooling, the relationship of formal schooling to out-of-school educational opportunities, the organization and structure of schools and their financing, and on how we prepare the educational professionals who staff them.

A complex of interrelated factors influences students' academic and social performance in school. Although the teacher assumes a pivotal role, student performance outcomes cannot be viewed solely in the context of teacher–student interaction patterns. Student expectations for school performance are also shaped by the influences of curriculum, school administrators and other related staff, parents and community members, the attitudes and values of society at large, peer groups, the school's culture and the student's own motivation. Arrangements which focus on governance patterns and empowerment strategies alone are not likely to engage the range of issues which educational theorists and policy makers must address if school reform is to be meaningful for the urban poor.

References

AMERICAN ASSOCIATION OF SCHOOL BOARD ADMINISTRATORS AND NATIONAL SCHOOL BOARDS ASSOCIATION (1991) 'Ten strategies for improvement', in American Association of School Board Administrators and National School Boards Association, *Beyond the Schools* (Arlington, VA: AASBA; Alexandria, VA: NSBA), pp. 18–28.

ARIAS, M. B. (1986) 'The context of education for hispanic students: an overview', *American Journal of Education*, 95, pp. 26–57.

ASTIN, A. S. (1982) *Minorities in American Higher Education* (San Francisco, CA: Jossey Bass).

BANKS, J. (1981) *Multiethnic Education: Theory and Practice* (Boston, MA: Allyn and Bacon).

BASTIAN, A. *et al.* (1986) *Choosing Equality: The Case for Democratic Schooling* (Philadelphia, PA: Temple University Press).

BERRUETA-CLEMENT, J. R. *et al.* (1984) *Changed Lives: The Effects of the Perry Preschool Program on Youths through Age 19*, Monographs of the High/Scope educational research foundation (Ypsilanti, MI: High/Scope Press).

BLOOM, B. S., DAVIS, A. and HESS, R. (1965) *Compensatory Education for Cultural Deprivation* (New York: Holt, Rinehart, and Winston).

BOWLES, S. and GINTIS, H. (1976) *Schooling in Capitalist America* (New York: Basic Books).

BOYKIN, A. (1986) 'The triple quandary and the schooling of Afro-American children', in U. Neisser (ed.) *The School Achievement of Minority Children: New Perspectives* (Hillsdale, NJ: Lawrence Erlbaum).

BROOKOVER, W. *et al.* (1979) *School Social Systems and Student Achievement: Schools Can Make a Difference* (New York: Frederick A. Praeger).

BROOKOVER, W. B. and LEZOTTE, L. W. (1977) *Changes in School Characteristics Coincident with Changes in School Achievement* (East Lansing, MI: Michigan State University, College of Urban Development).

Brown v. *Board of Education (Brown I)*, 347 US 483 (1954, 1955).

BUSH, G. (1991) *America 2000: An Education Strategy* (Washington, DC: US Department of Education).

CAHAN, Emily D. (1989) *Past Caring, A History of US Preschool Care and Education for the Poor, 1820–1965* (New York: National Center for Children in Poverty, Columbia University).

CARNEGIE COUNCIL ON ADOLESCENT DEVELOPMENT (1989) *Turning Points: Preparing American Youth for the 21st Century* (New York: The Carnegie Corporation).

CARNOY, M. (1974) *Education as Cultural Imperialism* (New York: D. McKay).

CELIS, William, III (1991) 'More schools being run by local panels', *New York Times* CXL, 48, 647, p. 14.

CHILDREN'S DEFENSE FUND (1989) *A Children's Defense Budget* (Washington, DC: Author).

CLUNE, W. H. and WHITE, P. A. (1988) *School-based Management: Institutional Variation, Implementation, and Issues for Further Research* (New Brunswick, NJ: Center for Policy Research in Education, Rutgers University).

COHEN, D. (1990) 'Governance and instruction: the promise of decentralization and choice', in W. H. Clune and J. F. Witte (eds), *Choice and Control in American Education*, Vol 1, *The Theory of Choice and Control in Education* (London: Falmer Press), pp. 337–386.

COLEMAN, J. S. *et al.* (1966) *Equality of Educational Opportunity* (Washington, DC: US Government Printing).

COMER, J. P. (1980) *School Power* (New York: The Free Press).

COMER, J. P. (1986) 'Parent participation in schools', *Phi Delta Kappan*, 67(6), pp. 442–446.

COMMISSION ON MINORITY PARTICIPTION IN EDUCATION AND LIFE (1988) *One-third of a Nation*, a Coleman report (Washington, DC: American Council on Education and Education Commission of the States).

CRONIN, J. M. (1973) *The Control of Urban Schools* (New York: The Free Press).

DAY, B. D. (1988) 'What's happening in early childhood programs across the United States', in C. Warger (ed.) *A Resource Guide to Public School Early Childhood Programs* (Alexandria, VA: Association for Supervision and Curriculum Development).

DENENBURG, V. A. (1970) *Education of the Infant and Young Child* (New York: Academic Press).

EDMONDS, R. (1979a) 'Effective schools for the urban poor', *Educational Leadership*, 37, pp. 57–62.

EDMONDS, R. (1979b) 'Some schools work and more can', *Social Policy*, 9(5), pp. 28–32.

EDMONDS, R. R. and FREDERICKSON, J. R. (1979) *Search for Effective Schools: The Identification and Analysis of City Schools That Are Instructionally Effective for Poor Children*, ERIC Document 170 396.

EKSTROM, R. B. *et al.* (1986) 'Who drops out of high school and why?', *Teachers College Record*, 87, pp. 356–373.

EPPS, E. (1974) *Cultural Pluralism* (Berkeley, CA: McCutchan).

FANTINI, M. D. (1970) 'Community control and quality education in urban schools', in H. M. Levin (ed.) *Community Control of Schools* (Washington, DC: The Brookings Institution), pp. 40–75.

FANTINI, M. and GITTELL, M. (1973) *Decentralization: Achieving Reform* (New York: Frederick A. Praeger).

FIRST, J. M. and CARRERA, J. W. (1988) *New Voices: Immigrant Students in US Public Schools* (Boston, MA: National Coalition of Advocates for Students).

FORD FOUNDATION PROJECT ON SOCIAL WELFARE AND THE AMERICAN FUTURE (1989) *The Common Good, Social Welfare and the American Future* (New York: Ford Foundation).

FUCHS, E. (1966) *Pickets at the Gates* (New York: The Free Press).

GAY, G. (1975) 'Cultural differences important in the education of black children', *Momentum*, 6, pp. 30–33.

GINSBURG, H. P. (1986) 'The myth of the deprived child: new thoughts on poor children', in U. Neisser (ed.) *The School Achievement of Minority Children: New Perspectives* (Hillsdale, NJ: Lawrence Erlbaum).

GOOD, T. L. and WEINSTEIN, R. S. (1986) 'Schools make a difference: evidence, criticisms, and new directions', *American Psychologist*, 41, pp. 1090–1097.

GOODLAD, J. I. and KEATING, P. (eds) (1990) *Access to Knowledge, An Agenda for Our Nation's Schools* (New York: College Entrance Examination Board).

GORDON, E. W. and WILKERSON, D. A. (1966) *Compensatory Education for the Disadvantaged* (New York: College Entrance Examination Board).

Green v. *County School Board of New Kent County*, 391 US 430 (1968).

GRUBB, W. N. (1987) *Young Children Face the States: Issues and Options for Early Childhood Programs* (New Brunswick, NJ: Center for Policy Research in Education, Rutgers University).

HAHN, A., DANZBERGER, J. and LEFKOWITZ, B. (1987) *Dropouts in America, Enough Is Known for Action* (Washington, DC: Institute for Educational Leadership).

HALE, J. (1980) 'Demythicizing the education of black children', in R. Jones (ed.) *Black Psychology*, 2nd edn. (New York: Harper and Row).

HENDERSON, A. T. (ed.) (1987) *The Evidence Continues to Grow: Parent Involvement Improves Student Achievement* (Columbia, MD: The National Committee for Citizens in Education).

HIRANO-NAKANISHI, M. (1984) *Hispanic School Dropouts: The Extent and Relevance of Pre-high School Attrition and Delayed Education* (Los Alamitos, CA: National Center for Bilingual Research).

HODGKINSON, H. (1989) *The Same Client: The Demographics of Education and Service Delivery Systems* (Washington, DC: Institute for Educational Leadership, Center for Demographic Policy).

HODGKINSON, H. L. (1991) 'How schools and communities must collaborate to solve the problems facing America's youth', in American Association of School Administrators and National School Boards Association, *Beyond the Schools* (Arlington, VA: AASA; Alexandria, VA: NSBA), pp 1–17.

HUNT, J. McV. (1969) *The Challenge of Incompetence and Poverty: Papers on the Role of Early Education* (Urbana, IL: University of Illinois Press).

JENCKS, C. *et al.* (1972) *Inequality* (New York: Basic Books).

JOHNSON, K. (n.d.) *Teaching the Culturally Disadvantaged: A Rational Approach* (Palo Alto, CA: Science Research Associates, College Division).

JOHNSON, W. B. (1987) *Workforce 2000: Work and Workers for the Twenty-first Century* (Indianapolis, IN: Hudson Institute).

JONES, J. M. (1983) 'The concept of race in social psychology: From color to culture', in L. Wheeler and P. Shaver (eds) *Review of Personality and Social Psychology*, Vol. 4, (Beverly Hills, CA: Sage), pp. 117–150.

KAGAN, J. (1973) 'What is intelligence?', *Social Policy*, 4(1), pp. 88–94.

KATZ, M. B. (1971) *Class, Bureaucracy and Schools: The Illusion of Educational Change in America* (New York: Frederick A. Praeger).

LABOV, W. (1970) 'The logic on nonstandard English', in F. Williams (ed.) *Language and Poverty* (Chicago: Markham), pp. 153–189.

LABOV, W. (1972) *Language in the Inner City* (Philadelphia: University of Pennsylvania Press).

Larry P. v. *Wilson Riles*, 343 F Supp. 1306 (N.D. Cal. 1972); No. C-71-2270 RFP (Oct. 1979), Order Modifying Judgement (Sept. 1986).

Lau v. *Nichols*, 414 US 563 (1974).

LEVIN, H. M. (1986) *Educational Reform for Disadvantaged Students: An Emerging Crisis* (Washington, DC: National Education Association).

LIGHTFOOT, S. L. (1983) *The Good High School: Portraits of Character and Culture* (New York: Basic Books).

LOPATE, C. *et al.* (1970) 'Decentralization and community participation in public education', *Review of Educational Research*, 40(1), pp. 135–150.

MATUTE-BIANCHI, M. (1986) 'Ethnic identities and patterns of school success', *American Journal of Education*, 95(1), pp. 233–255.

MAYOR'S ADVISORY PANEL ON DECENTRALIZATION OF THE NEW YORK CITY SCHOOLS (1969) *Reconnection for Learning: A Community School System for New York City Schools* (New York: Frederick A. Praeger).

MCCONE COMMISSION (1965) *Violence in the City – An End or a Beginning* (Los Angeles: College Book Store).

MCCOY, R. A. (1970) 'The formation of a school district', in H. M. Levin (ed.) *Community Control of Schools* (Washington, DC: The Brookings Institution), pp. 169–190.

MILES, M. B., FARRAR, E. and NEUFELD, B. (1983) *The Extent of Adoption of Effective Schools Programs*, report prepared for the National Commission on Excellence in Education (Cambridge, MA: Huron Institute).

Milliken v. *Bradley (Milliken II)*, 433 US 267 (1977).

MITCHELL, W. Pearl (1988) 'Interest groups in conflict: Equality of education, 1954–1979,' unpublished doctoral dissertation, University of California, Berkeley, CA.

MOSTELLER, F. and MOYNIHAN, D. P. (eds) (1972) *On Equality of Educational Opportunity* (New York: Random House).

NATIONAL COALITION OF ADVOCATES FOR STUDENTS, BOARD OF INQUIRY (1985) *Barriers to Excellence: Our Children at Risk* (Boston, MA: National Coalition of Advocates for Students).

NATIONAL COMMISSION ON EXCELLENCE IN EDUCATION (1983) *A Nation at Risk: The Imperative for Educational Reform* (Washington, DC: US Government Printing Office).

NATIONAL EDUCATION ASSOCIATION (1987) *Hispanic Concerns*, study commission report (Washington, DC: National Education Association).

NATIONAL GOVERNORS' ASSOCIATION (1986) *Time for Results: The Governors' 1991 Report on Education* (Washington, DC: National Governors' Association Center for Policy and Analysis).

OGUB, J. U. (1978) *Minority Education and Caste: The American System in Cross-cultural Perspective* (New York: Academic Press).

OGBU, J. U. (1986) 'Consequences of the American caste system', in U. Neisser (ed.) *The School Achievement of Minority Children: New Perspectives* (Hillsdale, NJ: Lawrence Erlbaum).

OLSEN, J. (1965) 'Challenge of the poor to the schools', *Phi Delta Kappan*, 46, pp. 79–84.

ORNSTEIN, A. C. (1980) 'Decentralization and community participation policy of big school systems', *Phi Delta Kappan*, 62(4), pp. 255–257.

PASSOW, H. A. (ed.) (1963) *Education in Depressed Areas* (New York: Teachers College, Columbia University).

PIERCE, L. C. (1977) *School-site Management* (Palo Alto, CA: Aspen Institute for Humanities Studies).

PURKEY, S. C. and SMITH, M. S. (1983) 'Effective schools: a review', *Elementary School Journal*, 83, pp. 427–452.

QUALITY EDUCATION FOR MINORITIES PROJECT (1990) *Education that Works: An Action Plan for the Education of Minorities* (Cambridge, MA: Massachusetts Institute of Technology).

RAMIREZ, M., III and CASTANEDA, A. (1974) *Cultural Democracy, Bicognitive Development, and Education* (New York: Academic Press).

REED, R.J. (1973) 'The community school board', *School Review* 81(3), pp. 357–364.

REED, R.J. (1975) 'Ethnicity, social class, and out-of-school educational opportunities', *The Journal of Negro Education*, XLIV(3), pp. 316–334.

REED, R.J. (1988) 'Education and achievement of young black males', in J.T. Gibbs (ed.) *Young, Black, and Male in America: An Endangered Species* (Doves, MA: Auburn House).

RESEARCH AND POLICY COMMITTEE OF THE COMMITTEE FOR ECONOMIC DEVELOPMENT (1987) *Children in Need: Investment Strategies for the Educationally Disadvantaged* (New York: Committee for Economic Development).

RICHARDSON, V. (1990) 'At-risk programs: evaluation and critical inquiry', in K.A. Sirotnik (ed.) *Evaluation and Social Justice: Issues in Public Education* (San Francisco, CA: Jossey-Bass), pp. 61–75.

ROSENHOLTZ, S.J. (1985) 'Effective schools: interpreting the evidence', *American Journal of Education*, 93, pp. 352–388.

ROSSMILLER, R.A. (1987) 'Achieving equity and effectiveness in schooling', *Journal of Education Finance*, 4, pp. 561–577.

ROWNA, B. (1985) 'The assessment of school effectiveness', in R.M.J. Kyle (ed.) *Research for Excellence: An Effective Schools Sourcebook* (Washington, DC: US Government Printing Office, National Institute of Education).

RUTTER, M. (1978) *Fifteen Thousand Hours: Secondary Schools and Their Effects on Children* (Cambridge, MA: Harvard University Press).

San Antonio Independent School District v. *Rodriguez*, 411 US 1 (1973).

SARASON, S. (1971) *The Culture of School and the Problem of Change* (Boston, MA: Allyn and Bacon).

SCHIFF, M. (1976) 'The educational failure of community control in inner-city New York', *Phi Delta Kappan*, 57(6), pp. 375–378.

SLEETER, C.E. and GRANT, C.A. (1987) 'An analysis of multicultural education in the United States', *Harvard Educational Review*, 57, pp. 421–443.

STEDMAN, L.C. (1987) 'It's time we changed the effective schools formula', *Phi Delta Kappan*, 69, pp. 215–224.

STEINBERG, L., BLINDE, P.L. and CHAN, K.S. (1984) 'Dropping out among language minority youth', *Review of Educational Research*, 54, pp. 113–132.

Swann v. *Charlotte-Mecklenburg Board of Education*, 402 US 1 (1971).

TRACHTMAN, R. (1991) 'Early childhood education and child care: issues of at-risk children and families', *Urban Education*, 26(1), pp 25–42.

US COMMISSION ON CIVIL RIGHTS (1971) *The Unfinished Education, Report II* (Washington, DC: US Government Printing Office).

WACQUANT, L.J.D. and WILSON, W.J. (1989) 'The cost of racial and class exclusion in the inner city', Annals of the American Academy of Political and Social Science, 501, pp. 8–25.

WARGER, J. (ed.) (1988) *A Resource Guide to Public School Early Childhood Programs* (Alexandria, VA: Association for Supervision and Curriculum Development).

WEBER, G. (1971) *Inner City Children Can Be Taught to Read: Four Successful Schools* (Washington, DC: Council for Basic Education).

WEIKART, D. (1989) 'Quality preschool programs: A longterm social investment', *Occasional Paper Number 5*, ERIC Document No. 312 033.

WELLS, H.G. (1920) *The Outline of History*, vol. 2 (New York: The Macmillan Company).

WILKERSON, I. (1991) 'Politics trip up Chicago school revolution', *New York Times*, CXL, 48, 647, pp. 1, 14.

WILSON, R. and JUSTIZ, M.J. (1988) 'Minorities in higher education: confronting a time bomb', *Educational Record*, 68/69, pp. 9–14.

WILSON, W.J. (1987) *The Truly Disadvantaged: The Inner City, the Underclass, and Public Policy* (Chicago, IL: The University of Chicago Press).

WOHLSTETTER, P. and MCCURDY, K. (1991) 'The link between school decentralization and school politics', *Urban Education*, 25(4), pp. 391–414.

WONG, K.K. and ROLLOW, S.G. (1990a) 'A case study of the recent Chicago school reform, Part I: The mobilization phase', *Administrator's Notebook*, 34(5), pp. 1–6.

WONG, K.K. and ROLLOW, S.G. (1990b) 'A case study of the recent Chicago school reform, Part II: Conflict and compromise in the final legislative phase', *Administrator's Notebook*, 34(6), pp. 1–4.

ZIGLER, E. and ANDERSON, K. (1979) 'An idea whose time has come: the intellectual and political climate for Head Start', in E. Zigler and J. Valentine (eds) *Project Head Start: A Legacy of War on Poverty* (New York: The Free Press).

ZIRKEL, P. A. and GREENWOOD, S. C. (1986) 'Effective schools and effective principals: effective research?' *Teachers College Record*, 89, pp. 255–267.

POLITICS OF EDUCATION ASSOCIATION YEARBOOK 1991, 167–179

11 *Politics and federal aid to urban school systems: the case of Chapter One*

*Carolyn D. Herrington and Martin E. Orland**

This chapter tracks the early effects of the 1988 amendments to the federal Chapter One programme on the policies and practices of four large urban districts (Atlanta, Chicago, Dade County and Dallas). Specifically, the article analyses reform efforts in the areas of programme co-ordination, parental involvement, school-wide projects and school performance accountability. Drawing on an historical analysis of the evolution of relations between the federal government and local school districts since the programme's inception in the 1960s, the authors argue that the apparently only modest impact of the 1988 reforms on the practice of Chapter One programmes to date is a result of a basic conflict between the intent of the reforms (to enhance educational effectiveness) and the political context as it occurs at the local level (an orientation toward bureaucratic and regulatory compliance).

Introduction

In 1988, four important provisions of the federal law governing Chapter One of the Education Consolidation and Improvement Act (ECIA) were changed in an effort to increase this programme's educational effectiveness. The Hawkins-Stafford Act amending Chapter One mandated 'programme improvement plans' in all schools with unsuccessful programmes, increased requirements for parent involvement and for programme co-ordination between Chapter One and regular instructional programmes, and made it easier for schools with very high proportions of poor students to use Chapter One as part of a comprehensive school-wide approach to educational improvement.

The Hawkins-Stafford amendments continue a 20-year federal tradition in the programme of relying on the policy instrument of regulation to influence the behaviour of states, school districts and schools. What most distinguishes these amendments from previous regulatory reforms, however, is their substantive focus. Earlier revisions to Chapter One's legal framework tended to centre on provisions for ensuring that programme monies were reaching their intended beneficiaries (low-achieving students living in low-income areas). The Hawkins-Stafford amendments, by contrast, attempt to use the policy lever of regulation to focus the attention of school districts and schools on Chapter One's instructional quality and effectiveness.

Given the recency of the amendments, there has been no national study to date of the impact at the district level. In the absence of macro-level data, the purpose of this paper is to track the early effects of the new Chapter One programme improvement reforms on the policies and practices of four large urban school districts. In each site, we examine the impact (or lack of impact) of the new regulatory changes in order to understand how the new requirements have influenced pre-existing administrative behaviours. In learning this, we hope to be able to make more general inferences about both the opportunities and

*The views expressed by Martin E. Orland are his own. No endorsement by the National Education Goals Panel should be inferred.

limits of a federal regulatory strategy for generating local attention to issues of programme quality and effectiveness.

The four urban school districts selected for study were Atlanta, Chicago, Dallas, and Dade County (Miami). All have had substantial histories with the Chapter One programme going back to its inception in the 1960s. Three of the four are among the largest ten districts in the country. All four have substantial mixes of race and ethnic groups. All four are involved in restructuring efforts: two in particular, Dade and Chicago, are involved in dramatic experiments in new government and management structures. Finally, all four are experiencing the fiscal and political stresses of urban life which have been accelerating over the last two decades (see table 1). Differences among the four exist in degrees of stress; responses among school administrators, district staff and constituent groups to reform efforts of the 1980s; and congruences of Chapter One priorities with state- or district-based initiatives.

Table 1. Selected characteristics in four urban school districts

	Rank order by[1] size of district Fall 1988	*Enrolment[2] Fall 1990*	*Eligible for free/[2] reduced price lunch 1987–88*	*Limited English[2] proficiency 1989–90*	*Percent[1] minority 1988*
Atlanta	43	60,711	69.5	1.4	N/A
Chicago	3	404,991	71.2	10.3	87.6
Dade	4	278,788	62.0	14.1	78.9
Dallas	10	132,730	70.2	16.7	80.9

Sources: [1]US Department of Education, National Center for Educational Statistics, Common Core of Data Survey, 1990.
[2]Council of the Great City Schools, 1991.

Data for this study were collected through a site visit to one district and from phone interviews with district staff involved in implementing Chapter One in the other three districts. Interviewees included associate superintendents for instruction, Chapter One programme directors and, when possible, research and evaluation staff and sub-district regional Chapter One programme directors. For each district, the interviews, lasting 60–90 minutes, were conducted using structured protocols. Follow-up telephone calls were placed to elicit additional information and verify responses. The interviews were conducted during the winter of 1990–91.

Background

Chapter One is the close cousin of Title One of the Elementary and Secondary Act of 1965, a cornerstone of Lyndon Johnson's War on Poverty. For 25 years the programme has been providing assistance to school districts for the purpose of delivering supplementary educational services to low-achieving students residing in areas with relatively high proverty concentrations. Chapter One serves over five million students nationwide, or about one out of every eight public school pupils. Nearly every school district in the country receives some support under this programme.[1] Urban school systems, however, tend to receive disproportionately large subsidies, since the funding formula is based heavily on local poverty rates. For example, a special analysis of programme appropriations in 1984–85 revealed that urban school districts housed 26% of all students in the nation but received 37% of all Chapter One funds (Birman *et al.* 1987).

Districts receiving Chapter One funds are required to target the assistance to schools with the highest concentrations of poverty. These schools in turn must then select for services students who are the lowest achievers (regardless of their individual family income), in the content area (i.e., reading, maths, language arts, etc.) designated for programme support.[2] Nearly all school districts provide Chapter One services in the elementary grades. Services to higher grade levels, while less frequent, are not uncommon. Programmes typically consist of remediation in reading and maths delivered to small groups of students (three to eight) on a daily basis for 30–50 minutes per day (Birman *et al.* 1987).

Chapter One is administered through state education agencies (SEAs) that are responsible for ensuring local compliance with all programme rules and regulations. SEAs review annual Chapter One applications and make site visits to monitor particular features of the programme. They also provide technical assistance to local districts in how to achieve regulatory compliance as well as how they might improve the quality of local programmes.

Regulations under Chapter One are both numerous and complex, providing standards for resource allocation (e.g., selecting schools and students), determining the content of programmes (e.g., conducting needs assessments, ensuring parent involvement) and programme evaluation. Districts are also subject to programme audit reviews (at both the federal and state levels) that could lead to fund paybacks should compliance violations be cited and sustained. Historically, large districts have been particular targets of federal compliance audits.

The well-developed regulatory framework for Chapter One was not initially present when the programme began in 1965. Regulations during the programme's early years were rather ambiguous about proper v. improper uses of Chapter One monies, and no infrastructure existed at either the federal or state levels to enforce compliance with the few standards that did exist (Bailey and Mosher 1968, Kirst and Jung 1982). The catalyst for regulatory tightening was the documented and well-publicized accounts by the NAACP Legal Defense Fund (Martin and McClure 1969) of programme monies going for 'general aid' to school districts rather than for targeted support to the educationally disadvantaged residing in low-income areas (Kirst and Jung 1982). Throughout the decade of the 1970s, groups such as the Legal Defense Fund, the Lawyers Committee for Civil Rights Under Law (LCCRUL) and other client-based advocacy organizations lobbied for the creation of stronger, more explicit, federal legal and regulatory standards to ensure that services to the programme's intended populations would not be sacrificed in favour of stronger constituencies within the school district.

These efforts proved almost uniformly successful in getting both Congress and the US Office of Education to build a tight federal regulatory framework around Chapter One (Kirst and Jung 1982). Prescriptive regulations were enacted or expanded in the areas of parent involvement, school and student selection, programme evaluation and school resource comparability, to name but a few. Systems were also created in each State Education Agency for monitoring local compliance with these regulations (chiefly through approving local applications and conducting periodic site visits). In addition, compliance monitoring was also conducted through site visits to states and school districts by the US Office of Education as well as federal compliance audits sponsored by the Department of Health, Education, and Welfare.

By the middle 1970s it was clear that administrative procedures for this programme were becoming institutionalized nationwide and that, in general, Chapter One programme services were reaching their intended beneficiaries (NIE 1977, Goettel *et al.*

1977, Peterson *et al.* 1986). Such procedures continued more or less unabated through the middle 1980s, even though some of the more prescriptive federal regulatory standards were removed when Chapter One was reauthorized in 1981. State and school district bureaucracies put in place during the 1970s to ensure that Chapter One was reaching the 'right' children generally behaved as though the old provisions were still in force (Birman *et al.* 1987, Farrar and Millsap 1986, Orland 1988). The behaviour of large urban districts proved to be similar to other local systems in this regard, although some marginal differences were noted.[4]

The 1988 reforms

When Congress considered the question of reauthorizing Chapter One in 1987, researchers and policy analysts were focusing increasing attention on the quality of instructional services being delivered under the programme. While studies convincingly showed that the federal government had succeeded in creating an administrative infrastructure that targeted programme services on the proper students (e.g., Farrar and Millsap 1986, Birman, *et al.* 1987), it was considerably less clear whether these students were benefiting much as a result of their participation. A 1986 study mandated by Congress to investigate the educational effectiveness of Chapter One concluded that the programme had small but positive short-term effects on the populations it served. The study also pointed out, however, that the achievement gains of Chapter One students did *not* move them substantially toward the achievement levels of their more advantaged peers, and that students who discontinued Chapter One gradually lost the gains they made when receiving services (Kennedy *et al.* 1986).

Other researchers questioned whether the programme's focus on regulatory compliance and fiscal integrity was sacrificing needed attention to questions of programme quality (Odden 1987), or encouraging districts to run 'clean' programmes at the expense of designs that were more likely to be instructionally effective (Smith 1987). The final report of the National Assessment of Chapter One (Birman *et al.* 1987: 176) suggests that '... strategies to improve Chapter One programs would involve incentives for administrators to pay more attention to the programme's quality and effectiveness'.

Congress and the Reagan administration were responsive to the idea of enacting new provisions in the 1988 reauthorization design to focus greater local attention on issues of programme quality and improvement. A broad spectrum of advocacy groups representing diverse constituencies (e.g., state educational agencies, the NAACP Legal Defense Fund) supported legislative provisions such as holding school systems and schools 'accountable' for the achievement outcomes of Chapter One participants.

A second reason for congressional and administration interests in programme improvement reforms was the absence of other types of issues to address. Historic concerns over the funding formula and regulatory compliance were not candidates for serious overhaul in 1988. No one wished to tamper much with Chapter One's basic funding formula which, by conveying universal benefits, had generated solid backing for the programme, through good times and bad, and from Republicans as well as Democrats. Nor was there any external impetus to change regulatory compliance provisions given their general acceptability among educators and continued success in facilitating service delivery to the intended target population (Birman *et al.* 1987). In this context, marginal regulatory reform to enhance programme quality was an appealing prospect; one that demonstrated constructive legislative and executive 'action', without alienating any of the programme's key constituency groups.

Four new provisions of the 1988 amendments in particular deserve mention in regard to improving the educational effectiveness of Chapter One programming:

1. *Program co-ordination*. One of the instructional weaknesses consistently identified in recent studies of Chapter One is the absence of adequate articulation between the services provided by the Chapter One specialist and that of the regular classroom teacher (Kimbrough and Hill 1981, Rowan *et al.* 1986, Birman *et al.* 1987). Congress now requires districts to assure their state education agency that their Chapter One projects '. . . allocate time and resources for frequent and regular co-ordination of the [Chapter One] curriculum . . . with the regular instructional program' (PL 100-297, section 1012). Increasing co-ordination between Chapter One and the regular instructional programme is also specifically noted as a potential area to be addressed in school improvement plans as well as in state programme improvement assistance (PL 100-297, sections 1020 and 1021).
2. *Parental involvement*. The new law did not bring back the former requirements for parent advisory councils, but it did stipulate procedures for involving parents in the Chapter One programme. These include written district policies for parent participation in the planning, design and implementation of Chapter One programmes and parent–teacher conferences with each Chapter One participant to discuss the child's placement and progress as well as how the parent can complement their child's instruction (PL 100-297 section 1016). As noted earlier, large urban districts were somewhat more likely to have retained their Chapter One parent advisory councils than other systems. It will be interesting to see whether these new provisions are effective in further energizing Chapter One parental participation.
3. *School-wide projects*. Responding to criticisms that Chapter One services in heavily impacted areas would be more effective if resources were targeted on improving the entire school instead of a subset of the lowest achievers within the school (see, for example, Smith 1986), Congress eased provisions for allowing such school-wide projects in schools where the incidence of poverty was 75% or greater (PL 100-297 section 1015). The new law, however, also requires that such projects develop an approved plan for how the funds will be used and that students in these programmes demonstrate, after three years, at least comparable levels of achievement to other Chapter One participants. It is assumed that large urban districts may be especially likely to take advantage of this new provision since most have at least a few schools with poverty concentrations at or above 75%.
4. *School performance accountability*. To prevent 'business as usual' in schools where Chapter One is not educationally effective, Congress is now requiring school districts to identify all such schools and develop and implement with them plans for programme improvement (PL 100-297 section 121). Large urban districts, with disproportionately high percentages of very low achievers, presumably will be especially affected by this provision.

The new provisions mark a new direction for the federal government toward Chapter One programme issues in encouraging close scrutiny of the programme's educational effectiveness. This focus on programme quality is encouraged through requiring certain process activities, (improvement plans and better programme co-ordination) and outcome analyses (identification of low-performing schools and comparison of students' progress with other students in Chapter One schools). However, the change in intent was not accompanied by a change in means. The federal government retains the same policy instrument utilized for the last 20 years in its administration of the Chapter One programmes, i.e., regulation. Documentation of compliance is still the primary mechanism by which the federal government is holding local districts accountable. For example, the second provision – parental involvement – is accompanied in the federal rules and regulations by three columns of suggested activities including convening parent conferences, informing parents of the programme objectives, training parents to work with children and many others. The problem, of course, is that a district could be in compliance by documenting its activities in some or all of these areas without necessarily changing the effectiveness of the programme.

Implementation of the 1988 reforms

The authors interviewed senior administrators with responsibility for Chapter One programming in each of the four districts. The primary question posed was: Are the 1988 amendments to the Hawkins-Stafford Act resulting in significant changes in the provision of Chapter One services? The answer in three of the districts was, clearly, no. In one district – Dade County – the amendments were seen as a catalyst for change, but on closer inspection, this was the case because the amendments further reinforced the directions in which the district was headed already.

In all four districts, respondents stated that the new provisions were not perceived as representing a major shift in policy for the federal government nor as requiring major shifts in programme direction at the local level. While stating that the reforms were on the whole positive and held promise for resulting in some achievement gains for students, none of the respondents saw the new provisions as resulting in major programme changes or realignments. At the time of the interviews, the law was two years old and the regulations had been out for over a year and a half. As an indication of the limited importance being attributed to the 1988 reforms, interviews revealed that many of the details of the law were still unclear to the district staff. On the other hand, in all four districts, changes that were occurring in the delivery of Chapter One programmes were attributed primarily to state and district policies oriented to meeting the needs of disadvantaged or at-risk children. The new federal law played only a secondary role.

With notable exceptions, one finds limited efforts to exploit fully the potential for programme improvement in the new laws. What emerges is a portrait of a highly stable, smoothly running programme, insulated from external pressures and cautious about changes that may disrupt the current balance of interests and power.

The next section of the paper looks more closely at the implementation of each of the four reforms separately.

Programme co-ordination: The programme co-ordination provision is a regulatory strategy to intensify the impact of the Chapter One-funded supplemental educational services by requiring better articulation with the student's regular instructional programme. The importance of viewing the student's educational progress as a whole was repeatedly stressed in the department's comments about the new 1988 provisions. For example, commenting on the requirement that local educational agencies include a review of the children's progress in the regular educational programme in their Chapter One evaluation, the department noted that it was insuffiicient for Chapter One children to make gains in the Chapter One programme if those gains did not translate into improved performance in the regular programme (US Department of Education 1989).

All four districts claimed to be pursuing integration of the Chapter One and regular instructional programme not only because of the 1988 federal provisions but because of the widely recognized benefits to the students. However, changes to date have been modest. Though a number of the districts were introducing other strategies, the 'pull-out' instructional model, which separates the Chapter One students from the non-Chapter One students, predominated.

In the main, programme co-ordination efforts preceded or exceeded the federal law. For example, in all four districts, the Chapter One teachers report to the building principal, not a Chapter One central administrator, a structural factor considered key to co-ordination among the two programmes. In Atlanta, local requirements for co-ordinating the regular and Chapter One programmes already existed, including collaboration among regular and Chapter One teachers in assessing students' progress. In Dallas, existing co-ordination requirements were more stringent than the new federal provisions, thus the federal provisions *per se* were having little impact. (It was reported that the additional paperwork required to document the programme co-ordination efforts for the federal government was strongly resented by the principals.)

Two districts were rethinking their instructional models in order to enhance programme co-ordination. Dallas was planning to increase the use of teacher aides and extend the length of the day. Dade was implementing a 'lead teacher' concept in a third of its Chapter One schools as part of its district-initiated teacher professionalization project. An important role of the lead teacher is to build strong ties between the Chapter One personnel at the school and the other school personnel. According to the Associate Superintendent for Instruction in Dade County, the district staff was trying to leverage the federal co-ordination provision into a mechanism to encourage principals to assign their best teachers as Chapter One teachers.

However, on the whole, the dominant instructional model was one of segregation. Most Chapter One students were 'pulled out' of their regular class for special supplemental instruction. Though some districts were planning to modify their reliance on 'pulling out', this was not necessarily as a result of the 1988 laws.

Parental involvement: All four districts retained the parental advisory councils in some form or another after the 1981 federal legislation repealed the requirement. Furthermore, all four districts were, on their own initiative, in some cases in very dramatic ways, increasing the role of parents as policy advocates and as teachers of their own children.

Atlanta and Dallas cited numerous examples of parental involvement being encouraged at the programme level and, through parent resource centres, home outreach activities, and equipment and materials loan programmes, at the level of the individual child as well. Dallas, for example, was conducting parent development programmes to enhance the effectiveness of parents as advocates for their children. In these two districts, there appeared to be much documentation of enhanced activity in pursuit of increased parental involvement; however, almost all of it seemed to be incremental extensions of existing strategies and there seemed to be no capacity in place to assess the effectiveness of the activities.

In Dade and Chicago, parental participation had moved beyond the more supplementary roles of assistance to the child and programme advocacy into more powerful and systemic roles of management and governance but this was not a result of the Chapter One programme. In Dade, the shared decision making/school-based management restructuring project carves out a major role for parents in policy and management decisions at some local school sites. In Chicago, parents comprise a voting majority of the newly initiated local school councils which are responsible for adopting school improvement plans, approving budgets and selecting principals. Thus, for Dade, the Chapter One initiatives were complementary to a more intensive role for parents in its site-based management and shared decision-making reforms and for Chicago, the Chapter One initiatives were virtually eclipsed by the much more pervasive role parents are playing in local school councils.

School-wide projects: Perhaps the most original of the reforms, the school-wide project provisions, directly addressed the concerns noted above regarding programme articulation and segregation of low-achieving students. The school-wide project concept allows the entire school to be the focus of the Chapter One supplemental efforts, not just a percentage of the students in the school. At the time of the interviews, only one district had pursued the option actively; the number of school-wide projects under way were negligible in the other three (see table 2).

Table 2. School-wide projects, 1989–90

District	*No. of school-wide projects, 1989–90*
Atlanta	3
Chicago	6
Dade	48
Dallas	3

Source: District administrators, personal interviews by authors, Winter 1990–91.

The Atlanta and Dallas districts, which has only three school-wide projects each, expressed considerable concern about the fiscal impact of serving all children in the school. Atlanta was allowing eligible schools to become school-wide projects only if their instructional goals could not be met otherwise because of the lack of additional classroom space. Dallas stated that it was not actively encouraging expansion of school-wide projects because the district could not afford more than a handful. Dallas was utilizing a computer-based integrated learning system for its Chapter One programmes and the staff development requirements were currently overburdening the system.

Dade County, alone, enthusiastically endorsed the concept and had 48 schools designated as school-wide projects. The appeal for Dade was that the school-wide approach reinforced the district's own orientation toward increased school-site management and deregulation at the building level. Dade County's self-initiated innovations identified the school as the unit of improvement and experimentation. Besides the 48 schools currently designated as school-wide projects, more were being planned for the upcoming years and expectations were high that the approach would produce student learning gains.

Within the law establishing the school-wide projects option, the federal government specifically encourages experimentation with alternative delivery models and lists two, serving pre-kindergarten students in Chapter One programmes and extending the length of the day for Chapter One students. Dallas was contemplating some use of the extended day and Dade had begun offering services to pre-kindergarten children. On the whole, though, we found limited enthusiasm in the districts for experimenting with alternative models.

School performance accountability: The school performance accountability provision was the most directive of the four new provisions in encouraging Chapter One administrators to analyse the effectiveness of their current approaches and, if outcomes are found unsatisfactory, to develop new strategies to improve performance. Presumably, the unwanted visibility brought to a school by failing to meet minimal standards of improvement and the actual process of developing a plan would lead to closer analysis of programme shortcomings and stimulate innovative or creative strategies for reform. However, the interviews gave no indication of this occurring. In three of the districts – Atlanta, Dallas and Chicago – school improvement plans were already required by either state of local mandate (or, in one district, both).[5] In a sense, school improvement plans were already part of the normal organizational apparatus and were not seen as threatening the status quo. In fact, in the main, the accountability provision was seen as another administrative requirement to be complied with. The additional paperwork was repeatedly cited as a disincentive.

Dade County was the only district that actively seized on the reform as an enabling agent, emphasizing that the reform did not just increase accountability but also placed more authority in the hands of the school-site administrator. Interestingly, Dade County expressed hope that the increased accountability required in the Chapter One programme might spill over to the regular instructional programme resulting in closer attention to all students' academic achievement.

The regulatory teeth in the school performance provision lies in the student achievement standards set by the state educational agencies. However, a recent survey of the state Chapter One offices indicated that, nationwide, states were opting for relatively low standards. One reason is that the states have limited capacity to deliver the technical assistance required for all schools not achieving the standards. Thus, the State Educational Agencies, another potential source of external pressure, are also reluctant to push too hard and are limited in their ability to provide assistance.

Insulation of Chapter One programme: Notably absent in the remarks of the district administrators about recent activities regarding Chapter One programmes in their district was any reference to interest groups in the community. Client-based advocacy groups such as the NAACP had been very influential in the early '70s in getting both Congress and the US Office of Education to build a tight regulatory framework around Chapter One (Kirst and Jung 1982). Also, in the 1980s business groups had been active in focusing attention on improving educational outcomes in many communities and in state governments.

However, with the exception of Chicago whose parent groups were politically well organized, no mention was made of outside groups pressing for reform in Chapter One programming. To check this impression, interviews were conducted with representatives of NAACP and the Urban League in the four cities to solicit information about their involvement in Chapter One policy development. Even though all had a slate of education issues, none identified the Chapter One programme as a priority. We also found no evidence of business or corporate involvement in Chapter One policy development.

Analysis

As has been established by other researchers, the Chapter One programme is well integrated into the political and organizational structure of most districts. The longevity of the programme, the stability of its funding and the tenure of its administrative and instructional staff compose a fixed and predictable programme. Information from the interviews provided no reason to suspect that significant design features of, or political supports for, the programme were being challenged or even reconfigured in any important way as a result of the 1988 reforms. All interviewees were aware of the 1988 changes to the law, but knowledge of the details of the law varied considerably. The reforms were viewed as marginal and incremental, not fundamental or restructuring (even though some staff did envision potential for more enduring change in the future).

The timing of the interviews, winter 1990–91, was almost two years after passage of the law. However, nothing of a dramatic nature had occurred yet as a result of the reforms. Only one district, for example, had chosen to pursue enthusiastically the option of school-wide projects. Enhanced parental involvement emanated from requirements of earlier Chapter One regulations or, in the cases of Dade and Chicago, were a result of district and state initiatives. School improvement plans were being crafted but for many schools this was just a repetition of an exercise already required by state or local regulations. One representative of the district staff commented that there may be more reaction and even resistance from school-based administrators if more attention is focused on the schools that do not meet their improvements goals, but that to date the reforms had provoked little resistance from school-level administrators. Attitudes toward the reforms were relatively consistent across all four districts. It was generally agreed that the reforms did create an opportunity, even if a modest one, to improve academic gains for low-achieving students. The reforms were also generally seen as creating an additional burden by increasing administrative reporting requirements at the classroom, school-site and district levels. In this sense, the federal objective of stimulating more critical scrutiny of the programme's educational effectiveness had occurred only marginally, if at all. No realignments of policy, administrative structures or service delivery had occurred as a result of the reforms.

Variation among the four districts in responses to the reforms appears dependent on the degree to which they aligned with existing local and state initiatives; federal leverage on the system was limited. The research on implementation conducted over the last two decades indicates the adaptation that occurs as policy objectives cascade down the mix of governmental levels and delivery-point providers (McLaughlin 1976). The federal initiatives were being circumscribed (or, in some cases, 'seized') by the local context.

In Atlanta and Dallas, the reforms were seen to be, at best, congruent and at worse, redundant with other district and state initiatives. The reforms were seen as a somewhat modest response to the acute stresses the school system is experiencing. Concerns about additional paperwork further reduced optimism about any significant impact to result from the reforms. In Dade County, the reforms aligned (and were nudged to further align) with the school-based management/shared decision-making restructuring campaign already in progress in the district. The tenets of increased accountability, school-wide decision making, and more parental involvement were prominent features of the district's reform thrusts. In Chicago, the local context also determined the implementation effects and context of the new federal reforms. However, in this locality, the local context overwhelmed and rendered insignificant the federal inititatives.

Conclusion

Why are the 1988 reforms not having a greater impact on the delivery of Chapter One programmes in the four districts under study? The thesis of this paper is that at least part of the answer lies in a basic conflict between the intent of the reforms and the political context as it exists at the local level.

The administrative environment that has grown up for the last 20 years around Chapter One (and its predecessor, Title One) programmes is one of regulatory compliance. The Chapter One programme administrative delivery system is the result of two decades of pulling and tugging among the affected parties and it has established a remarkably high level of accommodation among the groups. The amendments to the 1988 Stafford-Hawkins Act do not appear sufficiently dramatic to alter the political calculus as it has stabilized over the years at the local level.

To make the new reforms work, local administrators would have to be made to believe that they have more to gain than to lose by concentrating their attention toward programme quality. A continuing reliance on regulatory compliance may represent a lucid calculation on the part of local administrators of how to protect the programme from encroachment by other programmes or priorities within the district and avoid conflict between the district and the federal government. Habits of compliance-orientation no doubt change slowly even under strong pressures. Staying with a compliance approach provides the protection of a regulatory framework tested over time. The local administrators may be betting that they would have more to lose by risking an innovative approach whose outcome is uncertain than by introducing change to the system only when necessary, and then only gradually, and at the margin.

Finally, this situation raises the more general issue of how effective are the policy instruments currently available to government to force a focus on educational effectiveness rather than programme inputs. It is an issue many state governments are facing. What are the limitations of a regulatory approach? Can one stimulate introspection from the top with a local political context, developed over 20 years, that in the past has rewarded programme insulation and bureacratic compliance? The federal government was successful in changing behaviour of the districts in the early 1970s through the use of regulatory restrictions. However, it may be much more diffiicult for a government to encourage introspective and reflective professional habits through regulation. How can one document 'poor introspection'? What sanctions could one impose for 'not availing oneself of flexibility in the law' that would be as strong as those imposed for fiscal mismanagement? Given ingrained habits of compliance and unavailability of strong policy instruments to encourage innovation and experimentation, it may not be surprising that the 'shaking up' hoped for in Chapter One has not occurred yet.

Notes

1. To qualify, a system need only demonstrate that it has 10 poor students residing within their district.
2. Interestingly, despite the proportionately higher levels of student participation in Chapter One in urban districts, a typical school in an urban district is actually *less likely* than such a school in another type of district to receive Chapter One support. In 1985–86, 60% of elementary schools in districts enrolling 25,000 pupils or more (the great majority of which are urban) were Chapter One recipients. This compares to an average elementary school participation rate of 89% for all districts. The same pattern holds at the middle/junior high and high school levels (Williams *et al.* 1987). Several factors contribute to this phenomenon including almost universal district eligibility for Chapter One, regulatory

provisions allowing districts with only one school (or one school per grade span) to qualify automatically for the programme, and a desire among larger districts with severe compensatory education needs purposely to target greater levels of resources on their highest needs schools (and therefore fail to serve other schools that could technically qualify for the programme) in order to maximize the likelihood of overall programme impacts.

3. Throughout this section we use the terms 'urban interests' and 'urban constituencies' to refer to national organizations and interest groups who consider improving education in urban areas to be a significant part of their programme agenda. These include client-based groups such as the NAACP, Children's Defense Fund and the Lawyers Committee for Civil Rights Under Law, as well as more general-purpose interest groups representing the established public education system such as teacher and administrator organizations like the National Education Association and Council of Great City Schools.
4. The biggest differences between urban districts' behaviour patterns and other systems under the new Chapter One law were in the areas of school resource comparability and parent involvement. Urban districts found the pre-1981 comparability standards particularly onerous because they forced them to allocate instructional staff in ways that conflicted with their own resource allocation policies and disrupted regular school and classroom activities (Ellman *et al.* 1981). The proportion of large district (enrolling over 25,000 pupils) making resource reallocations under the new, more relaxed, comparability requirements declined from 16% (in 1981) to 8% (in 1986) (Birman *et al.* 1987). Conversely, large districts were somewhat *more likely* than other systems to retain Chapter One parent advisory councils (Orland 1988). In these districts, the parent councils were more likely to have been institutionalized as support mechanisms for the programme; channelling community demands in an efficacious manner (McLaughlin *et al.* 1988), and providing political support for disadvantaged programming within the educational bureaucracy.
5. Since the interviews, in May 1991, the state of Florida enacted statutes requiring improvement plans in all schools. So now all four districts have local or state requirements for school plans.

References

BAILEY, S.K. and MOSHER, E.K. (1968) ESEA: *The Office of Education Administers a Law* (Syracuse, NY: Syracuse University Press).

BIRMAN, B.B., ORLAND, M.E., JUNG, R.K., ANSON, R.J., and GARCIA, G.N. (1987) *The Current Operation of the Chapter 1 Program* (Washington, DC: US Department of Education).

ELLMAN, F., FERRARA, L., MOSKOWITZ, J. and STEWARD, S. (1981) *Utilization and Effects of Alternative Measures of Comparability* (Washington, DC: AVI Policy Research).

FARRAR, E. and MILLSAP, M.A. (1986) *State and Local Administration of the Chapter 1 Program* (Cambridge, MA: Abt Associates).

GOETTEL, R.J., KAPLAN, B.A. and ORLAND, M.E. (1977) *Synthesis Report: A Comparative Analysis of ESEA, Title I Administration in Eight States* (Syracuse, NY: Syracuse Research Corporation).

KENNEDY, M.M., BIRMAN, B.F. and DEMALINE, R.E. (1987) *The Effectiveness of Chapter One Services* (Washington, DC: Office of Educational Research and Improvement, US Department of Education).

KIMBROUGH, J. and HILL, P.T. (1981) *The Aggregate Effects of Federal Education Program* (Santa Monica, CA: Rand Corporation).

KIRST, M.W. and JUNG, R. (1982) 'The utility of a longitudinal approach in assessing implementation: a thirteen-year view of title I, ESEA', in W. Williams, R.F. Elmore, J.S. Hall, R. Jung, M. Kirst, S.A. MacManus, B. Narver, R.P. Nathan and R.K. Yin (eds) *Studying Implementation, Methodological and Administrative Issues* (Chatham, NJ: Chatham House).

MARTIN, R. and MCCLURE, P. (1969) *Title I of ESEA: Is It Helping Poor Children* (Washington, DC: Washington Research Project of the Southern Center for Studies in Public Policy and the NAACP Legal Defense Fund).

MCLAUGHLIN, M.W. (1976) 'Implementation and mutual adaptation', *Teachers College Record*, 77, pp. 339–351.

MCLAUGHLIN, M.W., SHIELDS, P.M. and REZABEK, D.J. (1988) *State and Local Responses to Chapter One of the Education Consolidation and Improvement Act, 1981* (Palo Alto, CA: Institute for Research on Educational Finance and Governance).

NATIONAL INSTITUTE OF EDUCATION (1977) *Administration of Compensatory Education* (Washington, DC: US Office of Education).

ODDEN, A. (1987) 'How fiscal accountability and program quality can be insured for Chapter 1', in D. P. Doyle, J. S. Michie and B. I. Williams (eds) *Policy Options for the Future of Compensatory Education: Conference Papers* (Washington, DC: Research and Evaluation Associates).

ORLAND, M. E. (1988) 'The black box and Chapter 1 policy: patterns of administrative behavior and their antecedents', presentation to the American Education Research Association, April 1988.

PETERSON, P. E., RABE, B. and WONG, K. (1986) *When Federalism Works* (Washington, DC: Brookings Institution).

ROWAN, B., GUTHRIE, L. F., LEE, G. L. and GUTHRIE, G. P. (1986) 'The design and implementation of chapter one instructional services: a study of 24 schools' (San Francisco, CA: Far West Laboratory for Educational Research and Development).

SMITH, M. S. (1987) 'Selecting students and services for Chapter 1', in D. P. Doyle, J. S. Michie and B. I. Williams (eds) *Policy Options for the Future of Compensatory Education: Conference Papers* (Washington, DC: Research and Evaluation Associates).

US DEPARTMENT OF EDUCATION (1989) *Federal Registry*, Vol. 54, No. 96, (Washington, DC).

WILLIAMS, D. I., THORNE, J. M., MICHIE, J. F. and HAMAR, R. (1987) *A District Survey: A Study of Local Implementation of ECIA Chapter One* (Washington, DC: Research and Evaluation Association).

POLITICS OF EDUCATION ASSOCIATION YEARBOOK 1991, 181–191

12 *Equity, adequacy and educational need: the courts and urban school finance*

Louis F. Miron, Patricia F. First and Robert K. Wimpelberg

Nearly two decades following the landmark *Rodriguez* decision in 1973, plaintiffs arguing on behalf of poor urban school districts have found an opening for financial redress. The supreme courts in several states, including New Jersey, Texas and Kentucky, have ruled in the last couple of years that all students are entitled to a 'minimally adequate' education. In *Abbott* v. *Burke*, in particular, the New Jersey court made reference to the special needs of inner-city students. In this chapter the authors trace the history of court cases related to urban school finance and analyse both the legal and conceptual basis for recent decisions that may benefit large-city districts.

Urban school districts lost out in the courts during the first round of state school finance reform. After the *Rodriquez* (1973) case was turned back by the US Supreme Court and district spending disparities in Texas were not found to violate the equal protection clause of the 14th Amendment to the US Constitution, a case in New York State (*Levittown* v. *Nyquist* 1982: 1983) was modified to raise an explicit argument on behalf of urban schooling. Plaintiffs claimed that the extraordinary competition for tax dollars for public services in urban districts like New York City made it significantly more difficult for urban than non-municipal districts to raise educational revenues. The problem was called 'municipal overburden'. Their petition was denied, however, as the New York Court of Appeals countered (and the US Supreme Court agreed) that, while urban districts are in competitive taxing environments, they are compensated by having access to additional sources of revenue not available to other kinds of school districts.

The earliest failure of the urban argument in state courts was re-enacted in Maryland (*Hornbeck* v. *Somerset County Board of Education* 1983) and Wisconsin (*Kukor* v. *Grover* 1986). Both states turned back petitions from their largest school districts, citing the *Levittown* court in their decisions. In losing the Maryland case, however, the plaintiffs extended the concept of overburden to include 'educational overburden' (or more properly, education-cost overburden), claiming that large districts with lower tax bases have the highest concentrations of students whose educational needs are the most expensive to meet.

The picture emerging in other states and over time, however, suggests that a partial reversal of fortune may be in the works. From the ashes of judicial failures in the first half of the 1980s and earlier, the seeds of new legal reasoning offer promise for judicial restitution for the educational costs and needs in America's largest cities. Certainly, few legal scholars are sanguine about the urban issues getting favourable attention from the *federal* courts; Verstegen (1990) is a cautious exception. Nevertheless, 'the judicial cauldron has continued to boil' in the state courts (LaMorte 1989: 3), and the educational conditions in large-city schools are producing a good bit of the heat.

In this chapter, we discuss the city systems' days in court and lay out the basis on which they appear to be gaining new ground. In the earlier period of state court cases, cities were unable to leverage the application of the principle of 'wealth neutrality' to their advantage and could not overcome the principle of 'local control' that protected state finance systems. However, a shift in judicial arguments that makes greater use of the principle of 'educational adequacy' has characterized more recent cases. Before describing the emergence of the adequacy construct, we lay out the context of disadvantages that have accumulated since the early 1980s for urban schoolchildren and their educators.

Worsening conditions in the cities

During the reform decade of the 1980s the balance among state, local and federal percentages of education funding shifted, on average, away from the dominance of local taxes to a stronger reliance on state revenue sources (Wong 1989). Furthermore, funding in both total and per pupil terms increased substantially during the 1980s. According to Odden (1980), the per pupil increase from 1980 to 1988, after adjusting for inflation, was around 30%. Hawkins (1989) reports that the funding gains were the result of a rising national economy together with strong state economies that provided the conditions for increasing revenues for governmental services, including education. Education support for children in urban schools, however, followed a dramatically different pattern.

Changes in federal and state aid to the cities

The general optimism of the 1980s hardly materialized for 'at-risk' children in urban schools primarily because of the changes in federal aid allocations. When the distribution of federal aid changed from a per capita categorical formula to the 'block grant' approach in 1981, the Council of Great City Schools (1982) – a coalition of the 28 largest municipal school districts – estimated that they lost 23% of their federal money in a two-year period (1980–81 to 1982–83). Davis and McCaul (1991) have documented that, between 1980 and 1989, spending on Chapter 1 decreased by 12%; on Chapter 2, by 62% and on bilingual education programmes, by 47%. These are the educational programmes designed to benefit 'at-risk' children (Levin 1988) – children who comprise the overwhelming majority of the enrolment of urban school districts and who are traditionally caught in a 'mismatch' between the resources of the home and community and the schools' expectations (Cuban and Tyack 1989, Levin 1988). Ironically, it is the original federal programmes of categorical aid that the New York Court of Appeals had in mind when it rejected New York City's argument for 'municipal overburden' by citing special revenues available to city schools that were not also available to non-municipal districts.

Not only have federal dollars been reduced, but those that have remained (and that at one time would have gone primarily to urban school districts) are now divided more frequently among all kinds of districts. In a review of the redistribution of federal funds, Monk (1990) found that the shift from categorical aid to block grants has benefited small districts in particular, because the allocational rules have relied more on student enrolments than special need as documented by socio-economic background. Monk notes, as well, that the switch to block grants has funnelled more federal money into private schools. He cites the state of Pennsylvania where block grants have lead to an increase of almost 150% in the money private schools have received from federal sources. Thus, while there is less federal money being spent on elementary and secondary schools, even less of that lower total is making its way to public schools in the largest cities.

The plight of some urban schools is hardly better when state funding is considered. Freedman (1990) shows that when the New York State Legislature apportioned its school aid for the 1987–88 school year, the largest concentrations of children needing the greatest number of special services were enrolled in New York City schools: for example, 80% of all state students with limited proficiency in English, 63% of those from impoverished families, 61% of those reading below minimum standards, and 54% of the handicapped. But for the 1987–88 school year, the neediest school children in New York State actually received fewer per pupils dollars than the less needy children. During political squabbles over its finance scheme, the New York State Legislature agreed on a formula in which each New York City pupil was counted as ninety-four one-hundredths of each pupil elsewhere in the state. Calling it the 'ivory soap solution' and recalling that the US Constitution once allowed a slave to be counted as three-fifths of a person, Freedman labelled this formula 'a perfect symbol of scorn: Financially or otherwise, New York City school children counted for less' (Freedman 1990: 115).

This formula brought $450 million less to New York City schoolchildren than they would otherwise have received. it meant in part 'that two in five high schools operated at more than 110 per cent of capacity and that the ratio of high school students to guidance counselors topped 600 to one, double the rate outside the city. A junior high school pupil had an average of twenty minutes during an entire year to discuss the choice of high schools with a guidance counselor, and 90 per cent of the elementary school students had no libarary available to them' (Freedman 1990:115).

Of course, the deprivations of urban children are rooted in problems deeper than those emanating from the schools. Urban scholars have begun to identify such sources as the restructuring of cities (Smith 1984, Fainstein and Fainstein 1989) resulting from global economic forces and internal demographic migration (Wilson 1987). Consequences for urban children are also exacerbated by federal policies since 1980 that lie outside the educational realm, policies that have largely benefited the middle and upper classes (Lemann 1991) whose proportions among city residents are comparatively low.

The anti-urban influence of the 'excellence' and 'effectiveness' movements

Besides the financial set-back for urban schools caused by new federal priorities that decreased aid to poor children, the 'excellence' and 'effectiveness' movements since the 1980s have also taken their toll. 'Excellence' has been rewarded in a variety of federal and state incentive programmes in the past decade or so. The problem it has posed for urban schools relates to the greater difficulty that urban schools have in garnering recognition that gravitates toward programme diversity and parental involvement that are easier for middle-class schools to accomplish. Further, the kinds of trademarks characteristic of 'schools of excellence' often result from institutions where the governance structure is unencumbered by large, multi-layered bureaucracies (Chubb and Moe 1988). Many urban schools have few if any children from the middle class, and they suffer debilitating inertia traceable to the large, complex organizations in which they are situated.

School effectiveness research has also muffled the argument for increased revenues for urban schools where it has been interpreted to mean that the amount of money spent on education should matter less than the organizational arrangements that determine how it is spent. Classic school effectiveness research compares schools that have similar student composition and community attributes but widely varying student achievement outcomes. Its goal is to identify the qualities and procedures internal to the high-performing school and to contrast them with similar aspects in less effective schools. Effective schools research, however, is misread and misused when its results are interpreted to mean that 'money doesn't matter'. Context differences among schools (by age range, size, urbanization, and socio-economic characteristics of the student body) redefine 'effectiveness' for each category of school (see Wimpelberg *et al.* 1989). Most important, effective schools research does not include interdistrict fiscal equity among the issues it addresses. Thus, to say that an urban school for the inner-city poor can become more effective if it puts in place those practices known to be effective in similar kinds of schools is not to say that it can provide educational opportunities deemed minimally adequate by comparison with state standards and higher spending districts. Neither does the effective schools research argue that gross levels of funding for more effective middle-class schools are defensible if they exceed levels of funding for more effective urban schools by a significant amount. The fiscal difficulties of urban schools, then, have been exacerbated by changes in federal aid policy and educational ideologies that emphasize 'excellence' and 'effectiveness' in such a way as to disadvantage urban schools.

The earlier period of school finance and the urban role

After Cubberley (1906) first identified the core elements of inequity in state school finance formulas, other education finance specialists developed approaches to state school aid distribution over the next few decades that attempted to balance local wealth and local interest in education with the state's constitutional mandate to protect its citizens equally or at least provide all children with minimal services (see, for example, Mort *et al.* 1960, Strayer and Haig 1923). State aid formulas devised by state legislatures and their administrative bureaux for education would come under the scrutiny of the state courts, and, with the California decision in *Serrano* v. *Priest* (1971) the strong and firm hand of the courts would have its influence. By 1977, some 25 states had enacted major reform, most of it as remedy for findings of inequities by state courts (Odden 1978). The guiding principle in most cases was 'wealth neutrality' – the proposition that expenditures for a child's education should not be a function of his parents' or his neighbours' wealth (Verstegen 1990). State finance systems that were held to be unconstitutional (according to *state* constitutions) under the equity principle of wealth neutrality were those where state revenues were not allocated in such a manner as to reduce significant variations in expenditures among local school districts that had resulted from differences in local property wealth.

While the momentum of the early 1970s spurred a majority of the states to reconsider their school aid formulas, the quest to attach the issue of educational equity and school finance to the *federal* constitution was destined to fail. In its five-to-four decision in *San Antonio Independent School District* v. *Rodriguez* (1973) the US Supreme Court ruled that expenditure differences based on variations in local property wealth and tax rates were not unconstitutional under the federal constitution. Applying the standard rules of judicial review, the court concluded, first, that education was not a fundamental interest within the federal constitution, although it described education as 'perhaps the most important function of state and local governments' (LaMorte 1989: 6). Second, the court did not find that children in Texas were grouped, uniformly, by poverty within school districts, hence no 'suspect classification' of children was created by the Texas system of state finance. Third, while the US Supreme Court acknowledged that expenditures varied from district to district, it was presented with no evidence that children were denied minimally adequate education in some districts because of lower expenditures. In sum, none of the conditions that could have invoked the 'strict scrutiny' of the court around the equal protection clause of the Fourteenth Amendment to the US Constitution was in evidence. Under these circumstances, the court applied 'a lenient form of review' (van Geel 1988: 634) by requiring the state of Texas merely to demonstrate that its school finance system supported a legitimate state purpose. The state offered the principle of 'local control', and the majority of justices accepted the state's interest in promoting that principle. Justice Powell concluded the majority opinion by acknowledging the financial disparities that would continue among Texas public school districts. The solution to such problems, he said, 'must come from the lawmakers and from the democratic pressures of those who elect them', not from the federal courts (411 US at 1348).

The seeming withdrawal of the federal courts after two decades of civil rights activism and its persistent refusal to interpret education as a fundamental *federal* constitutional right (though always 'important' or 'pivotal') gave way not only to state legislative reform but also increased state judicial activity over the next decade and a half (Hugg and Miron 1991).

The urban argument: from 'municipal overburden' to educational adequacy

Advocates for urban schools asked the New York courts for relief, claiming that city children were deprived of equal educational opportunity since the revenues for their schools had to come from a shrinking and overdrawn pool of general public tax dollars – a condition less common outside the municipal areas (Brazer and McCarthy 1986). 'Municipal overburden' meant that in America's larger cities the costs of sanitation services, police and fire protection, and public transportation strain the personal tax base that is maintained, on average, by poorer citizens. Because the courts were no more ready to declare education a fundamental constitutional right in the *Levittown* case than previous courts had been in *Serrano* or *Rodriguez*, the urban district had no standing in which the courts might apply rules of 'strict scrutiny' to the New York State finance system. Furthermore, the New York Court of Appeals rejected the municipal overburden argument because the courts said that cities were receiving special revenues to which non-urban district are not entitled. Similar cases in Maryland and Wisconsin were also unsuccessful. Nevertheless, in the language of the 1973 *Rodriguez* decision and the 'educational overburden' variant in the *Hornbeck* (1983) case, we find the basis for new decisions in several state courts that have found in favour of urban plaintiffs.

School finance and the courts in recent years: variations on the construct of adequacy

It is a salient shift in legal reasoning that the principle of 'wealth neutrality' as a constitutional criterion of equal opportunity has given way in increasing numbers of state cases to the principle of 'minimum adequacy' or 'basic education' provisions (Hugg and Miron 1991, LaMorte 1989, Verstegen 1990, van Geel 1988). The origins of adequacy can be traced to commentary in the *Rodriguez* (1973) decision, and its earliest applications in state court cases begin with *Seattle School District No. 1* v. *Washington* (1978). Since the *Seattle* case, at least five successful challenges to state school finance systems in state courts have applied one or another variant of the 'adequacy' construct. With increasing frequency, as well, these cases have cited the urban district as a prototype *in*adequate district. Our review of these cases suggests that three related issues arise: (1) the simple proposition that 'money matters'; (2) the quandary of defining 'minimum adequacy'; and (3) the related principle of 'educational need' (or 'vertical equity').

Money matters

As a brief preface to the more complex legal applications of adequacy in school finance, it is important to note that, unlike wealth neutrality, adequacy allows for the proposition that disparities among districts caused or permitted by state finance systems are not the only constitutional concerns of the court, but financing at a level that affords a basic or minimal set of educational activities to be carried out is also a constitutionally protected notion. Because minimal adequacy relates more easily to state constitutions in which responsibility for public education is attributed to state government, such an application of constitutional principle naturally gets exercised in the state courts. At the root of the minimal adequacy concept is the related issue of minimal funding.

The *Abbott* v. *Burke* (1990) decision in New Jersey was the first to reject the proposition growing out of the 'excellence' and 'effectiveness' movements that school quality need not depend on money. While the New Jersey Commissioner of Education, acting as defendant in the case, noted that some schools were found to be extraordinarily effective in producing achievement in poor, inner-city schools, the decision for the court asserted

> that the education provided depends to a significant extent on the money spent for it, and on what that money can buy in quality and quantity – and the ability to innovate. We do not dispute the Commissioner's proof about 'effective schools' except to the extent they are used to prove that disparity of expenditures does not count . . . (199 NJ 287, 575, A.2d at 359)

The roots of adequacy and its definitions

At the same time as the *Rodriguez* court upheld the state's purpose of enhancing local control, it 'left the door slightly ajar' (Hugg and Miron 1991: 949) by proffering the concept of minimal adequacy or 'some identifiable quantum of education' (411 US at 36) as a basis for potential constitutional challenge; the plaintiffs in *Rodriguez*, however, had not presented such an argument, hence it was not applied in that case. State courts did set about probing school finance systems, not only to compare inter-district variations in expenditures but also the nature of educational programmes in the lowest spending districts.[1]

Two cases a decade ago and four cases in the last few years have invoked the construct of adequacy in overturning state finance systems. In *Seattle School District No. 1* v. *Washington* (1978) a trial court held that providing a 'basic education' superseded all other requirements that could be placed on the Washington state department of education; the court also enumerated three kinds of programmes that should be included in a 'basic education' format: handicapped, bilingual, and remedial (see van Geel 1988). Similarly, a West Virginia trial court ordered the state board of education to develop a plan that would ensure adequate personnel, facilities and curricula for the state's children (*Pauley* v. *Kelly* 1979); After such a plan was drawn up (West Virginia State Board of Education 1984), the state's Supreme Court of Appeals ordered state officials to see to its implementation (*Pauley* v. *Bailey* 1984), although no timeframe was handed down (see LaMorte 1989). Some five years after the West Virginia cases, a Montana court found that the minimum foundation programme of state school financing fell 'short of even meeting the costs of complying with Montana's minimum accreditation standards' (*Helena Elementary School District No. 1* v. *Montana* 1989). This condition, coupled with an 8-to-1 ratio in spending among districts with similar numbers of pupils, led the court to invalidate the state's allocation system on the finding that it fostered unequal opportunity (see Hugg and Miron 1991). In the Montana case, 'minimum adequacy' was defined as programme characteristics that would gain a school or district state accreditation.

The three furthest reaching decisions in state courts came in Kentucky (*Rose* v. *The Council for Better Education, Inc.* 1989), Texas (*Edgewood Independent School District* v. *Kirby* 1989), and New Jersey (*Abbott* v. *Burke* 1990). In *Rose* the Kentucky Supreme Court thoroughly scrutinized the meaning of an efficient system of public schools (language in the Kentucky constitution) and concluded that the state must assume sole responsibility for effecting the court's detailed development of specific instructional goals designed to equip children for economic and social sufficiency. The *Rose* definition of 'efficient' included both adequacy and equity. The outcomes of interest to the court were seven:

(i) sufficient oral and written communication skills to enable students to function in a complex and rapidly changing civilization;
(ii) sufficient knowledge of economic, social, and political systems to enable the student to make informed choices;
(iii) sufficient understanding of governmental processes to enable the student to understand the issues that affect his or her community, state, and nation;
(iv) sufficient self-knowledge and knowledge of his or her mental and physical wellness;
(v) sufficient grounding in the Arts to enable each student to appreciate his or her cultural and historical heritage;
(vi) sufficient training and preparation for advanced training in either academic or vocation fields so as to enable each child to choose and pursue life work intelligently; and
(vii) sufficient levels of academic or vocational skills to enable public school students to complete favorably with their counterparts in surrounding states, in academics or in the job market. (790 S.W.2d 186 [Ky. 1989] at 212)

Rose concluded that the entire Kentucky pre-collegiate educational system was inadequate and cited data on average dropout rates, taxable property assessments, per pupil expenditures, and teacher compensation using statewide totals, rather than inter-district comparisons.

The *Rose* case was one of nine referenced in the Texas case, *Edgewood* v. *Kirby* (see Hugg and Miron 1991: 958). Although *Kirby* compared 'property poor' and 'property rich' districts – language that does not name 'urban' districts by classification, its analysis led to the conclusion that it would be virtually impossible for the poorer districts to emulate the wealthier districts without a revamping of the state school aid formula.

The *Rose* court isolated the specific areas in which the funding creates disparities in educational opportunity. It found, for example, that high-wealth districts were able to provide broader educational experiences for their students that included more extensive curricula, more up-to-date technological equipment, better libraries and library personnel, teacher aides, counselling services, lower student–teacher ratios, better facilities, parental involvement programmes and dropout prevention programmes. In contrast, the court found that poorer districts offered few or none of these advantages. The court listed even more specific programmes and services routinely found in schools in wealthier districts that were missing in poorer schools, such as foreign languages, pre-kindergarten programmes, chemistry, physics, calculus, college prep or honours programmes, and extra-curricular activities including band, debate or football. Furthermore, the court was presented with evidence that the combination of state aid and local revenues in the poorest districts was insufficient to meet the costs of the state-mandated minimum educational requirements (see Hugg and Miron 1991). Given its definition of adequacy, the *Kirby* decision is reminiscent of the *Helena* case (described above) that was tried in the same year.

One year after *Kirby*, the New Jersey Supreme Court (*Abbott* 1990) extended the construct of adequacy to include 'educational need' in grappling with the concepts of 'thorough and efficient' education in the state constitution. It also talked more explicitly than any other court before it about the condition of children in urban schools, commenting that the 'inadequacy of poor urban students' present education measured against their needs is glaring' (119 NJ at 302, 575 A.2d at 366). Urban school systems, it found, were offering science classes in such dilapidated labs that sinks had no running water and microscopes were unavailable. Testimony cited in the decision also noted that in some urban schools children ate lunch in the hallways or in a boiler room and that classes were held in closets and bathrooms. These inadequacies superseded the standard kinds of curricular disadvantages other courts had cited before *Abbott*: that students in the poorer districts had limited or no exposure to computers, biology, foreign languages, music, art, industrial arts, physical education and special education.

Educational need as a variant of adequacy

Perhaps as distinctive as the urban theme in *Abbott* is its explication of 'educational need' as a criterion of adequacy. Educational need constitutes a variant of educational adequacy because higher cost education, even if funded equally with 'regular' or lower cost education, would be inadequate for the high-need student. In the parlance of judicial finance, 'educational need' is interpreted as 'vertical equity' (Monk 1990). Simply put, the achievement of vertical equity would require that children with unequal needs be treated unequally. While the set of factors on which children's needs differ may include such characteristics as sex, race, religious belief and personal interests, the more compelling differences with educational consequences often include developmental age, language spoken at home, and mental and physical exceptionalities. The needs cited by the New Jersey court included basic nutrition, clothing and shelter, stable family support, community ties and models to emulate. The *Abbott* court attributed these special needs to urban poverty and the violence and despair it spawns, and it charged the state's financing system with some responsibility for the remedy. Attaching the concept of extraordinary education need to provisions in the New Jersey Constitution, the court claimed that children in poorer urban districts required more services than 'regular education' to achieve the 'thorough and efficient' mandate of the constitution.

Urban problems and judicial momentum

With three successful 'adequacy' challenges in the last two years, the hopes of the poor school district for redress in the state courts would appear to be enhanced. On the heels of *Abbott* with its explicit references to educational poverty in the largest cities, the urban district trying to educate our nation's neediest children may also be encouraged. The city school system in New Orleans, for example, has been exploring the potential of a legal challenge to school finance in Louisiana for a couple of years, building on a thorough reading of the particulars in post-*Rodriguez* legal precedent (see Hugg and Miron 1991, Miron 1991).

Successful equity challenges on behalf of big-city systems, however, are not automatically guaranteed. As LaMorte (1989) and Hugg and Miron (1991) have already noted, the constitutionality of current state school finance systems has been upheld slightly more often than it has been overturned, despite the *prima facie* disparities among district expenditures. Furthermore, we do not yet know the fiscal and educational results to come from systems that have been ordered to bring educationally inadequate programmes into compliance.

The future of urban school challenges will not necessarily be configured exactly like the cases we have observed in the past. Those looking into a suit on behalf of the public schoolchildren of New Orleans, for example, are considering an alliance with poor *rural* districts (Miron 1991). Also, the judicial history of 'minimal adequacy' includes cases argued for specific categories of educational need. Whether a partially deaf child must be provided her own signer or whether non-English-speaking Chinese-American children must be taught part of their school subjects in Chinese, with instruction phased in – these matters of educational adequacy have already gone to court and with mixed outcomes (van Geel 1988). The lesson to learn here is that adequacy adjudicated at the district level will not necessarily discourage individual claims for high-need children. And, as a related matter, the unit of analysis – district, v. school, v. student – can pose legal complications. As Monk (1990) points out, 'if the relevant class is defined as all students . . . who reside in a school district, a mixing will occur of individuals who vary along numerous dimensions to a substantial degree' (p. 36). Any interventions for a district (or school) that overlook variations among students, then, run the risk of treating 'unequals' equally.

Whether the 'adequacy' construct persists or gives way to other principles, whether the urban advocates continue to argue for city children or also reach out to their poor rural cousins, whether the needs of children with exceptionalities are represented as part of the urban educational mosaic or are championed on their own, the post-*Abbott* era in the state courts will be as diffiicult to anticipate as were the post-*Rodriguez* decades. To borrow LaMorte's characterization (LaMorte 1989:3) of court activity in the 1970s and 1980s, there are few reasons to believe that the judicial cauldron will quit boiling.

Note

1. As van Geel (1988) points out, state courts also challenged finance systems in order 'to alleviate what they have deemed an unfair burden on taxpayers in property-poor school districts' (p. 634).

References

BRAZER, H. E. and MCCARTHY, T. A. (1986) 'Municipal overburden: an empirical analysis', *Economics of Education Review*, 5(4), pp. 353–362.

CHUBB, J. E. and MOE, T. M. (1988) 'No school is an island: politics, markets and education', in W. L. Boyd and C. T. Kerchner (eds) *The Politics of Excellence and Choice in Education* (London: Falmer Press), pp. 131–142.

COUNCIL OF GREAT CITY SCHOOLS (1982) *Analysis of the Effect of the FY 82 and FY 83 Reagan Budget Proposals on Urban Schools* (Washington, DC: Author).

CUBAN, L. and TYACK, D. (1989) *Mismatch: Historical Perspectives on Schools and Students Who Don't Fit Them* (Stanford, CA: Center for Educational Research, Stanford University).
CUBBERLEY, E. P. (1906) *School Funds and Their Apportionment* (New York: Teachers College Press).
DAVIS, B. and MCCAUL, E. (1991) *The Emerging Crisis: Current and Projected Status of Children in the United States* (Orono, ME: Institute for the Study of At-Risk Students, University of Maine).
FAINSTEIN, S. S. and FAINSTEIN, N. (1989) 'The ambivalent state: economic development policy in the US federal system under the Reagan administration', *Urban Affairs Quarterly*, 25(1) pp. 41–62.
FREEDMAN, S. G. (1990) *Small Victories: The Real World of a Teacher, Her Students, and Their High School* (New York: Harper and Row).
HAWKINS, E. K. (1989) 'The effect of the reform movement on levels of elementary and secondary public school expenditures in the 1980s', paper presented to the American Educational Research Association, San Francisco.
HUGG, P. R. and MIRON, L. F. (1991) 'A hybrid theory for education reform', *Loyola Law Review*, 36(4), pp. 937–980.
LAMORTE, M. W. (1989) 'Courts continue to address the wealth disparity issue', *Educational Evaluation and Policy Analysis*, 11(1) pp. 3–15.
LEMANN, N. (1991) *The Promised Land* (New York: Alfred K. Knopf).
LEVIN, H. L. (1988) *Accelerated Schools for At-Risk Students*, CPRE Research Series RR-010, (Stanford, CA: Center for Policy Research in Education, Stanford University).
MIRON, L. F. (1991) 'Big city poor schools: a New Orleans case in the making', unpublished report, New Orleans, Urban Education Development Laboratory, College of Education, University of New Orleans.
MONK, D. H. (1990) *Educational Finance: An Economic Approach* (New York: McGraw-Hill).
MORT, P. R., REUSSER, W. C. and POLLEY, J. W. (1960) *Public School Finance*, 3rd edn (New York: McGraw-Hill).
ODDEN, A. (1978) 'School finance reform: emerging issues and needed research', in J. A. Thomas and R. K. Wimpelberg (eds) *Dilemmas in School Finance* (Chicago: Midwest Administration Center, University of Chicago), pp. 29–43.
ODDEN, A. (1990) 'School funding changes in the 1980s', *Educational Policy*, (4)1, pp. 33–47.
SMITH, M. P. (ed.) (1984) *Cities in Transformation* (Newbury Park CA: Sage).
STRAYER, G. D. and HAIG, R. M. (1923) *The Financing of Education in the State of New York: Report of the Education Finance Inquiry Commission*, Vol. 1 (New York: Macmillan).
VAN GEEL, T. (1988) 'The law and the courts', in N. J. Boyan (ed.) *Handbook of Research on Educational Administration* (New York: Longman) pp. 623–53.
VERSTEGEN, D. A. (1990) 'Invidiousness and inviolability in public education finance', *Educational Administration Quarterly*, 26(3) pp. 205–234.
WEST VIRGINIA STATE BOARD OF EDUCATION (1984) *Master Plan for Public Education* (Charleston: Author).
WILSON, W. J. (1987) *The Truly Disadvantaged* (Chicago: University of Chicago Press).
WIMPELBERG, R. K., TEDDLIE, C. and STRINGFIELD, S. (1989) 'Sensitivity to context: the past and future of effective schools research', *Educational Administration Quarterly*, 25(1) pp. 82–107.
WONG, K. K. (1989) 'Fiscal support for education in American states: the "parity-to-dominance view examined" ', *American Journal of Education*, 97(4), pp. 329–357.

Legal Citations

Abbott v. *Burke*, 575 A.2d 359 (NJ 1990).
Board of Education, Levittown Union Free School District v. *Nyquist*, 57 N.Y.2d 27, 439 N.E.2d 359, 453 N.Y.S.2d 643 (1982).
Edgewood Independent School District v. *Kirby*, 777 S.W.2d 391 (Tex 1989).
Helena Elementary School District No. 1 v. *Montana*, 769 P.2d 684 (Mont. 1989).
Hornbeck v. *Somerset County Board of Education*, 295 Md. 597, 458 A.2d 758 (1983).
Kukor v. *Grover*, No. 79 CV 5252 (Dane County Cir. Ct. June 21, 1986), *cert. granted*, No. 86-1544 (Wis., oral arguments heard 29 March 1988).
Board of Education, Levittown Union Free School District v. *Nyquist*, 453 N.Y.S.2d 643 (1982), appeal dismissed, 459 U.S. 1139 (1983).
Pauley v. *Bailey*, 324 S.E.2d 128 (W. Va. 1984).
Pauley v. *Kelly*, 255 S.E.2d 859 (W. Va. 1979).

John A. Rose v. *The Council for Better Education, Inc.*, 790 S.W.2d 186 (Ky. 1989).
San Antonio Independent School District v. *Rodriguez*, 411 U.S. 1, 93 S.Ct. 1278, 36 L. Ed. 2d 16 (1973).
Seattle School District No. 1 of King County v. *Washington*, 90 Wash. 2d 476, 585 P.2d 71 (1978).
Serrano v. *Priest*, 5 Cal. 3d 584 P.2d 1241 (1971).

POLITICS OF EDUCATION ASSOCIATION YEARBOOK 1991, 193–199

PART 4: EPILOGUE

Toward improved knowledge and policy on urban education

Charles E. Bidwell

The essays in this volume mark a watershed in the study of urban public education in the United States. By virtue of their intellectual breadth and substantive concern for the welfare of city schools and students, these papers forecast an integration of political and organizational analysis of education in the big cities – connecting the structures and processes of policy-making with the structures and processes that comprise the everyday lives of school administrators, teachers and students. These essays derive their theoretical and practical import from their ultimate focus on how city schools work and on the experiences that their students have in schools and classrooms. This focus on consequences for schooling as it is experienced in the city school marks a significant departure for students of urban school politics and policy in the US.

Past conceptions

The dominant social science analysis of urban education has been empirically and intellectually compartmentalized. Until almost the present day, those political scientists, sociologists and organizational analysts who worked on urban education have treated the big city public school districts as a nested hierarchy of closed systems: the board of education and its publics, the central district administration, the schools and classrooms within the district and the daily round of the students in these schools and classrooms.

Within this analysis the school board and its public form the arena of local school politics, so that they have become the principal subject-matter of the political scientists who are interested in the local politics of education. (See, for example, Bachrach and Baratz 1962, Dahl 1961, Hunter 1953, Kirby *et al.* 1973, McDonnell and Pascal 1979, Peterson 1981, Wirt and Kirst 1982.) In their work, the board of education appears as the one place where variously organized interests – including those of government bodies, business and occupational élites, and parents and taxpayers – compete or conspire. School board politics may differ in form and intensity according to the political culture and organization of the surrounding city and the conditions set by state and, at times, by federal policies. Nevertheless, whatever these differences, what the political actors seek to influence are the broad policies that purportedly provide the formal, long-term guidance of the urban school district.

At this point, the analysis is picked up by sociologists and other analysts of educational organizations. Direct political intervention into the inner workings of district or school has not been of great interest to the students of school politics, while the students of school organization have argued that the connection between board politics and policy and district organization and activities is at best tenuous (e.g., Bidwell 1965, Meyer and Rowan 1978, Weick 1976). Indeed, they have displayed no more interest in power and politics at any level of the school district than the students of school politics have shown in the workings of school organization. The omission of power and politics from work on urban school organization is remarkable, given the considerable interest of sociologists in the uses of power in other organizations and Max Weber's (1947) insistence on the importance of 'supreme authorities' for understanding how formal organizations mediate interests and services.

The organizational analysis of urban districts begins with the notion of bureaucratization. In this analysis, the diffusion of the 'one best' form for organizing big city education (Tyack 1974), the professionalization of school administration and the vast logistical complexities of supplying and accounting for the work of thousands of students and teachers in hundreds of schools have produced a thorough-going bureaucratization of system-level administration. However, at the boundary between school board and central administration, the story told is one of bureaucratic inertia, rather than of power and policy in bureaucratic politics. Superintendents come and go, we learn, victims of the shifting sands of school board politics, but the vast bulk of district administration remains – the associate and assistant superintendents, the bureau directors and managers who form an enduring administrative cadre. This cadre is said to be impervious by virtue of expertise, seniority and the formal rules and routines of work to school board policies and politics. Perhaps some district administrators are responsive to curricular or administrative doctrines promulgated in their own occupational associations and the schools of education, but not to the influence of local laity. Moreover, the inertia of the formal and routine in system operation suffices to overcome most such external professional influences, however earnest the administrator–innovators themselves.

Moving further into the internal structure and workings of urban school districts, the sociological and organization story becomes one of 'loose coupling' (Meyer and Rowan 1978, Weick 1976). This analysis has furthered the conception of these districts as internally closed by telling us that in city (and other) school districts bureaucratization does not imply strong organizational control of teachers' work or of other events in schools and classrooms. Although teachers are formally subject to standardized curricula and periodic performance evaluation, they are substantially autonomous in their own classrooms, as are school principals in their own schools. Formal curricula provide only broad templates within which quite different kinds of teaching can be done, without close administrative attention.

In the absence of effective organizational control, it would follow that events in schools and classrooms must be understood as conditioned primarily by local circumstances within schools – for example, the composition of staff and student body, the available material resources, and levels of trust between students and teachers. This interpretation leads to the expectation that in levels of instructional quality and rates of student achievement, the schools of an urban district are likely to vary in a way that corresponds to the distribution of students' social origins across these same schools. Because the district administration is closed against politics and policy, both local and nonlocal, while schools are closed against district administration and organizational control, we reach the conclusion that district politics and policy, on the one hand, and students' schooling, on the other, are essentially disconnected.[1]

Past and present conditions

Because it divorces politics and policy from organization and activities, this mode of analysis will no longer serve. One might argue with its cogency as an account even of the past nature of urban education, but one can see its origins in the not too distant past when the big city school systems were dominant locally, and highly and positively visible nationally. The bureaucratic city school district arose in a resource-rich, competition-thin environment. These districts grew and developed when the great cities that they served were themselves growing and developing economically and demographically. In this setting, the big city school systems came to dominate the local provision of education, and, correlatively, for the most part they came to enjoy ample revenues. Their cities could provide abundant tax revenues based on a concentration of valuable commercial and residential property.[2] Varieties of private education were present, but not even the Roman Catholic schools were strong competitors when the public schools could make credible claims to effectiveness. Moreover, the students who the big city districts enrolled were of sufficiently diverse social origins to justify specialized curricula and specialized schools and to allow the schools to supply virtually all of the city's labour force needs. No doubt this variety allowed the urban districts to satisfy varieties of demand from parents, employers and other constituents.

In comparatively abundant and comparatively placid environments of this kind, organizations often do not develop extensive ties from operating units to the outside world, and the impetus toward extensive, systematic internal monitoring of operations is weak. They look very much like classic Weberian bureaucracies, with routinized patterns of activity, hierarchical administrative structures, and at the top a chief executive and some sort of 'supreme authority', such as a board of directors that serves to absorb whatever shocks to the organizational system the environment manages to generate. Big city school districts presumably were no exception and took on a classic Weberian form, with external politics concentrated in the board of education and superintendency, thoroughgoing bureaucratization of administration and procedures, and, as Cibulka notes, the failure of district bureaux of evaluation to acquire the means for systematic assessment of district performance.

Although the history of urban education at the district level can be read in good measure as a history of partisan, interest-based politics, these interests contended and were more or less satisfied within a quite centralized, élite-dominated urban political structure. Contention in Chicago earlier in this century over the introduction of vocational education (Peterson 1985) is a case in point. Powerful demands were made for curricular and organizational change and controversy was sharp and sustained, but the principal actors were local élites – the professional leadership of the district, the leadership of the emerging craft and industrial unions and the principal figures of Chicago business and industry.

Now the realities of urban education have changed. Revenues bases have shrunk as economic activity and property values within big city limits have declined. This loss of revenue, often rapid and often drastic, means that city school districts no longer enjoy the budgetary slack that once permitted them substantial autonomy of operation, including the capacity to absorb inefficiencies that often were the costs of satisfying multiple clienteles and publics.

At the same time, the students enrolled in urban schools are very much more homogeneous socioeconomically now than they were in the balmier days of big city education. Before the Second World War, virtually the entire socioeconomic range of the metropolis was to be found within city limits, so that the city schools could both adapt to and exploit an extraordinary variety of student ambition, ability and life circumstance. The Chicago schools, for example, could justify claims to instructional effectiveness and responsive public service by pointing to élite high schools with strong records of college placement and victories in state or national Latin and mathematics competitions, to technical high schools with strong records of occupational placement, to high schools with teams of notable athletic prowess and to vocational programmes tightly connected to the requirements of skilled trades and easily able to place their graduates in stable, well-paying jobs. They could similarly point to elementary schools that provided equable climates for their students, that housed teachers who enjoyed high levels of parental and community trust and concomitant autonomy and that sent their graduates with little stress or strain further on into the system. Moreover, students who did not want to stay the course to high school graduation could find satisfactory places in a diverse, city-based economy or in marriage and child-rearing.

By the 1990s, much of the same demographic and economic diversity is to be found in Chicago and in other urban areas, but now it is spread across a metropolitan area, not concentrated within the core city, and in the central cities neither the student populations, nor the trusting local communities, nor the skilled jobs are to be found that once sustained the urban districts with ample tax rates or the external justification of claims to effectiveness. The policies of these districts now are thorough-going policies of redistribution which, while they may satisfy one or another of the interest groups active in local school politics, are hard to justify to the more affluent local taxpayers and increase the dependence of urban districts on nonlocal funds.

The upshot of this environmental transformation in urban education has been the simultaneous centralization and decentralization of the distribution of power to effect school district policies and, possibly, the work of teachers and the school lives of students. On the one hand, as the city districts have become increasingly dependent fiscally on federal, but especially on state sources, the power to intervene in broad district policies has shifted palpably from the local school board to higher levels of government. This trend almost certainly has been strengthened by the tendency of local interest groups to use the means provided by state and federal agencies and the courts to achieve their policy objectives on the local urban educational scene. Examples are many, notable among them the 1988 legislative mandate for a radical school district restructuring in Chicago and similar legislative interest and activity in the urban districts of such states as Kentucky, California and Arizona.

On the other hand, on the local level, one cannot now think of city school politics as élite-dominated. Local city politics generally is quite the reverse, as it has increasingly come to be a fragmented politics of interest groups, often populist in orientation and diversely anchored, for example, in ethnic communities and social action organizations. These local interest groups often enjoy a legitimacy and force that derive from the legal and ideological frames of civil rights, the expansion and upgrading of conceptions of citizenship (in the city no less than in the nation), and a concomitant stress on the broad public accountability of government. The urban school districts, perhaps because of the centrality of their work to both individual and public welfare, have been among the governmental bodies most exposed and vulnerable to this new politics, and it is a politics in which levels of interest group demand have perhaps intensified as a consequence of widely perceived inefficiency and ineffectiveness in the provision of educational opportunity. Moreover, loss of fiscal autonomy has opened the districts internally to influence by those entrepreneurial principals and teachers who, by virtue of their effectiveness in competitions for grants, school-business sponsorship and so on, acquire considerable power and independence within their districts.

In summary, as Wong argues in this volume, the contemporary local politics of urban education is a decentralized politics and is not one politics, but many. As centres of political power in education spread and diversify, the district administrators, school principals, teachers' unions and local school faculties and parent groups themselves take on the guise of political actors, and the guidance of educational activities across all the formal levels of the urban school district takes on the appearance of political action.

Future possibilities

These massive changes of environment, organization and structures of power in urban school districts call for a radically new approach to the study of urban schools. As many of the papers in this volume suggest, we must draw urban educational politics and organization into an integrated framework in a way that will relate to the nature of teachers' work and students' school lives and, thereby, to the educational life chances of students in big city schools. In this work of reconceptualization, we must do more than assert that boundaries have become more permeable. Those few writers who earlier sought to breach the boundary between politics and organizations did so by asserting that organizations are themselves politics (Blase 1991, Perrow 1979). However, as Wong notes in his paper, when these efforts were applied to urban school districts, there was a strong tendency to regard organizational politics and city educational politics as discrete and unrelated. Organizational politics remained within the closed boundary of district organization – an interplay of interests among the staff.

Let me suggest instead that we go beyond the now-confining intellectual limits of politics versus organizations as fields of study to think about urban education as a field of policy action, with the following components:

1. both individual and corporate actors, variously situated in geographical and social space (to include, for example, federal and state agencies and their staff members, district-level offices and bureaux and their incumbents, local schools and their administrators and faculties, local lay social movement organizations and parent organizations and their leaders, rank-and-file and hangers-on, local school councils, teachers' unions, and the students themselves);
2. the interests that characterize each of the actors in this field, including values and long-term goals of action in the field, as well as short-term objectives and immediate stakes in events in the city schools;
3. the resources that each actor commands, including their territorial and social locations, funds, legitimacy, and constituents' support;
4. formal structures relating the actors to one another, including legal provisions relating state or federal agencies to local school districts and the table of organization of a city school district;
5. informal structures of ties between corporate and individual actors, including coalitions among corporate actors and interaction networks among individual actors (e.g., the members of a school faculty or parent council or a superintendent and the school principals in the district); and
6. the activities of the actors in the urban education field, including both the strategic and tactical behaviour of movement organizations, the work activities of faculties, and the conduct and achievement of students.

In this policy field of urban education, observed states of any one of the components can be taken as the phenomenon to be explained, in the light of states on any subset of the remaining components. Thus studies of this field can embrace what to date we have thought of as urban school politics or urban school organization – for example, the analysis of relationships between interests, coalition formation, and policy influence or investigations into the correlates of structural change in urban high schools. Analysis of the field of urban educational action can span the 'political' and 'organizational' and deepen the understanding of phenomena on both sides of this artificial disciplinary division – for example, research into the sources of oppositional or cooperative action between school faculties and parent groups or local action organizations found in structures of social ties or in the capacity of each to mobilize allies both within the locality and externally (for example, regional or national umbrella organizations or courts or state agencies).

No less important, within the field of action frame, the investigator can consider how action to affect district or school-level policies or to influence their implementation affects what teachers and students do and, thereby, affects what students learn or accomplish – the great question of educational life chances. Similarly, the investigator can ask whether variation in politico-organizational forms (e.g., greater or lesser degrees of local school parental control) is related to gains or losses in schools' retention rates or levels of student learning and, if so, through the mediation of what forms and intensities of parent, teacher and student activity in the day-to-day lives of inner-city schools and inner-city families. So, too, the value becomes clear of closing the causal loop with studies that trace how change in schools' academic and other outputs affect the subsequent behaviour of actors within their field of educational action.

It will be immediately apparent that this approach entails at its centre studies that embrace relations that cross levels (at times, several levels) of sociopolitical aggregation. Where once our methods of data analysis made it virtually impossible to deal with multi-level explanatory structures, this limit no longer holds. It will also be apparent that central to the study of fields of educational action is an interest in change and in process that, on the one hand, will require long-term longitudinal or panel studies of educational events in the cities and, on the other, will require a good measure of field work which, alone among the tools in the social scientists' kit, permits the fine-grained analytical representation of social process.

This handbook has opened such possibilities by transcending the conventional disciplinary limits of politics, sociology and organizational studies and by stressing relationships between policies, policy making and events in schools and classrooms. It is a first step, but an important one.

Notes

1. By far the largest body of social science research on the outcomes of schooling, including questions of equity and effects on labour force and other forms of individual social participation, has essentially ignored the school and school district, their organization and the work of their teachers no less than politics and policies, to consider simply how years of school attained are related, on the one hand, to social origins, and, on the other, to later attainments in the world of work and other adult social arenas. This educational status attainment literature until very recently was perhaps the centrepiece of sociological research on education and life chances.
2. This earlier fiscal self-sufficiency of the urban districts no doubt has led analysts of state and federal educational policy to regard these districts as systems closed not only to the local environment, but also to policy actors and events at the state and federal levels. Thus, studies of educational policy-making and implementation at these levels for the most part have dealt with the policy-making side of things without much attention to linkages to the localities, while studies of the implementation of these policies have attempted to account for success or failure without extensive attention to events within the districts presumably affected.

References

BACHRACH, P. and BARATZ, M. (1962) 'The two faces of power', *American Political Science Review*, 56, pp. 947–952.

BIDWELL, C. E. (1965) 'The school as a formal organization', in J. G. March (ed.) *The Handbook of Organizations* (Skokie: Rand McNally), pp. 972–1022.

BLASE, J. (ed.) (1991) *The Politics of Life in Schools* (Newbury Park: Corwin Press).

DAHL, R. (1961) *Who Governs?* (New Haven: Yale University Press).

HUNTER, F. (1953) *Community Power Structure* (Chapel Hill: University of North Carolina Press).

KIRBY, T., HARRIS, T. R. and CRAIN, R. (1973) *Political Strategies in Northern Desegregation* (Lexington: Lexington Books).

MCDONNELL, I. and PASCAL, A. (1979) *Organized Teachers in American Schools* (Santa Monica: Rand Corp.).

MEYER, J. W. and ROWAN, B. (1978) 'The structure of educational organizations', in M. W. Meyer (ed.) *Environments and Organizations* (San Francisco: Jossey-Bass), pp. 78–109.

PERROW, C. (1979) *Complex Organizations: A Critical Essay*, vol. 2 (Glenview: Scott Foresman).

PETERSON, P. E (1981) *City Limits* (Chicago: University of Chicago Press).

PETERSON, P. E (1985) *The Politics of School Reform 1870–1940* (Chicago: University of Chicago Press).

TYACK, D. (1974) *The One Best System* (Cambridge: Harvard University Press).

WEBER, M. (1947) *The Theory of Social and Economic Organization*. Translated by T. Parsons and A. M. Henderson (Glencoe: The Free Press).

WEICK, K. (1976) 'Educational organizations as loosely-coupled systems', *Administrative Science Quarterly*, 21, pp. 1–19.

WIRT, F. and KIRST, M. (1982) *Schools in Conflict* (Berkeley: McCutchan).

References

BACHRACH, P. and BARATZ, M. (1962) 'The two faces of power', *American Political Science Review*, pp. 947–952.

BIDWELL, C. E. (1965) 'The school as a formal organization', in J. G. MARCH (ed.) *The Handbook of Organizations*, Chicago, Rand McNally, pp. 972–1022.

[illegible]

DAHL, R. (1961) *Who Governs?* New Haven, Yale University Press.

HUNTER, F. (1953) *Community Power Structure*, Chapel Hill, University of North Carolina Press.

[illegible]

Index

(v. = versus)